Christ Outside the Gate

Christ Outside the Gate

Mission Beyond Christendom

ORLANDO E. COSTAS

ORBIS BOOKS

Maryknoll, New York 10545

9-30-86

The Catholic Foreign Mission Society of America (Maryknoll) recruits and trains people for overseas missionary service. Through Orbis Books Maryknoll aims to foster the international dialogue that is essential to mission. The books published, however, reflect the opinions of their authors and are not meant to represent the official position of the society.

Manuscript editor: Lisa McGaw

Library of Congress Cataloging in Publication Data

Costas, Orlando E.
  Christ outside the gate.

  Bibliography: p.
  Includes index.
  1. Missions—Theory. I. Title.
BV2063.C658   1982   266'.001   82-7892
ISBN 0-88344-147-0 (pbk.)   AACR2

A
Rosin, Annette, y Dannette,
compañeras en la periferia

Contents

Acronyms

CCA	Christian Conference of Asia
CELAM	Conferencia Episcopal Latinoamericana (Latin American Bishops Conference)
CELEP	Centro Evangélico Latinoamericano de Estudios Pastorales (Latin American Evangelical Center for Pastoral Studies)
CEP	Centro de Publicaciones (Center for Publications)
CEVAA	Communauté Evangélique d'Action Apostolique (Evangelical Community for Apostolic Action)
CIA	Central Intelligence Agency
CISRS	Christian Institute for the Study of Religion and Society
CLAI	Consejo Latinoamericano de Iglesias (Latin American Council of Churches)
CLAME	Comunidad Latinoamericana de Ministerios Evangélicos (Community of Latin American Evangelical Ministries)
COWE	Consultation on World Evangelization
CWME	Commission on World Mission and Evangelism
E/D	Evangelism in Depth
EFMA	Evangelical Foreign Missions Association
FBI	Federal Bureau of Investigation
FMS	Federal Monetary System
FTL	Fraternidad Teológica Latinoamericana (Latin American Theological Fraternity)
IDB	Interpreter's Dictionary of the Bible
IFMA	Independent Foreign Missions Association
IISR	International Institute for the Study of Religion
IMC	International Missionary Council
IMF	International Monetary Fund
INDEF	Instituto de Evangelización a Fondo (Institute of In-Depth Evangelism)
IPLA	Instituto Pastoral Latinoamericano (Latin American Pastoral Institute)
IRM	International Review of Mission
ISEDET	Instituto Superior Evangélico de Educación Teológica (Evangelical Higher Institute of Theological Education)
JB	Jerusalem Bible

KJV	King James Version
LAM	Latin America Mission
LCWE	Lausanne Committee for World Evangelization
LTEG	Lausanne Theology and Education Group
MACC	Mexican American Cultural Center
MAP	Military Assistance Program
MARC	Missionary Advance Research Center
PACLA	Pan African Christian Leadership Assembly
PACTS	Pacific/Asia Center for Theology and Strategy
RSV	Revised Standard Version
TDNT	Theological Dictionary of the New Testament
WCC	World Council of Churches
WEF	World Evangelical Fellowship
WEFTC	World Evangelical Fellowship Theological Commission

Acknowledgments

Grateful appreciation is here expressed to the members of my family, friends, and colleagues who contributed in one way or another to the preparation and publication of this book:

My wife and colleague, Rose Feliciano Costas, who was not only a source of support at home and at work, but also spent long hours typing and revising the manuscript.

My friend and former colleague, Charles Troutman, with whom I tested many ideas on mission theory and for whose wisdom I shall be ever indebted.

Professors Thomas McDaniel and Douglas Miller from the Eastern Baptist Theological faculty whose encouragement, observations, and insights helped me to sharpen the argument of several chapters and improve the overall quality of the book.

The Rev. Luis Cortés, my assistant for Hispanic ministries, who served as an honest sounding board, and Joseph Smith, my student assistant, who prepared the index.

Elizabeth McClelland and Robin Songer, faculty secretaries at Eastern, who helped to type several parts of the manuscript.

The Rev. James Dekker, Christian Reformed Church missionary in Guatemala, who very generously and competently translated chapters four and six from the Spanish.

The many pastors, lay leaders, church and mission executives, theological institutions, and local congregations in the Americas and other continents with whom the reflections contained in this book were first shared and tested.

My daughters, Annette and Dannette, who have not only accompanied my wife and me in our pilgrimage throughout the Americas, but also are increasingly becoming partners in theological conversation.

Unless otherwise stated, all quotations from Scripture are taken from the Revised Standard Version, second edition (Nashville, Camden, and New York: Thomas Nelson Inc., 1971).

Prologue: A Personal Word

It all started in 1974 when I first published a book in English.[1] Although I had determined to do all my professional writing in Spanish,[2] I had come to realize the importance of establishing a communication link with the church in the English-speaking world, especially in Northern America,[3] and particularly that sector of it that has been traditionally connected with the missionary movement.

My wife and I had gone to Central America as missionaries with the Latin America Mission (LAM; a progressive, nondenominational evangelical[4] society with headquarters in Bogota, New Jersey). The greater portion of our financial support came from American churches and friends. Even so, we were not typical American missionaries. We were Puerto Ricans—native "Islanders" by birth and mainland "Ricans" by migration.[5] Soon after our wedding we had gone back to the Island to serve a pastorate at the First Baptist Church of Yauco, a charming southwestern town not far from my own birthplace of Ponce. It was in Yauco that I was ordained to the ministry. While there I completed my undergraduate studies at the Inter-American University with a major in Latin American history and politics. During this period I also had the opportunity to participate in several preaching missions in the Hispanic Caribbean and northern South America. My pastorate, studies, and travels enabled me to develop a deep Latin American identity, which in turn influenced my spouse's own self-understanding. When we returned to the mainland to pastor the Evangelical Baptist Church of Milwaukee, Wisconsin, and to pursue seminary studies in the Chicago area, we were a different family. We had found our roots.

Several years later, after completing two graduate degrees, we went to San José, Costa Rica, as missionaries with the LAM. Since we were Puerto Rican missionaries, we fitted nicely into the circle of Latin Americans who were serving in the various ministries of the LAM—in our case, the Evangelism in Depth (E/D) Team and the Seminario Bíblico Latinoamericano.

These were days of tremendous social, political, and cultural fervor. The LAM was beginning a self-initiated process of "latinization," which culminated in the organization of the Community of Latin American Evangelical Ministries (CLAME). The seminary became an autonomous school and the E/D Team was reorganized as the Institute of In-Depth Evangelism. My colleagues and I began to raise such questions as what did it mean to evangelize and educate theologically in the Latin America of the 1970s. We became an evangelical variant of the Latin American theological ferment of the decade.

But no sooner had we begun to take a few steps toward the development of a Latin American theology and a contextual missiological reflection than we began to feel the heat from Northern America, particularly the United States. Since I was one of the most vocal of the San José LAM-related theologians, I began to be quoted—and misquoted. The fact that our writings were mainly in Spanish complicated the matter further. Our so-called constituency was getting questionable reports from some missionary circles, often quoting us out of context. I decided to take the bull by the horns. I started to put in writing some of my developing missiological insights. I took advantage of an invitation from Gordon-Conwell Theological Seminary (Hamilton, Mass.) to serve as a visiting professor in January 1973 and organized my lectures into a full-sized book on mission.

The Church and Its Mission was addressed to the American Protestant "mission community"—missionaries, mission executives, pastors, and lay leaders. But it was situated in the experience of a Puerto Rican Christian who, having been helped by the Anglo-American church earlier in his life, now felt constrained to minister prophetically to it. I didn't dream that the book would have as wide a circulation as it did in evangelical circles, much less that it would have an impact on Hispanic pastors. The fact that I was one of their own apparently became a source of inspiration, even if the book didn't specifically address the issues of the Hispanic church and community.

From May 1974 to April 1976, my family and I lived in Europe, where I obtained a doctorate at the Free University of Amsterdam and served as research fellow at the Selly Oak Colleges in Birmingham, England. One day I received a call from a Hispanic pastor in New York, inviting me to spend a week with both the Hispanic and the Program councils of the Reformed Church of America. While I could not go immediately, I did so six months later. Thus began a renewed contact with the Hispanic church in the United States and the American mission community, which culminated in 1980 when I joined the Faculty of Eastern Baptist Theological Seminary in Philadelphia, Pennsylvania.

It was a move that I resisted for four years. From the moment we returned to Costa Rica in July 1976 (this time not with the LAM but under the sponsorship of the United Church Board for World Ministries) to resume our responsibilities with the Centro Evangélico Latinoamericano de Estudios Pastorales (CELEP), a ministry several colleagues and I had founded in December 1973, I found myself having to cope with an increasing demand of my time not only from the rest of Latin America, but also from other parts of the world, especially the United States. During that period it became clear to me that I had an important ministry to fulfill as a minority, Hispanic missiologist. I came to realize that there was a need in the United States for the interpretation of the Christian mission from the periphery—the perspective of the great absentees of the American missionary movement (oppressed American ethnic minorities: Asians, Blacks, Hispanics, and Native Americans). Consequently I returned to the United States after a decade of theological reflection in Latin

America. I came back, however, not to be one more professional in the growing American "missiological market" but, rather, to continue to do missiology from the periphery—this time, the periphery of the American metropolis.

The studies included in this volume reflect both the latter part of my work in Latin America and my new historical space. Some of them have appeared in full or in part in various publications;[6] others are being published for the first time;[7] yet others were originally written in Spanish and have since been translated and edited.[8] All have been revised for the present volume.

The point of these reflections is twofold. First, they demonstrate the contextual character of missiology as "a theology of the crossroads," or a critical reflection at the point where cultures, ideologies, religious traditions, and social, economic, and political systems confront each other, and where the gospel seeks to cross the frontier of unbelief.[9] As such they are not meant to be definitive theological statements, but essays on issues that emerge out of the heat and tumble of Christian mission among oppressed people today.

Second, these essays reflect the "thinking out loud" of an "outsider"—one who not only belongs to a marginalized community in the American metropolis and has lived and worked in an oppressed continent, but who has also situated himself theologically in the periphery of history. The fact that I teach at a graduate professional school of theology and write in the language of the "theological/missiological guild" is of little relevance. What is important is that I try to articulate the reality of rejection and marginalization of the Latin American peoples, the Hispanic community in the United States, and all oppressed women, men, and children everywhere. This is thus an effort to reflect on the Christian world mission not from the "inside" but from the "outside" of history, from the perspective of those who have been shaped by, and in many ways have suffered the negative impact of, the missionary movement.

I have begun these reflections with a personal word. In my opinion missiology should always start with a note of personal engagement. A missiologist is a "thinking missionary" (Winter); a man or woman of faith caught up in "the bottlenecks of life" (Verkuyl). This is where I am and have been.

Yet missiology must not only start with a note of personal engagement; it must land there. Missiological reflection demands a commitment to a more effective engagement in mission if it is to have integrity. Hence I have chosen to conclude with a sermon—the proclamation of Jesus Christ and his death as an event that took place "outside the gate" of the Holy City. Such a message issues a call to "move outside" the comfort and security of all Christendom projects, a call to come to Jesus, bearing the abuse he endured on behalf of an alienated world, building "tents" in the wilderness of history while marching, in the power of the Spirit, toward the everlasting city: the new heavens and new earth that God has promised the people of faith.

This is the message, the commitment, the task, and the goal of mission. This is my witness—and challenge. May it be received critically but prayerfully.

NOTES

1. See Orlando E. Costas, *The Church and Its Mission: A Shattering Critique from the Third World* (Wheaton, Ill.: Tyndale, 1974).

2. By 1974 I had published the following works: *La iglesia y su misión evangelizadora* (Buenos Aires: La Aurora, 1971);*¿Qué significa evangelizar hoy?* (San José, Costa Rica: Publicaciones INDEF, 1973); *Comunicación por medio de la predicación* (Miami: Editorial Caribe, 1973). In addition I had also written (in collaboration with members of the faculty of the Seminario Bíblico Latinoamericano and the Evangelism in Depth Team) *Hacia una teología de la evangelización* (Buenos Aires: La Aurora, 1973).

3. In this volume I shall be using the expression "Northern" (or "North") America for Canada and the United States, and "American" for people and organizations from the United States. To be sure, the term "American" applies to everyone who lives in the Americas, North, Central, South, and Antilles. But since the United States has no separate proper name, like Canada and Mexico, it makes it a lot easier to use the name "American" when referring to the United States.

4. By "evangelical" I mean specifically that spiritual movement with which many Protestant Christians in Northern America, and indeed around the world, identify themselves. In the United States evangelicalism functions as a subculture. In the words of James Wallis, "evangelicals have their own churches, organizations, schools, publications, leaders, financial support, and communication network—a formal and informal grapevine tying it all together" (*The Call to Conversion* [New York: Harper & Row, 1981], p. 22). For my own definition of the movement, see my *Theology of the Crossroads in Contemporary Latin America* (Amsterdam: Editions Rodopi, 1976), pp. 40ff.

5. Carl F. H. Henry chides me for joining (in 1974) in the call for "an authentic Latin American theology." He implies that I have no claim to speak on behalf of Latin America because I "was born in North America" (*God, Revelation and Authority,* vol. 4 [Waco, Tex.: Word Books, 1979], pp. 559-60). This is a very awkward statement, especially since Henry makes it in the context of his critical interaction with my *The Church,* where (pp. 11-12) I let it be known that I was not born in North America. I can only conclude that for Henry being born in Puerto Rico is equivalent to having been born in North America.

The point, however, is not a matter of geographic hegemony. (Puerto Rico is a Caribbean island, not part of the North American continent. No military or political conquest can change that.) The real issue with Henry's assertion is his ironic attempt to question my role as a Latin American. Henry should know, however, that Puerto Rico was part of Latin America long before it became a colony of the United States. Moreover, just as the Treaty of Guadalupe-Hidalgo established a political border between Mexico and the American Southwest, but not a cultural boundary, so the annexation of Puerto Rico at the Treaty of Paris officialized its colonial status but could not culturally pluck it from the Latin American world. Puerto Rico remains as much a part of Latin America as Namibia is part of Black Africa and Hong Kong of Asia. As for me, I remain a Puerto Rican, am still part of the Latin American world, and have become, again, a member of the Hispanic community in the United States.

6. Part of chap. 1 was first published in the *Journal of Theology for Southern*

Africa, no. 29 (December 1979): 23–30. I have also borrowed for this publication a small section from my chapter "A Radical Evangelical Contribution from Latin America," in *Christ's Lordship and Religious Pluralism,* ed. Gerald H. Anderson and Thomas F. Stransky, C.S.P. (Maryknoll, N.Y.: Orbis Books, 1981), pp. 133–56. The original version was presented at the South African Leadership Assembly, held in Pretoria, Republic of South Africa, in July 1979.

Chap. 2 is a translated and revised version of my chapter "Pecado y salvación en América Latina" in *América Latina y la evangelización en la década de los 80,* ed. Latin American Theological Fraternity (Cuernavaca, Mexico: FTL, 1980), pp. 271–89. It was originally prepared for the Second Latin American Congress of Evangelization, held in Huampaní, Peru, Oct. 31–Nov. 9, 1979.

Chap. 3 was first published in the *International Bulletin of Missionary Research* 5, no. 1 (January 1981): 2–8, out of an earlier version presented at a missiological consultation held in Buenos Aires, Argentina, in March 1976 under the sponsorship of the FTL. Parts of it were included in my article, "Nuestra misión y el crecimiento de la iglesia: Hacia una misionología de masas y minoría," *Ensayos ocasionales* 3, no. 2 (October 1976): 2–28. (English version in *Theological Fraternity Bulletin,* no. 4 [1976]: 3–24).

Chap. 4 was published in the symposium, "The Impact of the Third World on Mission," sponsored by the Southern Baptist Theological Seminary, Louisville, Ky., and published in its journal, *Review and Expositor* 74, no. 2 (Spring 1977): 183–97.

An abridged version of chap. 10 was published in *Missiology: An International Review* 8, no. 4 (October 1980): 395–405. It is a revised version of my inaugural address as Thornley B. Wood Professor of Missiology and Director of Hispanic Studies at Eastern Baptist Theological Seminary, February 20, 1980.

This article and the other previously published materials are included in the present volume with appreciation to their respective sources of publication.

7. See chaps. 8, 9, 11, and the epilogue. Some of the material in these chapters, however, has been used in public lectures: chap. 8 at a conference of the Coalition of Christian Colleges in Washington, D.C., in May 1981, and chap. 11 at an Evangelism Conference sponsored by the Andover-Newton Theological School, Newton Centre, Mass., in April 1981, the Pennsylvania State Pastor's Conference, Chapel Hill, Pa., in October 1981, and the Columbia Theological Seminary Forum, Decatur, Ga., February 1982. The sermon in the epilogue has been delivered in various versions at various places, the two most recent being the 1981 commencement exercises of Lancaster Theological Seminary, Lancaster, Pa., and the 1981 General Assembly of the Church of the Brethren in Indianapolis, Ind.

8. See chaps. 4 and 5, both of which were originally translated from the Spanish by my friend and colleague, the Rev. James Dekker. They were then edited and revised by me. Chap. 4 was first published as "La empresa misionera, ¿un instrumento de domesticación?" *Taller de teología,* no. 5 (1979): 39–53. Chap. 6 appeared in the Latin American/South African tribute to J. Verkuyl published by *Occasional Essays* 6, nos. 1–2 (December 1979): 24–37.

9. Costas, *Theology of the Crossroads,* pp. 9ff., 325ff.

Part I

FROM THE LATIN AMERICAN PERIPHERY

1

Contextualization and Incarnation: Communicating Christ amid the Oppressed

A lay missionary colleague stopped me one day at the entrance to my office and said, "I need to ask you a question."

"Well, let's see if I can answer it."

She then asked, "What is this business of contextualization?" She had been hearing and reading about it in sermons, informal conversations, mission programs, and articles without actually knowing what it was all about.

This colleague was not alone. Contemporary Christianity is increasingly concerned about contextualization. It stems from the growing awareness of the importance of "context" in the church's understanding of itself, its faith, and its mission in the world. The long-range universal formulations of the older theologies have had to give way to shorter-range, situation-oriented discourses which, though shorter in life span, are more relevant to the life-in-mission of the church.

These contextual theologies are not the direct outgrowth of the traditional theological factories: the world of academia. They stem, rather, from the peculiar situation in which many Christians find themselves as they try to live out their faith and fulfill their vocation in their respective life circumstances. This situation has led theologians to give increasing attention to the "now of history," especially to their own historical reality. This does not mean that those who are trying to be consciously contextual in their theologizing have entered into a new captivity but, rather, that they have at last begun to rediscover the true nature of theology, namely, reflecting on the faith in the light of one's historical context.

The contextualization of our theological reflection is not only imperative because the life and missional situations of Christians the world over so demand it; it is especially necessary because this is what theology *should* be, and

3

in fact has always been, namely a contextual reflection on the action of God in history. To pretend to be anything else is but an illusion, and a very dangerous one for the church.

The Language of Contextualization

Let us consider the language of contextualization. Just what do we mean by "context"?

The word "context" has its roots in the Latin *contextus,* which means "weaving together." Another way of looking at its etymology is by dividing the word: *con,* which can be associated with the Latin *cum* ("with") and *text,* which is rooted in the Latin verb *texere* ("to weave"). From *texere* we derive the concept of a literary structure. "Context" stands, then, for everything that accompanies or surrounds a text.

This is congruent with the two definitions that *Webster's New Collegiate Dictionary* gives to the term. A context, it says, can be either "the parts of a discourse that surround a word or passage and can throw light on its meaning" or the "interrelated conditions in which something exists or occurs: environment."[1]

This word represents a conceptual category. It refers to the *time-space* boundaries of understanding. The context is the stage where all comprehension takes place. It is the reality that ties together, and therefore shapes, all knowledge.

There is no such thing as timeless or nonspatially related knowledge, since knowledge is a fundamental part of life, which is, in turn, a complex, interrelated phenomenon. The Spanish philosopher José Ortega y Gasset used to say, "I am me and my circumstances." In other words, I do not exist outside my circumstances. Neither do I know outside historical reality. Everything that I am, everything that I know is intrinsically bound to everything that I do. Because knowledge is contextual, it is also practical. It is human sensorial activity, shaped by reality and geared toward its transformation.

As a category the concept of "context" stands for the psychological and social foundations of human communication. In communication people come together about a given piece of information. They weave together (or interrelate) ideas, attitudes, values, and feelings. This interrelation leads to some form of change. Communication is thus a practical endeavor, a form of human activity. It is shaped by reality and profoundly affects it.

 Every human enterprise is contextual in that it is informed and shaped by factors outside itself. The context involves both the presuppositions and the settings of understanding and communication. It refers not only to all the baggage people bring with them when they share and interpret reality to one another, but also to the situation wherein they reflect upon their practice.

The term "context" represents not only a concept but a processual reality. It stands for what has been, what is, and what will be. In other words, it faces the future. It is always becoming because it confronts us with the transforming challenge of the text that one is dealing with. To contextualize is then not only to ask about the past and present of a text in the light of the past and present of its readers and hearers, but especially to ask about its future, its transforming effect upon those who will come into contact with it.

The context, then, is reality in all its dynamics. It is constantly changing and affecting change. We all participate in it, actively or passively. Not one of us can claim to stand outside it. The question is whether or not we can consciously and critically incorporate it into our efforts to interpret and communicate the gospel. This is what we do in contextualization.

The Theological Roots of Contextualization: The Incarnation

The contextualization of the gospel is not a new theological phenomenon; it has been around from the earliest moments of the Christian faith. It is evident throughout Christian history, though it has not always been acknowledged as such. It does not take much effort to show how theology—from the patristic writings to the present—has been situational through and through. Indeed it has been generally bound to the experiences and categories of western culture. Nor need we do much research to be convinced of the pressure that the social milieu has put historically on the Christian world mission for a contextual interpretation and communication of the gospel.

What is harder to accept for some, however, is the contention that the roots of contextualization take us to the Bible itself. We have become so used to reading the Bible in the vernacular that we have forgotten the distance that separates us from its actors and writers. When we take a close look at its pages, however, we note that the Scriptures are contextual from beginning to end.[2]

Biblical contextualization is rooted in the fact that the God of revelation can only be known in history. Such a revelation comes to specific peoples in concrete situations by means of particular cultural symbols and categories. It is not possible to read the Old Testament without being struck by the human character of its revelatory claims. Theology in the Old Testament appears as a culture-bound, historically situated reflection on the God who is known in human language. In the New Testament, however, this revelation reaches its peak: God is known in human flesh.

The Incarnate Word

The New Testament witnesses to the fact that the Word, which was from the beginning with God and is God, has become flesh in Jesus of Nazareth (Jn. 1:3, 14). In him God's Word has been "heard," "seen," and "touched" with human hands. As the Son of God, Jesus not only "reflects the glory of God and bears the very stamp of his nature" (Heb. 1:3), but has definitely, once and for all, made God contextual. Through the life of Jesus of Nazareth, God has come within the reach of every woman, man, and child. God has become one with us: Emmanuel (Mt. 1:22–23).

This act, which in the structure of at least three of the Gospels (Matthew, Luke, and John) appears as the starting point of New Testament faith, is nevertheless Christologically the point of arrival. As Raymond Brown has pointed out:

> . . . one may speak of the Gospels as developing backwards. The oldest Christian preaching about Jesus concerned his death and resurrection, as may be seen in the formulas of Acts 2:23, 32; 3:14–15; 4:10; 10:39–40; and I Cor. 15:3–4. Not only did these events constitute the clearest instance of God's salvific action in Jesus, but also it was through them that the disciples came to a more adequate understanding of who Jesus really was.[3]

Indeed, it was not until the resurrection that the disciples were able to understand the cross as a revelation of God rather than a tragic accident, as Luke tells us they originally thought (Lk. 24:18–26; Acts 2:32–36). The Easter event made theological sense of the cross and confirmed the understanding that the disciples had developed of Jesus through the years they had spent with him. Only through the experience of the resurrection did the early church discover the meaning of the cross. Only by the resurrection of the crucified Jesus was it able to interpret the theological significance of his life and ministry. And faith in him led it to the conclusion that God had become human in the man Jesus while remaining true to himself.[4]

The Man Jesus

The New Testament teaches that Jesus was a thorough human being. He was a Jew, the son of a modest family, who grew up in an insignificant town in the province farthest from the capital and the most culturally backward. He spoke with a Galilean accent, had a limited formal education, and was a carpenter by trade. He was aware that he belonged to a "unique people, although one humiliated for centuries by foreigners."[5] Yet he was misunderstood by his family, his friends, his disciples, and the religious leaders of his country. From the time he left his home to become an itinerant preacher, he lived a poor and lonely life with no permanent abode. He so identified himself with the poor and the oppressed that he dedicated himself to a suffering service in their behalf. It is this poor, humble, enigmatic, lonely Jewish preacher who fearlessly defended the cause of the hurt of his society whom the Christian faith confesses as the Son of God.

The Crucified Son

It is in his death on the cross, however, where the mystery of Jesus as the Son of God is most densely revealed. The New Testament traditions converge not only in the identification of the risen Lord with the man Jesus who was crucified, but also in the description of his suffering and death as that of a poor and oppressed man. Jesus died between two thieves. He was unjustly condemned. He was betrayed by a friend and was sold for thirty pieces of silver. He had no one to defend him; his friends left him. He did not even have a grave of his own.

These facts were no mere accident as far as early Christians were concerned. They saw in them God's hand. Therefore they did not hesitate to link Jesus' suffering with the Suffering Servant of Isaiah who "was taken away . . . by oppression and judgment," had to share "his grave with the wicked," and was "numbered with the transgressors" (Isa. 53:8–9, 12). Apparently they saw Jesus accepting the role of the Suffering Servant once he became conscious of the inevitability of his death (Mk. 8:31; 9:31; 10:32–34; Mt. 20:17–19; Lk. 18:31–34). Peter, especially, saw in Jesus God's servant (Acts 3:13, 26; 4:27, 30) who "bore our sins in his body on the tree" (cf. 1 Pet. 2:22–24). According to Luke, Philip's conversation with the Ethiopian eunuch revolved around the interpretation of Isaiah's fourth Servant Song in the light of Jesus' death (Acts 8:26ff.). Paul, for his part, takes the servant motif to develop his own theology of the cross (1 Cor. 1:25, 27; Phil. 2:8).

The interpretation of Jesus' suffering in the light of Isaiah's Suffering Servant situates the cross on the side of the poor and the afflicted, the sick and the oppressed. Such contextualization is carried even further in Paul's linkage of the cross with the incarnation. According to Paul, Jesus takes the form of a slave in his incarnation, becoming totally identified with humanity in its lowest form. The cross is the ultimate test of this identification: Jesus became obedient unto death (Phil. 2:8). The fact that Paul makes this affirmation in the same passage where he affirms Jesus' exaltation by God as Lord is indicative of the fact that, for Paul, the risen Christ is associated with the same people with whom Jesus was identified in his death.

This is carried a step further in Hebrews 13:13 where Jesus' death is located "outside" the Holy City—the place where the leftovers of the cultic sacrifices were thrown. Interestingly enough, however, Jesus' death appears in this passage in connection with his exalted role and future history. The fact that the community of faith is to go to him "outside the camp" and "bear the abuse he endured" indicates that for the writer of Hebrews the risen Lord is to be located in the battles and heat of history, among the nonpersons of society.

The cross of Jesus underscores the dissimilarity between the lordship of Christ and the lords of this world. This is evident in what the New Testament calls the scandal of the cross. This scandal lies in the fact that the man Jesus, who came proclaiming the nearness of the kingdom of God "with mighty works and wonders and signs" (Acts 2:22), ended his life condemned as a blasphemer and a political rebel.

The God-Human

But the scandal of the death of Jesus is not so profound as the Easter faith, which affirms that the so-called blasphemous and rebellious preacher who was forsaken and abandoned by his God and Father had indeed risen from the grave by the power of God's Spirit, and that he had been enthroned as the Lord of heaven and earth. This identity between the risen Lord and the crucified Jesus led early Christians to formulate the doctrine of the incarnation: the affirmation that the poor and oppressed preacher who died on Calvary was none other than the Son of God.

Hence writers like Luke saw Jesus' entire life, from his annunciation to his death, from the perspective of the poor. The announcement of his birth is linked with the hope of the poor and disfranchised (Lk. 1:51ff.). He is born in a stable (Lk. 2:8) and his parents can only afford to fulfill the requirement of the law with the offering assigned to the poor (Lk. 2:24; Lev. 12:8). He locates his own mission among the poor, the captives, the sick, and the oppressed (Lk. 4:18). He calls the poor the heirs of the kingdom (Lk. 6:20). He seems to insinuate an identification with both the wounded man in the parable of the Good Samaritan (Lk. 10:30ff.; cf. 21–28, 38–41) and poor Lazarus in the story of the rich man who went to hell (Lk. 16:19ff.). He praises Zacchaeus for returning fourfold what he had stolen from the poor (Lk. 19:1–10), and points to his healing and heralding ministry as signs of the messianic age (Lk. 7:22–23).

The point behind Luke's theology (substantiated by the other Gospels and the epistles of Paul) is that Jesus is not a lord like Caesar, Herod, or the religious rulers of Israel. He does not rule as a despot or an oppressor, but as a liberating servant. He says, "I am among you as one who serves" (Lk. 22:27).

Just as the Gospels and the epistles look backward to the theological life and work of Jesus in the light of the Easter experience and arrive at the conclusion that the one who came and died had to be the incarnation of the Son of God, so the book of Revelation looks forward to the eschatological revelation of the risen Lord and anticipates his sovereign presence in the course of history. Nevertheless it maintains Jesus' identity as the one who was crucified.

In one of the most important visions of the book, John of Patmos is told that the only one who "is worthy to open the scroll" in the hands of the Father (which contains the secrets of history) is the Lion of the Tribe of Judah. This is a messianic title, which the author applies to the risen Lord. It is linked to his universal authority. Through his resurrection Jesus prevailed over sin and death. This means that he also conquered the evil one, Satan, and all earthly powers. The vision is one of royal power: Jesus is the conquering Lord; there is no other Lord who can match his authority in and over history. It is therefore very significant that, following the announcement of the conquering Lion of Judah, John sees a totally different image: "a Lamb standing, as though it had been slain" (Rev. 5:6). To be sure, it has "seven horns" and "seven eyes," implying that it has absolute universal authority. Even so, its fundamental characteristic is the fact that it was *slain*. Hence the new song, which the representatives of earth ("the four living creatures") and heaven ("the twenty-four elders") sing:

> Worthy art thou to take the scroll
>   and to open its seals,
> for thou wast slain, and by thy
>   blood didst ransom men for God,
> from every tribe and tongue and people and nation,
>   and hast made them a kingdom
>   and priests to our God,
> and they shall reign on earth [Rev. 5:9–10].

This apocalyptic vision and Christological doxology is meant to be a definite contrast between the lordship of Christ and that of the political and economic lords of this world, specifically between him and Caesar. The lordship of Christ is not grounded on military might, but on sacrificial love. It is not oppressive and emasculating, but creative and liberating. It is not totalitarian, but communal and fraternal. It facilitates the formation of a new world community on the basis of love and service.

Christ's authority has been earned through suffering and death. It has been invested in him by the Father who raised him from the dead by the power of the Spirit. The redeemed community shares in his reign on earth, but it does so by intercession and service to the Father ("a kingdom and priests," Rev. 5:10). The Father remains the ultimate mystery. Jesus reigns in his behalf and is forming the new world community for the Father's praise and service.

The cross of Jesus qualifies his role as the Christ of God and Lord of the world. It tells us why one man could be the anointed of God or be "God's faithful covenant partner" (Berkhof). Moreover it explains how it is that he could be given authority on heaven and earth and have sovereignty over all of life.

Throughout the New Testament we find multiple references to the suffering death of Jesus as having its root in the action of God himself. Paul says that God "did not spare his own Son, giving him up for all of humanity" (Rom. 3:25). Elsewhere Paul states that God made Jesus "to be sin for us" (2 Cor. 5:21). John's Gospel refers to him as the Lamb of God, implying that he is God's sin-offering for the world (1:29). At Pentecost, Peter states that Jesus' death was not an accident; he died in accordance with God's plan and foreknowledge (Acts 2:22).

Why did the Father offer the Son as a sin-offering? The answer to this question lies in Paul's assertion that "God was in Christ reconciling the world unto himself" (2 Cor. 4:17). Jesus was made to be sin in order to take upon himself the death that belonged to every human being (2 Cor. 5:14; Rom. 5, passim). Death, in this context, is the consequence of sin (Rom. 6:23). Sin is ungodliness and unrighteousness; death is separation from God's fellowship (Rom. 1:18-3:23). Since all have sinned, all are subject to death (Rom. 5:12). Accordingly Jesus died not just as the righteous and innocent Jew wrongly accused of being a blasphemer (Mk. 14:64; Mt. 26:65; Jn. 19:7). He died especially as the innocent *man* who took upon himself the *universal blasphemy* of humankind (Rom. 2:12ff.). Therefore he died the death of every human being (Rom. 5:6ff.).[6]

Paradoxically, in Jesus' death as the forsaken Son, God is revealed as passionately affected by suffering. God becomes accessible to humankind through the suffering of Jesus. In the words of Kazoh Kitamori, the cross reveals "the pain of God."[7] This leads Jon Sobrino to conclude that suffering is "a mode of being belonging to God."[8] We must not forget, however, Jürgen Moltmann's qualification that "the Father suffers with the Son, but not in the same way."[9] At the cross we see the Father suffering the death of the Son even as we see the Son suffering his forsakenness by the Father. Therefore we can appreciate the fact that the distress and trouble of Jesus on the cross (Mk. 14:33), the "loud cries and tears," which according to the epistle to the Hebrews (Heb. 5:7) accompanied his death, and his desperate quotation of Ps. 22:2, "My God, my God, why hast thou forsaken me?" (Mk. 15:34), were not simply expressions of Jesus' passion, but also of the Father's own suffering over the forsakenness of the Son.

The Pauline expression "God was in Christ" refers not just to the fact that God delivered the Son and became thereby personally accessible to humankind, but also to the fact that God participated in the passion and suffering of the Son for the world. God refused to be identified at the cross by his power and glory. Rather, God was revealed in the helplessness and weakness of Jesus. The cross was both the culmination and the test of the incarnation. It was the point where the self-emptiness of the Son was revealed in its crudest form. Therefore the experience of the cross must be seen as the foundation upon which the criterion for the judgment of the nations at the eschaton is established (Mt. 25:31ff.). Jesus Christ not only suffered on his own cross, but continues to suffer on the millions of human crosses around the world. These crosses are represented in the images of the orphan, the hungry, the naked, and the prisoner in the parable of the Judgment of the Nations. Thus the Father suffers with Jesus the pain of sinners and the outcast. The nations will be judged at the end of history on whether they acknowledged the crucified Lord hidden in the suffering of their oppressed members and saw them as the Father's suffering ones. Seen in this perspective, is it any wonder that in the New Testament many Greeks and Jews would consider the cross a "foolish" and "scandalous" event? Is it any wonder that in our day many continue to consider it a "foolish" and "scandalous" sign? It not only challenges all human strategies of salvation, but especially the traditional concepts of God (as power and impassive). Because of this, God cannot be manipulated by human reason or religious tradition, and the salvation of humanity cannot be bought or earned: it is given by grace alone and can be appropriated only by faith.

Thus Jesus' death and suffering *opens the way to God* and *makes God accessible to humanity. It also opens the way to humankind* and *makes men and women available to the kingdom of God.* The Easter community confessed Jesus not only as the Son of God, but also as the Son of man. This title, which has its origin in the Old Testament prophecy of Daniel, is not meant to portray Jesus as "an ideal superman."[10] Rather, it speaks of him as the true human because, like the Son of man of Daniel, he does not proceed from the chaos and deformity of human history. He has not been defiled and overtaken by the "beasts," which have dehumanized history (Dan. 7:1ff.). The Son of man is the symbol of humanity in its fullest potentiality. Therefore he proceeds from God (Dan. 7:13), the only one who can restore humanity to its creative potential. The Son of man is the revealer of a new humanity. He is not only the One from heaven but the Person of the future. He is the bearer of justice and liberation.

The fact that the New Testament Gospels refer to Jesus as the Son of man (either as a self-designation or as a title) is indicative of the intimate connection between the role that the Son of man is called to fulfill in Daniel and the role that Jesus fulfilled. He is seen as the embodiment of the Son of man: in his proclamation of the imminent manifestation of God's kingdom, in his commitment to justice and liberation, in his challenge to the powers of this world (represented in the Jewish religious structure and the Roman empire), and in his dedication to the liberation of history from its bondage and deformity.

However, unlike Daniel's Son of man, Jesus does not reveal his unique identity first and foremost in a cataclysmic event (coming with power in the clouds), but on the cross. He reveals his triumph in his weakness, his righteousness in his blasphemous death, his authentic humanity in his inhuman suffering, and his liberating power in his total surrender. He does not transcend the predicament of human history by avoiding its perils but, rather, by taking upon himself the infirmities and corruption of deformed humanity. He reveals and restores true humanity by dying as the representative of the nonhumans. As the crucified Son of man, says Moltmann, Jesus reveals his power

in the impotence of his grace, in the reconciling force of his passion, and the sovereignty of his self-emptying love. His kingdom lies in the inelegant fraternity with the poor, the prisoners, the hungry and the guilty. Those who have been exiled by the kingdoms of this world are transformed in his community into the bearers of the human kingdom of the Son of Man.[11]

The cross reveals Jesus as the man for others and in so doing locates authentic humanity in being at the service of others. This is why, in the New Testament, humanization is possible only through self-denial, obedience, and death. One must deny oneself, take up the cross, and follow Jesus through the wilderness of life (Mt. 16:24; Heb. 13:13). Men and women discover and recover their true humanity in the process of discipleship. In the same process they become aware of the fact that the Father has given Jesus sovereignty over the world (Mt. 28:18), that in his presence the lords of this world lose their dominion, and that those who are in communion with him not only participate in the hope of the kingdom (cf. Mt. 16:25ff.; Heb. 13:14), but are already its firstfruits (Rom. 8:23; Eph. 1:11–14, 22). In discipleship the crucified Son of man's eschatological identity is made apparent. Just as the crucified Son of man is the sign of authentic humanity, so his eschatological identity is a sign of the final redemption (and therefore of the absolute humanization) of humankind. This soteriological and eschatological reality is confirmed by the resurrection. The event of the resurrection is the authentication of the cross as the central sign of the Christian faith. Hence the experience of the resurrection involves sharing the sufferings of Jesus (Phil. 3:10), and suffering with him implies anticipating in life God's coming kingdom (1 Pet. 4:13–14).

The incarnation bears witness not only to the fact that God has become part of history in the man Jesus, but also to the fact that this man reveals authentic humanity. This fact led Karl Barth to state that "since God Himself became man," humanity has become "the measure of all things."[12] In the incarnation not only has God's true self been revealed, but also the true identity of women and men. This means that humankind discovers its authentic identity in Jesus Christ and comes to know the true God through him. The incarnation turns theology proper and anthropology into a Christological issue. It also makes contextualization an inevitable and indispensable process for a proper understanding and communication of the Christian faith.

For Christians contextualization is a theological necessity in the sense that it is not possible to understand God or humankind without the mediation of the God-human Jesus Christ. In the history of Jesus we discover the fullness of God and the fullness of humankind. "Human like [Jesus] can only be God," says Leonardo Boff. The opposite is no less true: divine like Jesus can only be the whole, faithful, and authentic human—the one and only person who has lived totally for others and for the Great Other (God).[13]

It follows from what has been said that, because of the incarnation, we cannot think of God as an abstract being, removed from human experience, faceless and personally unidentifiable. God has a historical identity: that of Jesus, the carpenter from Nazareth and the prophet from Galilee who suffered death on a cross and was raised from the dead by the Spirit. God is not absent from human history, but continues to be present in the Spirit of the risen Christ (2 Cor. 3:17) who indwells the life and witness of the church.

Missiological Implications of the Incarnation

This reality has several implications for the communication of the message of Jesus Christ in our contemporary world, and especially among its poverty-stricken, oppressed, and powerless majority. Indeed, it was out of the mystery of the incarnation, to which Jesus' resurrection and death bear witness, that the early Christian community began to understand its mission as participation in the continuing mission of Jesus Christ. The church is to follow the pattern of the incarnation because it is the body of Christ indwelled by his Spirit: the new people of the God whose Son became flesh in Jesus of Nazareth by the power of the Holy Spirit.

Experiencing the Incarnation in Contemporary History

The first missiological implication of the incarnation is that of a new and fresh experience of Jesus Christ from within the harsh reality of the hurt, destitute, and marginated of the earth. This proceeds from the fact that, in Jesus Christ, God became related with humanity in a radically new way. This meant that the Son of God humbled himself to the extent that he took the form of a servant and thus the identity of the poor, powerless, and oppressed. This identity reached its climax at the cross where Jesus died as a rejected criminal, suffering not only *for* but *with* humanity in the lowest and most horrible form of death.

If the cross is not only a part of reality, but, as Hebrews 13:13 reminds us, an ongoing challenge in the missional experience of the church; if, following the implications of this and other texts, Jesus Christ has not only died once and for all but continues to bear upon himself the affliction and oppression of all human beings and shall continue to do so until the day of the final redemption—if all of this is Christologically true, then it must also be true that Jesus Christ is today one with the outcast and oppressed of the earth. Wherever there is oppression, there is the Spirit of Christ incarnated in the *experience* of the oppressed; there is God contextualized in the present history of the nonpersons of society.

Insofar as Christ has assumed the identity of the hurt, he is one with them. We can affirm, accordingly, that Christ today is a black Southern African, a Latin American peasant, a Cambodian refugee, a homeless Palestinian, a persecuted Russian Jew, an orphan and homeless child, a humiliated female person. He is all of these things because he is truly human and truly God, the one for others, "God of the oppressed."[14]

It should not be a shock to us to hear it said that Christ is black or brown, persecuted or poor. For centuries he has been identified with Western symbols and categories. He has been thought of either as a white savior, the great European conquistador, the justifier of the rich and powerful, or the soother of the guilt-ridden conscience of oppressors. Why should it be such a shock to think of him as the poor man from Nazareth in whom the eternal Son of the Father has been revealed, the man who has been made Lord and Christ through his resurrection (Acts 2:36) in accordance with the Holy Spirit (Rom. 1:4). He is present among the naked and the prisoners, the thirsty and the hungry, the strangers and the sick (Mt. 25:42ff.). Why should we not emphasize the identity which, according to the Gospel of Luke, Jesus took upon himself at the outset of his ministry, affirming the Spirit's anointment to be the liberator of the captives, the healer of the blind, and the bearer of good news to the poor (Lk. 4:18)?

Nor should those who may not be black or brown, poor or persecuted feel threatened when they hear it said that Christ today is to be found among the wretched of the earth. For this does not mean that he has rejected people just because they happen to be white and thus benefit from the privilege of white domination, or that God has turned his face from them just because they happen to be middle and upper class and thus enjoy the material goods of life. God still loves the whole world (Jn. 3:16) and does not wish "that any should perish, but that all should reach repentance" (2 Pet. 3:9). Instead of feeling threatened, people should see in the Incarnate Word a reminder of the scandal of the gospel and the radical nature of conversion. The good news of salvation does not come via the wise and mighty but, rather, by way of the ignorant and downtrodden (1 Cor. 1:18ff.). Neither is the call to conversion an invitation to soothe guilty consciences, to reinforce one's privileged status, and to give one strength to continue to be part of an oppressive social system. It is, rather, to turn from personal sins and from alliances with the oppressive structures of this world, to join the struggle of God's kingdom against the forces of evil, of injustice, exploitation, and repression.

Contextualization and incarnation are basic to the Christian mission. The incarnation of Christ in the context of our racist, sexist, colonialistic, profit- and war-mongering, success-crazy, manipulative, and poverty-stricken world will enable Christians today to find Christ anew. But why should Christians need to find Christ anew?

Christians need to find Christ anew because, in the world in which we live, in this complex and confused "global village" (McLuhan) of which Christians are part, Christ's *real* identity has been hidden from the eyes of an overwhelming number of Christians. How else can we explain the fact that in his name millions are being subjected to a continuous process of humiliation, suffering, and death? In Africa, Asia, Latin America, and the Caribbean, for example, many nations are subjected to brutal military dictatorships and thousands upon thousands are suffering torture, imprisonment, harassment, and exile. These people live in a perpetual state of terror. This is justified in some countries that consider themselves Christian by a fanatic insistence that at stake is the defense of a "Christian civilization" from godless forces that want to destroy it. So, in the name of Christ, these "powers and principalities" are oppressing rather than liberating, murdering rather than protecting lives, separating human beings from their loved ones rather than reconciling them with one another; in short, they are inflicting horror rather than bringing hope.

The Christ propagated by the oppressive powers of this world is not the true Christ. It is, rather, the Antichrist of whom the New Testament speaks.[15] It is imperative, therefore, that Christians learn to differentiate the true Lord from the false lords of this world.

This differentiation can be done only when we discover Christ's real identity in our respective historical situations. Without such a discovery, it is possible neither to verify our knowledge of the biblical Christ nor communicate the gospel relevantly in an oppressed world. Since Christ is the heart of the gospel, it follows that effective evangelism is not possible where his liberating presence is not being experienced and his true identity is being distorted. In order to communicate him effectively to the world, we need to know experientially who he really is, where we may find him, and on what basis we can be related to him.

Evaluating Our Experience in the Light
of the History of Jesus Christ

Another missiological implication of the incarnation is the historical evaluation of our experiences. It has already been noted that in our world Jesus Christ has been distorted (we might add "beyond recognition") by oppressive powers and principalities.[16] How then can we be sure that the Christ we experience in the context of the poor and disfranchised is not another distortion of his true identity? How can we be sure that this is a *real* experience and not an illusion, the projection of an ideologized view of Christ? This is where the life and ministry of Jesus of Nazareth as witnessed by the New Testament documents need to be borne in mind as a test of the identity we discover when we experience him from "below."

The true identity of Jesus Christ is not determined by our cultural reality. The Christ we experience in the world of the disfranchised is not the product of the so-called culture of poverty. Nor is he an offspring of Marxist ideology, a consequence of the so-called scientific analysis of the historico-economic process of society, which detects its inherent contradictions and posits the means for its solution, guaranteeing thereby the ultimate liberation of the oppressed.

The true identity of Christ is, rather, defined by the life, ministry, and death of Jesus Christ as witnessed to by the New Testament. For the New Testament constitutes the basic source of information about his history. It also underscores its theological relevance for the church's mission and its historical significance for the confession of faith in his name. Any other basis for the identity of Christ is simply illusory and unsustainable.

The criterion of the life, ministry, and death of Jesus Christ permits us to identify him today. This criterion leads us not only to discover who he is (the

Lord and Savior of the oppressed), but where he is to be found today (among the poor, the powerless, and the oppressed), and what he is doing (healing their wounds, breaking their chains of oppression, demanding justice and peace, giving life, and imparting hope).

Transforming Reality

This brings us to a third missiological implication of the incarnation for the contextualization of the gospel in the world of the oppressed. Not only must our experience of Christ from below be tested against a past historical criterion (the life, ministry, and death of Jesus), and vice versa, but it must also be verified in the transformation of the present situations of the oppressed. This proceeds from the very character of Jesus Christ as Lord and Savior of the world. He did not suffer and die to leave things as they were but, rather, to bring a new order of *life*. He both proclaimed and embodied the kingdom of God, the new order of love, freedom, justice, and peace which aims at the total transformation of history and demands a radical conversion as condition for participation in it. To incarnate Christ in our world is to manifest the transforming presence of God's kingdom among the victims of sin and evil. It is to make possible a process of transformation from personal sin and corporate evil to personal and collective freedom, justice, and well-being.

Earlier I said that Christ continues to be present in history in the life and ministry of the Spirit. In the New Testament the Holy Spirit is presented as embodying the community of faith. The church is considered to be both the temple of the Spirit and the body of Christ. It is the body of Christ insofar as it is indwelt by the Spirit. Christ's transforming power is mediated by the work of the Spirit in the life and witness of the church. To incarnate Christ in our respective situations of oppression, the church, collectively and through its members, must become immersed in them and work for their transformation.

In the course of our discussion, we have stressed the relevance of context for theology, the dynamic nature of contextualization, its theological roots in the incarnation and the imperative of incarnating Christ in our respective contexts of oppression for a meaningful communication of the gospel in the world of the oppressed. The point, however, is not a matter of theological precision and missiological awareness but, rather, of commitment and practice. The real issue is whether or not we as Christians are willing to be immersed in the concrete situations of the disfranchised of our societies and witness to the lordship and saviorhood of Christ from within, a commitment that will have to be verified in our participation in the concrete transformation of these situations. Anything else is pure talk, and the kingdom of God "does not consist in talk but in power" (2 Cor. 4:20).

NOTES

1. "Context," *Webster's New Collegiate Dictionary,* ed. Henry Bosby Wolf (Springfield, Mass.: G. & C. Merriam Co., 1973), p. 245.

2. Cf., e.g., Daniel von Allmen, "The Birth of Theology: Contextualization as the Dynamic Element in the Formation of New Testament Theology," *International Review of Mission,* no. 253 (January 1975): 37–52.

3. Raymond Brown, *The Birth of the Messiah: A Commentary on the Infancy Narratives in Matthew and Luke* (Garden City, N.Y.: Doubleday Image Books, 1979), p. 26.

4. We are confronted here with the classical question of the deity and humanity of Jesus Christ. Is he "truly God and truly man," as the Chalcedonian Confession (A.D. 451) states? The answer of the New Testament seems to me undisputably affirmative. Yet the ontological language in which the Chalcedonian Confession is framed has been a source of problems for numerous scholars during the last several centuries. How can there be two natures in one person? The point of Chalcedon, however, is not explaining "how" but affirming *that* Jesus Christ is truly God and truly human, "without mixture, without change, without division, without separation." Chalcedon's concern is not philosophical, even though it speaks in ontological categories (the only ones available at the time), but soteriological. The deity and humanity of Christ are for Chalcedon essential "for our salvation." Here again Chalcedon does nothing more than reaffirm the witness of the New Testament. For a discussion of the background of the problem in Western theology (prior to the mid-1950s) and a sober clarification (from a Reform perspective) of the intent of the Chalcedon Confession, see G. C. Berkouwer, *The Person of Christ,* trans. from Dutch by John Vriend (Grand Rapids, Mich.: Wm. B. Eerdmans, 1954), pp. 21ff. A discussion of the problem in the light of its Alexandrian and Antiochian background with an attempted clarification for the Latin American Catholic context is to be found in Leonardo Boff, *Jesus Christ the Liberator: A Critical Christology for Our Time,* trans. from Portuguese by Patrick Hughes (Maryknoll, N.Y.: Orbis Books, 1978), pp. 187ff.; and in Jon Sobrino, *Christology at the Crossroads: A Latin American Approach,* trans. from Spanish by John Drury (Maryknoll, N.Y.: Orbis Books, 1978), pp. 328ff.

More recently, H. Berkhof has attempted to move beyond the language of Chalcedon and its fundamental assertion through a Christology that stresses the humanity of Jesus Christ as the basis for his unity with God. He states that "the Chalcedonian formula becomes much more intelligible if we remove it from the framework of the static notion of 'nature' that governed the thinking of the Greek church fathers and that of many centuries after them. The New Testament speaks a different language, also, when it speaks of the duality of the structure of the being of Jesus' person. It does not speak of the two structures as being found statically on top of each other but as historically following each other. See Acts 2:22–36; Rom. 1:3f.; Phil. 2:8–11; Tim. 3:16; Heb. 5:7–9. The New Testament shows us a history in which the man Jesus, because of his total obedience even to death, may share in the life and rule of God. In this history, Jesus transcends the boundaries of what we understand as 'human.' However, he does not lay aside the 'human'; but, in the way of a progressive obedience and glorification, he exhibits more and more new, and, to us, unknown dimensions of the divinely intended humanity. One who wants to express that comes understandably and dangerously close to dualistic-sounding formulations like 'God-man' and 'two natures' " (*Christian Faith,* trans. from Dutch by Sierd Wovdstra [Grand Rapids, Mich.: Wm. B. Eerdmans, 1979], p. 288).

Berkhof attempts to overcome the latter problem by speaking of Jesus only as the Son of God and God's faithful covenant partner. He argues that "that which is entirely unique in Jesus' relationship to us is as a rule not expressed with the word 'God' but with names like: lord, savior, firstfruits." Moreover, the word "God" does not express "as a rule . . . that which is entirely unique in Jesus' relation to us." Nor is this notion of "God becoming man" an expression "which is . . . derived from the New Testament. There the terminology is that of God's *sending* of his son, and of the *Word* (God's creative speaking) which became flesh and, there, a few times, on account of the intimate union of God and man in him, Jesus is called 'God' (. . . John 20:28; Tit. 2:13; and I John 5:20), but then only for the purpose of capturing in an accentuated formula Jesus' uniqueness and instrumentality relative to us." He further argues that "what is at stake in these passages is Christ '*the* representative of God in the world and in history . . . himself the bearer of the divine office. . . .' What we have here is a covenantal functionality which, only in this way, agrees with the numerous statements in which Jesus distinguishes himself from God, or is distinguished from God by the writers" (ibid., p. 290).

Berkhof's insistence on taking the Old Testament "covenantal" and "Sonship" language as a basis for a Christology (from "behind") that is neither bound to the pitfalls of classical formulations (from "above") or more recent critical Christologies (from "below") is well taken. It certainly does more justice to biblical language and overcomes the abstractions of Chalcedon. Its "functionality" makes more sense to modern (Western) people for whom abstract formulations make little sense. (For a similar attempt, from the perspective of a biblical scholar, see John A. T. Robinson, *The Human Face of God* [London: SCM Press, 1973], chaps. 5 and 6.) Interestingly enough, in this effort Berkhof comes quite close to Latin American (liberation) Christological thought (see especially Sobrino, *Christology,* pp. 386–88). Like Sobrino and Robinson, Berkhof takes very seriously the humanity of Jesus. Indeed, in so doing he pushes to the limits the *vere homo* of Chalcedon.

My problem with Berkhof is his tendency toward a one-sided Christology. He does not feel comfortable with the other side of the Chalcedonian affirmation: the *vere Deus.* His response to the problem of language in the Chalcedonian Confession takes us back to Schleiermacher (for whose Christology Berkhof shows a qualified admiration; cf. *Faith,* p. 291; Friedrich Schleiermacher, *The Christian Faith,* vol. 2 [New York: Harper & Row, 1928], par. 94). Like the latter, Berkhof concentrates his Christology on Jesus the man and underscores his likeness to the rest of humanity. However, he locates the uniqueness of Jesus, not in an abstract "God-consciousness" but, rather, in faithfulness to God. (Here Berkhof overcomes the pitfall of Schleiermacher's German idealistic categories by working within a covenantal framework.) However, Berkhof avoids the startling assertion of the doctrine of the incarnation, namely, that, in the man Jesus, in this particular man, God became part of history *while remaining true to himself.* Thus, in spite of his concern to keep close to biblical faith, Berkhof seems more prepared to accommodate Christology to the Western technological (functional) mind-set, which has little patience with "mystery," than to explain the doxological language of faith that permeates the biblical message. Could this not be the reason why he makes such a painstaking effort to demonstrate bibli-cally that the designation of Jesus as God is neither exegetically valid nor theologically correct?

Berkhof's admirable effort to show a more biblical way to Christology is creative and stimulating, but not thoroughly convincing. For in the New Testament not only are there direct (even if few) references to Jesus as God, as he is quick to admit, but also passages where Jesus is indirectly called God. (Cf. for instance the prologue of John's Gospel, which identifies Jesus with the Word and the latter with God.) Rather than trying to make these direct and indirect references to the identification of Jesus with God agree with those passages that stress the difference between Jesus and the Father (as if doxological language would have to meet the test of scientific logic in order for its truth to be verifiable) through sophisticated exegetical "maneuverings," what is needed is a model that explains the New Testament claim of Jesus as God and human without resorting, on the one hand, to the two-nature scheme, or, on the other, to a one-sided formulation.

It seems to me that the unity of Jesus with God can be better explained with a "trinitarian framework in an eschatological key." In the New Testament the deity of Jesus is expressed in the context of his particular relationship with the Father and the Spirit. Jesus was possessed by the Spirit in his ministry and lived a life of total depen-dence on the Father. As James Dunn has noted, Jesus "experienced God as Father in prayer" and "found God as Spirit in mission" (*Jesus and the Spirit* [London: SCM Press, 1975], p. 90).

It is as Son that Jesus is called God, and his Sonship is declared in the resurrection "according to the Spirit." It is within the framework of the trinitarian fellowship (the tri-unity of God) that Jesus is called God, and this unity is affirmed in the resurrec-tion. As Pannenburg has well stated: ". . . Jesus' unity with God . . . is . . . decided retroactively from the perspective of Jesus' resurrection for the whole of Jesus' hu-man existence on the one hand . . . and thus also for God's eternity, on the other. Apart from Jesus' resurrection, it would not be true that from the very beginning of his earthly way, God was one with this man." Hence we can only perceive the unity of Jesus with God "from the perspective of its result, from the perspective of Jesus' historical reality. Jesus is no synthesis of human and divine of which we can only see the human side in the historical Jesus. Rather, as this man, Jesus is God." In other words, "as *this* man . . . Jesus is not just man, but from the perspective of his resur-rection from the dead . . . he is one with God and thus is himself God" (Wolfhart Pannenburg, *Jesus, God and Man,* trans. Lewis Wilkins and Duane A. Priebe [Lon-don: SCM Press, 1968], pp. 321, 322–23).

By limiting himself to a perspective "from before," Berkhof is not able to allow the eschatological starting point ("from ahead") of the Easter community to inform his own Christology significantly. Moreover, he condemns himself to the failure of all Christologies that try to explain the unity of Jesus with God from the perspective of either his humanity or his deity. Above all, he does not deal adequately with the real, decisive point of the Christian doctrine of the incarnation, expressed so vividly in classical Christological doxologies like Chalcedon, namely, that in Jesus, God became one with us while remaining true to himself, and that through his life and death he became one with the Father while remaining truly human, thus enabling us to become one with God. The incarnation is the doctrine that witnesses to this twofold reality: God becoming human, and men and women becoming divine.

I conclude this note with a summary statement from Boff, with whom I stand in full agreement: "If we accept in faith that Jesus was a human being who could relate to God and be in God to the point of being his Son (i.e., the personal identity of Jesus with the eternal Son), and, if we accept in faith that God can empty himself of his own self (cf. Phil. 2:7) in such a way that he fills the complete openness of Jesus to the point of becoming himself human, then we accept and profess what Christians profess and accept as the Incarnation: the unconfounded, immutable, indivisible, and inseparable unity of God and humanity in one and the same Jesus Christ; God remains God and the human being radically human. Jesus was the creature that God wanted and so created that he could exist totally in God, so created that the more he became united to God, the more he became himself, that is, human.

"Hence, Jesus is truly human and also truly God. The inverse is also valid: . . . God becomes more himself the more he is in Jesus and assumes his reality. . . . The man-Jesus is God himself who enters the world and becomes history. . . (John 1:14). God undergoes *becoming* while losing nothing of his being. When God *becomes* and makes himself history and becoming, there appears the one we call Jesus Christ, Word Incarnate" (*Jesus Christ,* pp. 197–98).

5. José Comblin, *Jesus of Nazareth: Meditations on His Humanity* (Maryknoll, N.Y.: Orbis Books, 1976), p. 15.

6. Pannenburg, *Jesus,* p. 263.

7. Kazoh Kitamori, *Teología del dolor de Dios,* trans. into Spanish by Juan José Coy from *Theology of the Pain of God,* 5th English ed. of the Japanese original (Salamanca: Ediciones Sígueme, 1974), passim.

8. Cf. Jon Sobrino, *Christology,* p. 195.

9. Jürgen Moltmann, *The Crucified God,* trans. R. A. Wilson and John Bowden (London: SCM Press, 1974), p. 203.

10. Jürgen Moltmann, *El hombre: antropología cristiana en los conflictos del presente,* trans. from German by José M. Mauleón (Salamanca: Ediciones Sígueme, 1976), p. 153. English trans.: *Man: Christian Anthropology in the Conflicts of the Present* (Philadelphia: Fortress Press, 1974). According to J. Jeremias the title "Son of man" belongs to the tradition of the sayings of Jesus and can be traced back to Jesus himself. Cf. *Teología del Nuevo Testamento,* vol. 1, trans. Constantino Ruiz-Garrido (Salamanca: Ediciones Sígueme, 1974), p. 310. English trans. by John Bowden: *New Testament Theology* (London: SCM Press, 1971).

11. Moltmann, *El hombre,* p. 153.

12. Cf. Karl Barth, *Against the Stream: Shorter Post-War Writings 1946–52* (New York: Philosophical Library, 1954), p. 35.

13. Cf. Boff, *Jesus Christ,* pp. 178ff.

14. Cf. James Cone, *God of the Oppressed* (New York: Seabury Press, 1975), pp. 108ff.

15. Cf. the two papers on "Cristo y anticristo en la proclamación" by René Padilla and Valdir R. Steuernagel in *América Latina y la evangelización en los años 80,* ed. Fraternidad Teológica Latinoamericana (Mexico, D.F.: FTL, 1981), pp. 219–31, 233–47.

16. On the concept of "powers and principalities," see chaps. 2 and 4.

2

Sin and Salvation in an Oppressed Continent

Sin and salvation are two fundamental themes in the communication of the gospel. On the one hand, the gospel is a *saving* message; on the other, it is a message addressed to a *sinful* world.

Neither sin nor salvation appears in a vacuum, however. They are not abstract concepts but concrete realities. To be sure, our knowledge of them is informed by revelation, particularly the witness of Holy Scripture. Still, the gospel can be communicated relevantly only when the scriptural witness about sin and salvation is understood in concrete historical situations.

In this chapter I propose to analyze these two themes in the context of Latin America. There are at least two justifications for choosing this specific context. The first is obvious: as a Latin American Christian it is natural that I should be concerned with the content of the gospel that is communicated in this region. But there is a deeper justification: the fact that Latin America is a region where sin has revealed some of its cruelest expressions, where the proclamation of the gospel in general, and its salvific content in particular, has often been distorted beyond recognition. Since Latin America is the one "Christian" section of the third world, a discussion of sin and salvation in its context should be relevant not only for those of us who live and work among its people but also for those who are located in similar historical situations.

Sin: Its Manifestation and Consequence

In the Bible sin is not a topic for speculation; it is a question of relationships. It manifests itself in the relationships between humankind and God, neighbors, women and men, and the environment. We cannot speak of sin without referring to its consequences. The Bible presents sin as a destructive force that thwarts and deforms human life. Accordingly the problem of sin cannot be understood and explained; it is possible only to register its presence and its consequences.[1]

Disobedience to the Lordship of God: Revelation of God's Wrath

From the first book of the Bible to the last, sin is described as disobedience to the lordship of God. Whether it be the first human couple (Gen. 3:1ff.), Cain (Gen. 4:3ff.), the nations at Babel (Gen. 11:1-9), Sodom and Gomorrah (Gen. 18:16ff.), or Jacob's sons (Gen. 37:2ff.), the kings of Israel and the people themselves (e.g., Jer. 2:4, 11ff.; 3:6ff.; 15:6; 17:20ff.), the Jews of Jesus' day (Jn. 8:42ff.), the philosophers in Athens (Acts 17:16-32), the principalities and powers of which Paul speaks (Eph. 1:21-22; 3:10; 6:12; Col. 1:16; 2:15), or the totalitarian state of Revelation 13 (the beast), the case is always the same: disobedience to the Lord of history. Disobedience is the open rejection of the Word of God. Those who disobey become deaf, their minds are closed, they refuse to dialogue with God. Since they do not listen to God, since they refuse to follow God's instructions, since it is the same to them whether God speaks to them or not, it is natural that they should distort revealed truth (Rom. 1:18). They are obsessed with themselves and they obey their own capricious desires and pride; they give greater glory to the creature than to the Creator.

For this reason a basic consequence of sin is the "wrath of God" (Rom. 1:18). This phrase expresses the divine displeasure and indignation over human disobedience. This displeasure is evidenced, on the one hand, in the state of death into which human beings have fallen (Eph. 2:1-3). Death signifies separation from the fellowship (and direction) of God. To speak of death is not only to refer to the physical separation of the human body from the world of the living (the end of corporeal activity), but also to the absence of the divine presence from human life. To live in a state of death is to live far from God, to be alone in the world. Hence Paul associates wrath with unbridled conduct—to live under the control of one's desires, will, and fleshly thoughts (the "I" apart from God) (Eph. 2:3). Because women and men did not recognize God as God, they were given up to (or allowed to fall into) "the lusts of their heart to impurity. . . to dishonorable passions . . . a base mind and to improper conduct" (Rom. 1:24, 26, 28). This situation of death in which all human beings find themselves immersed (Jn. 3:36) is but the prelude to the coming wrath that will fall on all the "disobedient." It will be an experience of "tribulation and distress" that will be carried out in God's "just judgments" (Rom. 2:5-9, JB). This tribulation and distress represent eternal separation from fellowship with God. Sin, insofar as it is disobedience to God's lordship, brings as a consequence present and future separation from fellowship with God. Therefore to disobey God is to *reject* God's love, and to suffer the wrath of God is *to be left outside* the sphere of God's kingdom of love.

Injustice and Alienation

In the second place, sin means injustice. It is the opposite of God's dealings with creation. God is just in all judgments. Human beings are by nature unjust in all their relationships. Sin represents a deliberately aggressive action against others. If disobedience implies rejection of the lordship of God, injustice signifies hatred and repudiation of the neighbor. Sin, then, is every unjust act—every lack of consideration for the well-being of one's neighbor, every insult to human dignity, every act of violence done by one to someone else.

For this reason Paul calls wickedness every act of "fornication," "perversity," "envy," "murder," "strife," "deceit," and "malignity" (acting in bad faith) (Rom. 1:29). He adds that gossipers, "slanderers, haters of God, insolent, haughty, boastful, inventors of evil, disobedient to parents, foolish, faithless, heartless, ruthless" (Rom. 1:29ff.) are also unjust. This catalogue of vices has the characteristic of reflecting aggressive conduct toward others. Injustice is a distortion of the "just" truth of God. God's justice is distorted when the only thing that matters in life is what one desires, and not the good of others. From that moment everything that results is offensive judgments (actions). These offensive judgments are synthesized and summarized in the abuse of the weakest neighbor—the poor (the widow, the orphan, the foreigner, the oppressed) (Jer. 22:3, 13–17). The prophets, therefore, described the true knowledge of God in terms of doing justice to the poor (Jer. 22:16; Mic. 6:8).

Injustice alienates people; it makes them strangers to themselves; it leaves them morally deformed; it makes them deviate from their vocation as God's creatures. Sin is represented by traveling on the wrong road, wandering without a set course; it is conduct that is completely out of place and disordered. So it is that sin obliterates the original goal of humankind, which was created in the image and likeness of God (to live for eternity), dissipates the deep meaning of that eternal life (to serve the neighbor in love), and makes men and women lose the confidence and assurance that they were given in creation.

We see this truth clearly illustrated in the biblical story of the first human couple. According to Genesis, Adam was given "the breath of life" (Gen. 2:7). He was placed in a garden with many fruit trees from which he could take his daily sustenance. In this garden was placed the "tree of life" (Gen. 2:9), the fruit of which could give him eternal life. Adam's life was incomplete, however, and God gave him a companion with whom to share his life and ministry as steward of the earth (Gen. 2:20ff.; 1:27–30). Their vocation was not to live for themselves, but for God (in the cultivation of the earth). They were created male and female in order to serve God in mutual love. God provided them with the resources necessary for a full life. The first human couple, then, moved within the garden with confidence and assurance, two persons who had nothing to fear, who felt no anxiety, who were not ashamed of themselves. With the entrance of sin, death also entered in all its dimensions (Gen. 3:3, 8ff.). Adam and Eve not only suffered separation from God (Gen. 3:23–24) and the threat of an eventual physical separation from each other (Gen. 3:19), but their sin also brought on the cursing of the earth and affected the future of their own descendants.

Thus sin is an act of violence not only against one's neighbor, but also against oneself. It brings about total alienation of women and men—because it cuts them off from their neighbors, from creation, from their Creator, and from themselves.

Unbelief and Idolatry

In the third place, sin means unbelief. Those who reject the kingdom of God and turn their backs on their neighbor do this because they do not believe in God. Faith is an ethical question, not an intellectual one. It is commitment substantiated in daily life. To believe in God is to do God's will. Not to believe is to refuse to follow God's precepts. This refusal results from what Paul calls being "futile in their thinking" and having their "senseless mind darkened" (Rom. 1:21), which prevents people from being consistent with themselves as they see God's glory reflected in their surroundings but do not honor God as God. Their minds have been made senseless; their hearts have lost all capacity for discernment. Why? Because they wanted to know more than God; they were not happy to be creatures—they wanted to take God's place (Rom. 1:22–23). Unbelief is no confidence, no openness, no dedication to the other due to a superconcentration on oneself (vanity), a lack of sensitivity toward one's neighbor (egoism), and closed-mindedness (foolishness).

Unbelief leads to idolatry. No confidence in God based on *self*-confidence leads people to create their own gods. Paul says that since humankind was insensitive to the glory of God reflected in nature, it ended up giving glory to human images (Rom. 1:23). The absence of God leads to the invention of gods. Idols are false gods because they conceal the truth, namely, the absence of God. Idols are thus projections of human vanity and its deifying presumption.

The first step toward reestablishing faith in the true God is the destruction of false gods. One must become *a*theistic (denying the existence of the gods) in order to become a believer in the true God. This was the battle raged by the prophets of Yahweh against idolatry; the idols represented Israel's no confidence in Yahweh. To follow Yahweh it was necessary to become atheistic, that is, to deny that the gods had any real power. This is the logic behind the Second Commandment (Ex. 20:4) and the reason for Jesus' insisting on the spiritual reality of God (Jn. 4:20). The true God is above and beyond the gods, is not the fruit of the imagination, and therefore cannot be manipulated. In order to believe in this God, it is not sufficient to be religious or to renounce the gods. One must recognize that the living God is above all a mystery, and thus qualitatively different from men and women.

As unbelief, sin is the practical denial of the reality of God; it is the logical conclusion of disobedience and injustice. Therefore it leads to the creation of false gods. Idolatry is the means by which people project their pride and manipulate their neighbor. It is the culmination of their corruption and alienation.

Personal Action, Collective Guilt

Disobedience, injustice, and unbelief are not generic concepts; they are personal actions. The Bible teaches that sin is a reality in the life of every human being. Paul, quoting various psalms, states it radically and emphatically:

> None is righteous, no, not one;
> No one understands, no one seeks for God.
> All have turned aside, together they have gone wrong;
> No one does good, not even one.
> Their throat is an open grave,
> They use their tongues to deceive.
> The venom of asps is under their lips.
> Their mouth is full of curses and bitterness.
> Their feet are swift to shed blood,
> In their paths are ruin and misery,
> And the way of peace they do not know.
> There is no fear of God before their eyes [Rom. 3:10b–18].

The reality of this affirmation is manifest in daily experience. We are sinners because we sin, not necessarily because the Bible says so. History itself confirms the reality of sin as a universal human experience.

To say that sin is personal, however, is not to say that its consequences are limited to the individual. In biblical faith, that which is personal is never individualistic, isolated from others. On the contrary, that which is personal is intrinsically related to that which is collective. Men and women find their personality in society. For this reason, too, every personal action affects the community. Personal sin brings with it collective guilt.

The Old Testament is full of examples of collective guilt due to the sin of individuals. One of the most prominent cases is that of Achan, son of Carmi. He took advantage of the spoils of the battle for Jericho and stole money and a mantle against Yahweh's specific command. As a consequence of this personal sin, "the anger of the Lord burned against the people of Israel" (Josh. 7:1) and he did not "turn from his burning anger" (Josh. 7:26) until Achan and *his whole family and his property* had been totally destroyed. The sin of one involved the others.

Paul employs a similar argument in the Adam analogy. He says, "As sin came into the world through one man and death through sin, and so death spread to all . . . because all . . . sinned" (Rom. 5:12). The sin of one man affected all, because "all" were represented already in the one. Therefore guilt and condemnation have passed to all. All are guilty of sin, not just because they personally sin, but because they are part of Adam. Thus sin is both personal and social.

Structural Action, Personal Responsibility

The opposite is equally true, however. Sin is structural as well as personal. It is structural in the sense that it answers to the "logic" behind collective behavior.[2] Society is not the sum total of its members; it is composed of a complex network of interpersonal, cultural, and institutional relationships. The totality of these relationships makes up the personality of society. The community, at the same time that it socializes personal actions, generates its own actions, the fruit of the interests of the totality in all its relationships. This is why in the Bible there are examples of both personal sins and corporate sins. The Old Testament gives us not only the spiritual history of the Israelites but also the history of Israel as a nation; it not only speaks to us of men and women, but also of kingdoms, peoples, tribes, clans, and families.

Institutions disobey God, act unjustly, and set themselves up as gods. This is clearly demonstrated in the history of Israel. It is also evident in the secular state that, according to the New Testament, has been ordained by God to execute justice (Rom. 13:1ff.). Sometimes, however, the state rebels against the sovereignty of God (blaspheming God's name), oppresses the just and the innocent, and sets itself up as a god (Rev. 13:1-8). The same thing happens with what Paul calls the "principalities and powers" that operate in "heavenly places" (Eph. 1:21; 2:2; 3:10; 6:12ff.).[3]

Structural sin affects people. When the government of a nation becomes demonic, its citizens suffer the consequences and bear the responsibility of the sins of the nation. Thus, for example, Isaiah feels the weight of the sin of his people and considers himself dead before the presence of Yahweh (Isa. 6:5). The same thing is true of Paul in the face of Israel's disobedience (Rom. 9:3ff.). We could cite numerous additional cases in which the sin of a people, a tribe, or a family decisively affects the life of its members. Therefore Paul warns, "Do not be deceived; God is not mocked, for whatever a man sows, that he will also reap" (Gal. 6:7). This is applied both to the individual and to society. Just as personal sin affects the community, social sin also affects the individual.

Salvation: Its Basis and Effects

Because sin is a universal problem, its eradication must be radical. It is impossible to speak of a purely personal salvation, because that would leave social sin intact. Nor is it possible to speak exclusively of social salvation, because that would leave untouched the personal root of sin. Salvation, to be truly effective, must be salvation "of the soul and of the body, of the individual and society, of humanity and of 'the whole creation . . . groaning in travail together' (Rom. 8:22)."[4] I understand this affirmation to be precisely what the Bible teaches; and it is what I shall attempt to demonstrate in the second part of this chapter.

The Gospel, Saving Power

From the perspective of the New Testament, salvation is grounded in the gospel, which comes from God (Rom. 1:1). The gospel is the good news of God's merciful action for the salvation of the world. Therefore Paul describes it as God's saving energy (Rom. 1:16). By this he means that the gospel is God's most creative historical event. Indeed it reaffirms God's redemptive purpose for the world and opens up a new horizon of hope and fullness of life.

The gospel must be understood in the light of its Old Testament heritage. The God who sends the good news is the same God who in the Old Testament is revealed as Israel's creator and redeemer (Isa. 43:14-15); the one who freed Israel from Pharaoh's hand and made them a holy people in order to give light to the nations, open the eyes of the blind, and set the captives free (Isa. 42:6-7). In Israel's liberation the pattern is established for the re-creation of humanity. It confirms Abraham's inheritance and the historical calling of his descendants. Abraham's call is seen to be God's answer to the chaos of the nations (Gen. 12:1-2). In its experience of salvation Israel discovers God the creator. Thus the Old Testament views creation from the perspective of redemption (cf. Pss. 74, 89, 93, 95, 135, 136; Isa. 44:24; Amos 4:12; 5:8f.; 10:16; 27:5; 32:17; Mal. 2:10). It is the beginning of a great eschatological project—the kingdom of God. Sin is the great disorder that tries to frustrate the work of God; salvation is the re-creation that overcomes sin and regains control of God's great plan.

Israel's liberating and re-creating memorial is the foretaste of the gospel of Jesus Christ. It is a foretaste in that God's plan has to do with all humanity, not with one people alone (cf., e.g., Isa. 19:18ff.). The whole of history—not the history of Israel alone—constitutes the sphere of the kingdom of God. This requires the presence of a new Moses—one who would be greater than Abraham and even greater than Adam himself. These are the great themes dealt with in the epistles to the Hebrews and the Romans, and in the four Gospels: Jesus Christ is the final, definitive, redemptive Word that God has communicated to the world. In him and through him Israel's mission is fulfilled and universalized. Jesus Christ is, then, the gospel of God. He is the center and the secret of salvation: "And there is salvation in no one else, for there is no other name under heaven given among men by which we must be saved" (Acts. 4:12). Our question, then, is this: What is the meaning of this salvation that God provides in the person and work of Jesus Christ? Without attempting to exhaust the topic, we may outline a threefold response.

Salvation as Obedience to the Kingdom

Salvation implies, in the first place, obedience to the kingdom of God. Some may be surprised at this statement, because in many Christian circles obedience is customarily associated with the *conditions* for salvation and not with its *content*. It is said that in order to be saved it is necessary to obey the gospel. With the help of the traditional translation of Romans 1:5 ("obedience to the faith," KJV), it is thought that obedience is a means by which faith is expressed. What has not been taken into account is that for the apostle Paul obedience is already the fruit of the saving grace of the gospel, and that faith is not conditioned obedience but, rather, obedience is itself faith in action. A more careful translation of Romans 1:5 would bring forth this fact. Thus the RSV translates the same phrase as the "obedience of faith."[5] Of even greater importance than the grammatical construction of the text is the Old Testament background of the concept of "obedience" and the way the apostle Paul uses it in Romans.[6]

In the Old Testament tradition, to obey means to listen to, or to pay attention to the Word of God. The Old Testament considers obedience a blessing because it is the foundation of the Covenant between Yahweh and the people. To listen to Yahweh, to pay attention to God's voice, is to follow God's statutes or to do God's will. Thus obedience is the basic motif of the exodus: "Let my people go that they may serve me" is Moses' favorite appeal to Pharaoh. Service, in this context, implies worship, and worship means the response of love to, and celebration of, Yahweh's word of liberation. When Israel arrives at Sinai, the first thing Yahweh says to the people is "You have seen what I did to the Egyptians, and how I bore you on eagles' wings and brought you to myself. Now, therefore, if you will obey my voice and keep my covenant, you shall be my own possession . . ." (Ex. 19:4–5). The "if you will obey my voice" of this passage is not a condition to becoming Yahweh's "own possession"; rather, it is the characterization of *being* Yahweh's possession. Being the Covenant People *is* living as a redeemed people—in obedience (in submission and in a state of alert) to the Word of God. Israel must be distinguished from the other nations by its obedience to Yahweh. The liberation from Egypt is a sign of their special relationship with God. Israel will be the redeemed people that obeys the voice and follows the precepts of the Lord of history.

The problem, of course, is that Israel does not follow Yahweh's ways; they rebel against Yahweh; they refuse to obey God. The means of grace given to them to enable them to follow Yahweh are insufficient to resolve the basic problem, what Jeremiah calls deceit and corruption of heart (Jer. 17:9). Israel will need, therefore, a new heart on which the law of Yahweh can be written (Jer. 31:33). Then obedience to Yahweh will be possible.

The New Testament tells us that this new heart is now possible through the perfect obedience of Jesus Christ: "For as by one man's disobedience many were made sinners, so by one man's obedience many will be made righteous" (Rom. 5:19). Jesus' obedience (Heb. 5:8–9) makes it possible for all those who follow him to break with the control of disobedience that produces injustice and to submit themselves to the obedience of the kingdom of God and its justice (Rom. 6:16). By the saving grace of Jesus Christ we acquire the gift of obedience to the Lord of history; we are enabled to submit ourselves to the Word of God and to be directed by the Holy Spirit (Rom. 8:1ff.; 15:18–19; 16:25–26).

Obedience to the kingdom of God is, then, the fruit of the grace revealed in Jesus Christ. It is not a precondition to the experience of salvation, but part and parcel of that salvation. Thus it is not only one of its *visible* fruits, but also its historical *confirmation*. Jesus said, "Not everyone who says to me, 'Lord, Lord,' shall enter the kingdom of heaven, but he who does the will of my Father who is in heaven" (Mt. 7:21). The apostle John, for his part, states that "by this we may be sure that we know him, if we keep his commandments . . . whoever keeps his word, in him truly love for God is perfected. By this we may be sure that we are in him . . ." (1 Jn. 2:3, 5–6a). Further on he adds, "Little children, let no one deceive you. He who does right is righteous, as he is righteous" (1 Jn. 3:7). All these texts underline the fact that salvation in Christ is confirmed by obedience to God's lordship (following Christ and putting his Word into practice). This is what Paul calls the "work of faith" (1 Thess. 1:3), and James, faith that works (Jas. 2:18ff.). In other words, the salvation that is manifest in the gift of obedience is confirmed by obedient action.

Salvation as Justification and Liberation

In the second place, salvation means justification and liberation. According to the apostle Paul the good news of salvation includes the revelation of God's justice (Rom. 1:17).[7] Justice is not a secondary topic in God's economy. We learn in the Old Testament that justice is a fundamental question in God's relationship to humanity (e.g., Mic. 6:8). God deals with all creatures on the basis of justice and expects just dealings among them. Upon this principle has God established human society. When there is not justice, when there is not consideration for others, what rules is egoism and, therefore, injustice.[8]

The justice that God reveals in the gospel is grounded in grace (Rom. 3:21–22). It lifts up the fallen ones and restores them to a right relationship with their neighbors. It is a redemptive justice, revealed in the person and work of Jesus Christ (Rom. 3:22), the just man who took the place of the unjust and was made thereby the justice of God (2 Cor. 5:21). Thus the gospel justifies every sinner who trusts in Jesus Christ, making just the unjust, straightening out their lives and changing their relationship with God, their neighbors, and all of nature.

The justification that comes through faith in Christ (Rom. 1:17; 3:22; 5:1) frees sinners from their guilty conscience and from their state of death (Rom. 8:1–2). The gospel proclaims the forgiveness (or cancellation) of every debt (of sin). To be in Christ is to be free from the power of sin and death. Justified and liberated, women and men are able to dedicate themselves freely and unconditionally to the cause of justice. Thus justification and forgiveness, far from being exhausted in the gracious action of a transcendent God, are confirmed by the practice of justice and the liberation of others.

Salvation as justification and liberation from sin is not just a personal spiritual experience. Justification and liberation are not exhausted in our personal practice of justice (Mic. 6:8) nor in the forgiveness that we proffer to those who offend us (Lk. 11:4). "As evil works both in personal life and in exploitative social structures which humiliate humankind, so God's justice manifests itself both in the justification of the sinner and in social and political justice. As guilt is both individual and corporate, so God's liberating power changes both persons and structures."[9]

To be sure, this dimension of justice and liberation can be confirmed only eschatologically, since history is conflictive and frequently obscures the truth. Social and political justice and the structural and cosmic liberation implicit in salvation are not clearly discernible in history. We must seek their verification in the future—the distant future (the definitive consummation of the kingdom of God) and the near future (social and political events that clear up the fog of doubts that surround our frail human existence and keep alive hope in the emergence of a new and just world). The near future is always a foretaste of the distant future. We do not have to wait for the consummation of the kingdom in order to discern its justice in the social and political sphere and the presence of its liberating power in social structures. The Holy Spirit is showing us already signs of social and political justice and structural liberation in many places and situations. We know that an event is a sign of the justice of God when it enables the poor and oppressed to experience a measure of economic, sociocultural, and political liberation. We know that liberation is "evangelical" when it tears down the structures that perpetuate divisions among peoples, among men, women, and children, and between the human family and nature—divisions that promote hate, hostility, and resentment, instead of love, well-being, and freedom. Every movement that dignifies human life, that promotes equitable economic relations, and that encourages solidarity among individuals and peoples can be said to be, therefore, a manifestation (though partial) of the saving power of the gospel.[10]

Salvation as Reconciliation and Communion

What was said above introduces a third implication of salvation. Since sin has alienated men and women not only from God and their neighbor, but also from the rest of creation, the salvation that is proclaimed in the gospel includes the reconciliation of all creation. According to the apostle Paul, "it pleased the Father" that in Jesus Christ "all the fullness of God" should "dwell," in order "to reconcile to himself all things, whether on earth or in heaven, making peace by the blood of his cross" (Col. 1:19-20). For Paul, the whole universe finds its harmony in Jesus Christ. That is, the whole creation can fulfill its assigned task to the extent that it is grounded in Christ. He is the one who reunites, reintegrates, and reconstitutes men and women into God's cosmic order; they enter into communion with the Father through the Son in the power of the Spirit.

It is interesting to note how Paul bases this great truth on the experience of the cross. The reconciliation that Christ effects is not an idea, the result of contemplating the universe. It is a *concrete reality* based on nothing less than his suffering on the cross. It is the fruit of a real (historical) confrontation of the Son of God with the forces of evil. To achieve the reconciliation of the universe to himself it was necessary for the Father to *give up* his Son (Rom. 8:32) to death and for the Son to shed his blood, suffering and being forsaken by his Father, bearing the universal blasphemy of humankind, and dying the death of a sinner. It is this that Paul refers to when he says that "God was in Christ reconciling the world to himself," at the same time that he was made sin "for our sake" (2 Cor. 5:19, 21). In the epistle to the Colossians, Paul adds that in this work of reconciliation there was a cosmic confrontation between Christ and the rebel principalities and powers, who refuse to submit to his lordship. Christ was crucified because of these rebel forces, but in his vicarious suffering he emptied them of all authority, publicly demonstrating their impotence and definitely triumphing over them (Col. 2:15).

Interestingly, in spite of the fact that the reconciliation effected by Christ embraces the whole cosmos, it is focused on the elimination of human alienation. In the first chapter of Colossians, precisely in the place in which Paul refers to the reconciliation of "all things," we read, "And you, who once were estranged and hostile in mind . . . he has now reconciled in his body of flesh by his death . . ." (Col. 1:21–22a). In the next chapter, before referring to the defeat of the powers, Paul returns to the theme and affirms, "And you, who were dead in trespasses and the uncircumcision of your flesh, God made alive together with him, having forgiven us all our trespasses, having cancelled the bond which stood against us with its legal demands; this he set aside, nailing it to the cross" (Col. 2:13–14). Though the Father wanted to reconcile the whole cosmos to himself by means of the death of Jesus Christ, and, in spite of the fact that to accomplish this a life-and-death confrontation with the powers of this world was necessary, the basic problem in this reconciliation was human sin. Thus the sign of the reconciliation of the universe lies in the restoration of the communion between God and humanity, and within humanity (Eph. 2:14–16). The restoration of the universe revolves around the reconciliation of humankind. As Paul also puts it in the epistle to the Romans, "The creation was subjected to futility, not of its own will but by the will of him who subjected it in hope; because the creation itself will be set free from its bondage to decay and obtain the glorious liberty of the children of God" (Rom. 8:20–21).

Now we can understand why it is that the New Testament places such emphasis on the communion among those who experience reconciliation by faith in Christ. The fellowship of faith (the church) is not only the fruit of God's work of reconciliation in Christ; it is also a sign of the coming kingdom. If the kingdom of God represents the definitive reconciliation between God and humanity, between individuals, peoples, sexes, generations, and races, and between humanity and the rest of creation—a promise that will be fulfilled in the second coming of Christ—then the communion of God's people is an overriding necessity, in order that the world might understand what the salvation that God offers in the gospel really is. An equally imperious need is that the church seek communion with all of humanity and with the environment. The hope of the final reconciliation of creation must be demonstrated not only in the internal communion of the people of God, but also in a continuous effort for peace and reconciliation among nations and their inhabitants.

It is not without significance that we read in the Beatitudes, "Blessed are the peacemakers for they shall be called children of God" (Mt. 5:9). The search for peace (or well-being in all its dimensions) should be a characteristic of every Christian and a responsibility of the whole People of God. Peace and reconciliation among peoples is not a question that has to do only with the future (or consummation) of the kingdom of God. It is a challenge that is always before the community of faith, because it has been called to be an agent of peace among the peoples. Furthermore, if as Christians and members of the People of God we anxiously await the new heaven and new earth where peace shall reign, we cannot remain with our hands folded when the world is torn apart by wars and strife.

Therefore, Jesus also says, "Blessed are those who are persecuted for the sake of justice, for theirs is the kingdom of heaven" (Mt. 5:10, JB). Peace is always the fruit of justice, which is attained only through suffering and sacrifice. Peacemakers are, then, those who pay the price of justice, and the "blessed" are those who do their best to make peace and justice.

Reconciliation is always an experience and a promise. In Christ we are reconciled to God, to our neighbor, and to nature, but we still await the final reconciliation of all creation. This hope impels us to commitment. Hope of the final reconciliation of all things through Christ finds its concrete expression in the search for the unity of the People of God as well as for a more fraternal world community, and an increasingly harmonious relationship with nature. Concern and commitment to a more humane life, a more just society, and a healthier environment (rivers, seas and fish, air and birds, land and animals) are not foreign to the experience and the hope of salvation; they are part and parcel of it.

We have said that salvation is the great work of grace that is announced in the gospel of Jesus Christ. The good news includes a new dialogue (a new relationship) between God and humankind. In this new relationship men and women are declared just before the Father, set free from the power of sin and death, and reconciled to God, their neighbors, and the rest of creation. This places women and men in a new situation in the world. First, it makes them faithful pilgrims of the kingdom of God, disciples absolutely and unconditionally committed to Christ's mission in history. Second, it places them in the service of justice and the integral liberation of all creation. Third, it prepares them to live in communion with the Father, by the grace of the Son and the power of the Holy Spirit—a communion that is substantiated in the fellowship of the church and in its efforts to achieve the reconciliation of a divided world in process of ever greater disintegration.

Since such a great salvation is a work of grace, the only way it can be appropriated is by repentance. Repentance involves at least a twofold process: first, turning from idols, injustice, and selfishness; and, second, unconditional commitment to the gospel.[11] Commitment to the gospel implies putting one's confidence in Jesus Christ and becoming an ally in his cause, or in simpler terms, following the way of the cross: a mission of sacrificial service. Repentance places salvation in the perspective of mission and service, not allowing it to be diluted into escapism or individualism. The gospel offers a salvation that liberates for mission and transforms life into a great service to God, humanity, history, and the entire creation.

Sin and Salvation in Latin America

I now turn to the specific burden of this chapter. It was necessary to engage in a discussion of the biblical message of sin and salvation before analyzing its meaning in the concrete situation of Latin America. On the one hand, as an evangelical Protestant it is my conviction that in doing theology we must first let the canonical Scriptures of the Old and New Testaments speak. On the other hand, as a missiologist I am interested in understanding the Christian *message* concerning sin and salvation for the church's mission. It is essential, therefore, that we seek to hear first and foremost what the fundamental Christian source of knowledge has to say about this subject. In so doing, we also limit the field of discussion so that it becomes clear that my intent is not to describe sin and salvation as psycho-social phenomena or as psychological or philosophical problems, or even less as mere religious topics. Rather, it has been made unquestionably clear that my attempt has been to understand sin and salvation as conveyed in the biblical kerygma. But, having undertaken such a task, I must go on to explore what sin and salvation mean within the Latin American reality, in as much as this is the missional context with which this chapter is concerned. This is not only the place where we must proclaim the message, but also the situation from which we must understand it.

How have sin and salvation *historically* appeared in Latin America? Without pretending to be either exhaustive or rigorously scientific, I shall seek to answer this question by way of several observations, which I believe are historically verifiable.

A Continent Born in Sin, but Saturated with the Message of Salvation

We need to bear in mind, first of all, that Latin (or more precisely, Iberian) America is a continent conceived in sin. The Spanish and Portuguese presence begins with the conquest and the domination of the aboriginal peoples living on the continent. This is not to deny, of course, that these peoples had their internal wars before the arrival of the Spanish and Portuguese. But what we, today, know as Latin America does not begin with the pre-Columbian peoples, but with their conquest and exploitation at the hand of the European invaders. With the discovery of the Americas, the great motherland (Bolivar) became the scene of one of the greatest rapes recorded in human history. This has included not only the genocide of millions of aborigines, but also the enslavement of Africans and their descendants, the exploitation of natural resources, the political and cultural domination of the emerging societies, and the continually increasing impoverishment of its peoples. Stated in other terms, since its birth Latin America was made (as a block) exploitative nuclei. Its economy was structured for the advantage of the European metropolis (represented during the first three centuries by Spain and Portugal, but later by Great Britain and the United States, which in the final analysis is an extension of northern Europe). As such, Latin America has been incorporated into the world economy to provide two things—raw materials and cheap labor. This has left it not only an exploited continent, but also one that is dominated by the economic policies of the countries of the new economic metropolis (Western Europe, North America, and Japan), oppressed by governments and national oligarchies allied with the former and multinational corporations, and dependent on the goodwill of the international market.

From this situation spring many of the evils suffered by different sectors of the population. I am thinking of the rural *peasants*, who either own no land and are forced to sell their labor to landholders who control them by means of the miserable salaries they pay, or else are forced to sell the produce of the little land they own at unjust prices. I am reminded of the *workers* who populate the urban areas, many of them affected by unemployment, and when they find permanent work their salary provides the smallest part of what they need to live modestly. Then there are the pockets of *marginated peoples* who struggle to survive, abandoned to the shantytowns, undernourished, without medical attention or the possibility of education for their children, living in anguish and misery. There are the *children* who wander the streets of the great cities without a home, barefoot, undernourished, with no possibility of a decent education, condemned to vice, promiscuity, crime, a premature death, in short, to an uncontrolled and alienated life. I cannot forget the *young people*, besieged by drugs, the hedonism of the consumer society (which defines life in terms of pleasure), the scarcity of opportunities to study, and the lack of work. I have in mind millions of *women*, relegated to the role of second-class persons by a male-dominated culture, exploited as sex objects by consumer programs, and oppressed by the male population that sees them only as servants rather than partners in life and work.

We know that the basis of this whole situation is the perversity of the human person—disobedience, injustice, and unbelief. No matter how much we review the situation of sin that has historically characterized the Latin American continent, we cannot escape Paul's verdict, "No one does good, not even one" (Rom. 3:12b). This profound and indisputable reality does not obscure or take the place of social sin; rather, it finds expression in that situation. To understand the heart of Latin Americans, one must observe the whole of their actions and sufferings. There is an inseparable relation between personal reality and social situation; both have been distorted and corrupted by sin.

The irony of Latin America is that it was not only born in sin but also has been saturated with the message of salvation. Europeans arrived with the cross as well as the sword. They enslaved the indigenous and African populations while announcing the message of salvation. They whipped people with their structures of exploitation and at the same time anointed them with the balsam of the gospel. The landholders that arose along the way were concerned that their laborers should be baptized and instructed in the faith. And with the penetration of the new Euro-North American powers and the neo-colonization of the continent came Protestant missionaries who brought along the Bible, preached a personal gospel, and formed evangelical churches.

This ironic and contradictory history caused, among black and indigenous peoples, the emergence and growth of syncretistic sects and practices, whose structure and content reflect an energetic protest against such an alienating and oppressive evangelization. Among the majority population arose a "popular religiosity" as a response to a rigid and alienating Iberian Catholic church. Within Protestantism similar situations were doubtless one of the sociological causes of the growth of the Pentecostal movement, especially in its autochthonous branch.

It can be said, therefore, that throughout Latin America's history the gospel has always had its witnesses (though they have left a lot to be desired). In this respect Latin America is not like other continents in the third world—it has been a continent born in and stratified by sin, but at the same time it has been saturated by the saving message of the gospel. Notwithstanding the fact that the face of Christ has been disfigured by injustice and oppression, his name is not foreign to the ears of the majority of Latin Americans.

A Christian Continent but Corrupted by Idolatry

Latin America is thus a continent formed (and deformed) by Christianity. Its language, customs, symbols, and values, its institutions and lifestyle have been profoundly affected by a sociocultural vision situated within the Christian tradition. The majority of its inhabitants have been baptized and identify themselves as Christians, albeit in many instances by name only. Words such as "gospel," "sin," "salvation" are familiar terms to Latin American men and women. Hence it can be considered a Christian continent.

It cannot be denied, however, that Christianity in Latin America has been corrupted by idolatry. The God and Father of our Lord Jesus Christ, who is totally other and cannot be represented by "any graven image" (Deut. 5:8), has been replaced in Latin America by unjust social, economic, and political structures; by images shaped by human vanity and pride. The most ironic aspect of Latin American societies is that the more religious they feel, the more they deny God. How can one explain the fact that practically all the Latin American dictators profess to be Christians, defending the Christian cause? How can one explain the economic injustice of a continent rich in natural resources that claims to follow the Lord who was identified with the poor and dispossessed of the earth in his birth, in his life, in his ministry, and in his death? How can one explain torture, imprisonment without trial, and persecution in countries where so much has been said and is being said about the gospel of love? Is Latin America less idolatrous than those continents on which gods of plaster and wood are worshiped? Is it less pagan than the most pagan continents of planet earth? Does it have fewer atheists than the most secular societies of Western or Eastern Europe, North America, or Asia? No!

A Suffering but Hopeful Continent

Latin America is a suffering, yet hopeful, continent. Its people bear on their brows the marks of the affliction of social and personal sin. It suffers the genocide of thousands of Nicaraguans, Salvadorans, and Guatemalans killed by bloody dictators, oligarchies, and armies. It suffers a long history of fratricidal wars. It suffers the bitterness of exile and torture, hunger and poverty, alcohol and drugs, prostitution, and illiteracy.

Yet Latin America is a continent that has never lost hope. Where sin abounds, Paul says, grace abounded all the more (Rom. 5:20)—there abounds the grace that is common to all; there abounds the grace that is revealed in Jesus Christ. God's grace keeps hope alive in every Latin American country and their respective communities—a hope that is reflected in the continuing struggles of its peoples, in popular music, in their very religiosity, and even in football games! We know, however, that this hope has ultimate meaning only when it is interpreted in the light of the gospel and when it is rooted in Jesus Christ.

Evangelization in a Situation of Sin and Salvation

How does the church evangelize in a situation of sin and salvation such as that of Latin America? How does one proclaim the gospel in a continent of hope amid suffering, where the cross has traditionally accompanied the sword and where people call themselves Christians but live in idolatry? The answer to this question is not easy. However, I would like to offer three suggestions.

Overcoming Historical Contradictions

To evangelize effectively in such a situation it is necessary to overcome the historical contradictions that have characterized the proclamation of the gospel. The good news of salvation cannot be announced with credibility without denouncing the surrounding sinful situation, nor can injustice, disobedience, and idolatry be denounced without announcing God's call to obedience, justification by faith, and reconciliation to God, neighbors, and nature. One cannot evangelize, either, if one is bound to sin in any of its dimensions or withdraws from the pain and suffering of those who are to be evangelized. Evangelization demands, above all things, authenticity. Therefore, in order to evangelize effectively, one must have experienced liberation from the power of sin and death, communion with God, neighbors, and the rest of creation, and be earnestly and passionately involved in the search for a just peace among the nations and their inhabitants. In brief, those who are evangelizing must consider themselves and conduct themselves like servants of the crucified Son of God. As the Lausanne Covenant puts it: "A Church which preaches the Cross must itself be marked by the Cross" (article 6).

This implies that it is impossible to bring good news of salvation in a poor and oppressed continent if one is allied to structures that disregard life and perpetuate injustice. To do so would be to perpetuate the contradiction between the sword and the cross. It would mean sharing the liberating message of the gospel with one hand and justifying domination and exploitation with the other.

This also implies that methods must be consistent with the message that is proclaimed and the God in whose name evangelization is done. It is not possible to witness to the living God from the altar of an idol. Thus when the personality of the evangelist is made the center of the evangelistic event; when the hedonistic philosophy behind the consumer society (with its emphasis on pleasure and escape from the problems of life) is allowed to inform the content of the message; when evangelization contributes to the alienation of women and men by the denial of their cultural values and the affirmation of the cultural penetration of dominant societies through advertising, music, language, and style of communication, what is transmitted is a domesticating religious ideology, not the liberating gospel of Jesus Christ. This proceeds from the fact that the manner in which one communicates is as powerful as what one says. Methods are never ethically or theologically neutral.

Avoiding False Dichotomies

To proclaim the good news faithfully and effectively in the Latin American situation of sin, false dichotomies must be avoided. Latin America has lived through a history of senseless polemics. Some have emphasized personal sin; others have stressed social sin. Some have proclaimed a spiritual salvation; others, a political one. Some have said that only in the light of the personal and spiritual can the social and political dimension of salvation be discovered; others have taken the opposite position, emphasizing that only through the social and political can the personal and spiritual side of the saving power of the gospel be found.

These dichotomies are as false as they are senseless. If sin is personal and social, spiritual and historical, then what is accomplished by these dichotomies is to cut its trunk and dilute its effects. If salvation is personal, cosmic, and public, present and future, spiritual and corporal, to set one dimension against the other or to subordinate one to the other is to limit its unity and efficacy. In such case, free reign is given to what the Bible calls the enemy, Satan, the evil one, who tries by every possible means to frustrate the transforming effect of the gospel. For evangelization to be authentic and deep, it must set aside such false dichotomies, taking seriously the wholeness of salvation and the radical nature of sin.

Critically Evaluating the Contents of Evangelization

Effective and authentic evangelization in the Latin American context demands, finally, a critical evaluation of the contents of its practice. Criticism is never pleasant; it disturbs, frightens, threatens, especially when it touches the very content of a task. But without criticism movements become monuments, communities become ghettos, messages become enslaving ideologies. Unfortunately, in Protestant evangelistic circles there has been a tendency to shun theological criticism. Many evangelists, pastors, and lay persons have felt rejected by the former. This is unfortunate. Perhaps one must accept it as inevitable. But it is the church that has had to pay the price, and it is its evangelizing mission that will suffer even more in the future.

A critical evaluation of the message, especially insofar as it touches the problem of sin and salvation in Latin America, is crucial for effective evangelization. On the one hand, the evangelizing community must be continually confronted with the Word of God in order to see to what extent it is being faithful to the gospel in its proclamation. On the other hand, sin is dynamic, not static; it takes different forms at different stages of history. It is not sufficient, then, to speak of human sin in universal terms; to do so is to fall into useless abstraction. Sin must be seen in its specific character for the gospel to be able to make a positive impact. Likewise, salvation is an experience, not an idea; it is a dynamic present reality, not simply a promise for the future. What the gospel announces is a salvation *of* the past, *in* the present, and *for* the future. Therefore it cannot be abstracted from the concrete context of those being evangelized without losing its transforming efficacy.

In a continent surrounded and permeated by sin, the only way to evangelize effectively is to announce "in season and out of season" a salvation that is concrete and global, present and future, personal, public, and cosmic, the result of the redeeming grace of Jesus Christ, appropriated in faith through the power of the Spirit, for the glory of the Father. To be satisfied with less would be to declare the gospel impotent and unable to solve the problem of sin in the Latin American nations, among their people, and in their history of injustice, unbelief, and idolatry. We know, however, that the gospel is the efficacious power of God for salvation, and that it is the foretaste of the total transformation of history and the creation of new heavens and a new earth. The question is whether the People of God in general and the Protestant communities in particular across the length and breadth of their continent will be willing to recover the totality of the saving message and proclaim it faithfully by the power of the Holy Spirit. This is the challenge that lies before Latin American Christians in the 1980s.

NOTES

1. See G. C. Berkouwer, *Sin*, trans. from Dutch by Philip C. Holtrop (Grand Rapids, Mich.: Wm. B. Eerdmans, 1971), pp. 130ff.

2. See Rubem Alves, *Tomorrow's Child* (New York: Harper & Row, 1972), pp. 62ff.

3. On the concept of principalities and powers, see further chap. 10.

4. World Conference on Salvation Today, "Salvation and Social Justice: Report of Section II of the Bangkok Conference," *IRM* 62, no. 246 (April 1973): 199.

5. John Murray, in his commentary on *The Epistle to the Romans, The New International Commentary of the New Testament,* vol. 1 (Grand Rapids, Mich.: Wm. B. Eerdmans, 1965), p. 13, admits that "it is not impossible to think of obedience to faith as the commitment to oneself to what is involved in the act of faith," but he goes on to state that "it is much more intelligible and suitable to take 'faith' as in opposition to 'obedience' and understand it as the obedience which consists in faith. Faith is regarded as an act of obedience, of commitment to the gospel." Cf. also F. F. Bruce, *The Epistle of Paul to the Romans*, Tyndale Bible Commentaries, vol. 6 (Grand Rapids, Mich.: Wm. B. Eerdmans, 1963), p. 74.

6. Cf. F. W. Young, "Obedience," *IDB*, vol. K–Q, George Arthur Buttrick, general ed. (Nashville, Tenn.: Abingdon, 1962), pp. 580–81.

7. Most English Bibles prefer the term "righteousness" over "justice" in their translation of the Greek work *dikaiosynè* (Rom. 1:17; 2:6; 1 Jn. 3:7). The latter is the term used most often by the Septuagint to translate the classical Hebrew hendiandys *mišpat usᵉ dakah* (right and justice). While righteousness can be an adequate translation for the idea behind *mišpat,* when used in reference to the hendiandys it may obscure the fact that it "is the most clearly technical term that the Old Testament uses to signify justice for the poor and oppressed, social justice" (José P. Miranda, *Marx and the Bible: A Critique of the Philosophy of Oppression*, trans. from Spanish by John Eagleson [Maryknoll, N.Y.: Orbis Books, 1974], p. 93). This is perhaps the reason why the Jerusalem Bible translates *dikaoisynè* in Rom. 1:17; 2:6, as "justice" rather than "righteousness." (For a thorough discussion of the problem and a bold defense of the concept of "justice" as the central organizing principle of God's economy, see Miranda, *Marx and the Bible*, especially pp. 111ff.) The term "righteousness" may be stylistically preferable but it is ideologically dangerous. Indeed the history of modern exegesis reflects a tendency to cover up its socioethical content and to highlight the religious, spiritual dimension, a practice that not only goes contrary to the Old Testament background but reflects a historic tendency in Western theological circles to split ethics and theology, or the horizontal from the vertical dimension, which in turn has served to justify oppression in far too many situations.

8. On the biblical concept of "justice" (which in most English Bible dictionaries appears under "righteousness"), see, in addition to Miranda (above), G. Schrenk, *"dikaiosúnē" TDNT 2,* ed. Gerhardt Kittel, trans. and ed. Geoffrey W. Bromiley (Grand Rapids, Mich.: Wm. B. Eerdmans, 1964), pp. 192ff.; E. R. Achtemeyer, "Righteousness in the Old Testament," and P. J. Achtemeyer, "Righteousness in the New Testament," *IDB,* vol. R–Z, pp. 80–85, 91–99.

9. Bangkok Conference report, p. 199.

10. There are those who, while agreeing with the personal and spiritual dimension of salvation, are hesitant to link it with social and political events. One theologian who has expressed such hesitancy is Carl F. H. Henry: "Salvation . . . is primarily God's business, or rather, God's grace. The Christian (one might also say, the church) is not the Savior of the people. God's Messiah is the crucified and risen Jesus, while we— though a minority in any generation—are first called out of the world, and then thrust back as light and salt. We are sent first and foremost as servants, not as leaders of movements. We are sent to nourish the global grapevine with a rumor of hope: the risen Lord is present and at work" (*God, Revelation and Authority,* vol. 4 [Waco, Tex.: Word Books, 1979], p. 566).

Henry and I agree that salvation is the business of God's grace, but we disagree that its only historical manifestation is the church. We agree that the church is a servant community, sent into the world to be light and salt and to bear witness to the fact that "the risen Lord is present and at work," but we disagree as to *how* it is to carry out its witness and service, *where* Jesus Christ is at work, and *what* he is doing in history.

Henry has no other way of explaining God's action in history except in traditional dualistic terms: God is active in creation and judgment, in providence and redemption. Yet Henry does not adequately explain what is the relationship between the God of providence and the God of redemption, between creation and the new creation, between the one through whom "all things were created, in heaven and on earth," in whom "all things hold together," the "head of the body, the church . . . the firstborn from the dead," the one in whom "all the fullness of God was pleased to dwell, and through him reconcile to himself all things, whether on earth or in heaven" (Col. 1:15–19) and "the God who made the world and everything in it, being the Lord of heaven and earth, . . ." who "will judge the world in righteousness . . ." (Acts 17:24, 31).

Indeed Henry is quick to chide me for falling into "generalities" when it comes to the discernment of the historical signs of the messianic age, but he seems blind to the concrete statements that I make in reference to the church's role in the struggles of history. He leaps over my reference to the church as a prophetic eschatological community of salvation, called to witness to God's justice and messianic peace by *demonstrating* it in its life and mission, and *discerning* its signs and *interpreting* their meaning in the struggles of history "in the light of the gospel" (*The Church and Its Mission* [Wheaton, Ill.: Tyndale, 1974], p. 206, n. 83).

It is my contention that God in Christ has not only saved the church from sin and death, but has promised to save the world from corruption and decay; that history, in spite of all its contradictions and failures, is being moved by the Holy Spirit toward the final consummation of God's kingdom; and that the church is not only the firstfruits of the new creation, but a witness to its final fulfillment and historical anticipations. Therefore the Church should not spare any opportunity to discern the presence of the kingdom in history and interpret its signs to the world in the light of biblical revelation.

It is ironic that theologians like Henry would be so hard-nosed when it comes to historical manifestations of God's eschatological salvation, when in fact they formally hold to the now/not-yet dialectic of the kingdom. In a previous chapter, Henry states that "The gospel resounds with good news for the needy and oppressed. It conveys assurance that injustice, repression, exploitation, discrimination and poverty are dated and doomed, that no one is forced to accept the crush of evil powers as finally determinative for his or her existence. Into the morass of sinful human history and experience the gospel heralds a new order of life shaped by God's redemptive intervention. It trumpets Christ's fulfillment of the messianic promise . . . (Matt. 11:5, KJV)" (*God, Authority and Revelation*, p. 542). He holds that the "gospel is comprehensively liberating" and argues that "from its very first pages the Bible extends to the burdened and downtrodden, the alienated and brokenhearted, the poor and afflicted the prospect of redemptive source" (ibid., p. 543).

In spite of these forthright prophetico-eschatological statements, Henry cannot seem to move beyond the life of the church when it comes to the concreteness of the messianic promise of justice and liberation. "The church" is for Henry, "*the* sign of God's redemptive presence in the world [italics added]. The church evidences that in fallen history a new humanity and a new society can arise where reconciliation and righteousness, hope and joy replace the rampant exploitation and oppression of fellow humans and their despair of survival" (ibid.).

Why is Henry so reluctant to see in history the same messianic signs that were present in Jesus' proclamation of the kingdom? Why is he so unwilling to let the church interpret Christ's redemptive presence in the struggles of history even if such interpretation is done under the guidance of the Spirit and in the light of the gospel? Why does he confine the kingdom to the church?

Neither time nor space allows an exhaustive answer to this question. But surely one obvious response is found in Henry's separation of the doctrine of creation and salvation. Henry isolates the history of salvation from secular history. He relates the saving power of the gospel to personal life and afterlife, or to the life and mission of the church and the final consummation of the kingdom, while leaving the affairs of secular history and the nations to God's providence and judgment. Without stating it in so many words, Henry ends up in the two-kingdom scheme of traditional Lutheran theology, which, as Carl E. Braaten has noted, "is supposed to do the job of relating eschatological salvation to world history, saving faith in God to loving action in the world, God's redemptive role in Christ to his political purposes in Caesar's realm." The problem with that scheme is that it has cut off the gospel "from the substance of political and social life," as the Lutheran track record in matters of church and state so clearly shows. While it is true that the love, justice, peace, and freedom of the eschatological kingdom of God are "not of this world," they are, nevertheless, "*in* it, not fully and perfectly, but partly and provisionally, backed by the promise of God to transform the structures of life within the sequences of history" (Carl E. Braaten, *The Flaming Center: A Theology of the Christian Mission* [Philadelphia: Fortress Press, 1977], pp. 57, 58, 62).

Henry's implicit two-kingdom scheme is undergirded by a sociology centered on the individual. Society in general and the church in particular are the sum total of individuals. History stands or falls by the actions of individuals. In the economy of salvation what matters is that individuals are brought into the saving knowledge of Jesus Christ. "The New Testament first of all deals with the rescue of persons from sin, and with their restoration to a new relationship to God and neighbor; from this restoration and reconciliation flows the deepest social concern" (*God, Revelation and Authority*, p. 576).

One can understand why an Anglo-American theologian would maintain such views: it is the ideological presupposition of those who have been on the side of social, economic, and political power and have been, thus, historically against revolutionary change. Though Henry holds that the church is called "to challenge and contain the powers of evil: . . . to resist the Evil One, . . . to indict rampant injustices and support the afflicted and oppressed, . . . to sensitize moral conscience against wrong and for the right, . . . to exhibit the purpose of God in a new life and a new community. . ." (*God, Revelation and Authority*, pp. 545–46), he warns, nevertheless, against confusing "the warped social situation with the fixed and inviolable order of creation," which can lead to the repudiation of "the divinely given constants for evolutionary or revolutionary alternatives" (ibid., p. 544).

One is flabbergasted, however, to see how Henry, with such a clear ideological stance, vehemently criticizes those who are honest enough to recognize their ideological commitment to the poor, the powerless, and the oppressed (cf. ibid., p. 569). Henry would do well to bear in mind Jesus' stunning question: "Why do you see the speck that is in your brother's eye, but do not notice the log that is in your own eye?" (Mt. 7:3).

11. Thus defined, repentance is synonymous with conversion. Elsewhere I have defined conversion as repentance (turning from) and faith (turning to) (see Orlando E. Costas, *The Integrity of Mission: The Inner Life and Outreach of the Church* [New York: Harper & Row, 1979], pp. 8–9). Gabriel Fackre, in his *Word in Deed: Theological Themes in Evangelism* (Grand Rapids, Mich.: Wm. B. Eerdmans, 1975), pp. 84–98, formulates this twofold process along four steps: (1) from sin (and self), (2) to God, (3) into the church, (4) for service in the world. But, as I have argued, conversion is more than an initial moment; it is a lifelong process (see Orlando E. Costas, "Conversion as a Complex Experience: A Personal Case Study," in *Gospel and Culture*, ed. Robert Coote and John Stott [Pasadena, Calif.: William Carey Library, 1979], pp. 240–62; and *Down to Earth*, ed. Coote and Stott [Grand Rapids, Mich.: Wm. B. Eerdmans, 1980], pp. 173–91).

3

Church Growth as a Multidimensional Phenomenon

The Christian mission is grounded in the mission of the triune God. There is no other mission than that which originates in the purpose and action of God in history. The Christian mission participates in that purpose and action, since its central point of reference is God's revelation in Jesus Christ, and is carried out in the power of the Holy Spirit (see chap. 6, on mission of the triune God).

God's mission has as its ultimate and definitive goal the full manifestation of the messianic kingdom, understood as a new order of life characterized by love, freedom, justice and peace. The church is the firstfruits of that new order: it anticipates the messianic kingdom in its life and proclaims it in its mission.[1]

There is much debate, however, as to the place the church occupies in the eschatological horizon of the mission of God. Is its origin and growth part of the very objective of God's mission or is it an unanticipated fruit, one of the many "surprises" related to God's working in history?[2] Should we expect church growth, seeing it as a sign of the presence and future revelation of the messianic kingdom and using it as a measuring stick for our missionary faithfulness? Or ought we to consider church growth as a gift that is to be received with praise and thanksgiving, but not necessarily expected? Put it another way: Can we speak of the objectives of the mission of God only in terms of the ultimate and definitive character of the kingdom, or may we speak of one or more penultimate and provisional goals that can be demonstrated here and now and that can verify our evangelistic faithfulness and testify to the present reality of the coming kingdom?

My own view is that church growth *is* a sign, a provisional and penultimate goal of the mission of God. In other words, the category of growth is basic to a correct interpretation of the Christian mission in general and the church's evangelizing ministry in particular. The problem, however, is what kind of growth may be associated with the mission of God and what kind of growth may be expected as an authentic result of the church's evangelistic endeavor.

43

While church growth can and must be considered as a sign and provisional goal of the mission of God and a proper fruit of evangelism, not every kind of growth is related to this mission and to evangelism.

My first objective in this chapter will be to establish the preceding thesis in biblical and theological terms. This in turn will lead us to consider not only the fact of church growth but also its multidimensional nature and thus enable us to become conscious of that type of growth which may be identified with the mission of God and which may be expected from the work of evangelism.

The first objective makes a second task necessary: dissociating the kind of growth reflected in biblical theology from that which may be found today in some Protestant circles. In the second part of this chapter I want to examine a concrete case from Latin America, which demonstrates how the biblical model of church growth can be mutilated and deformed, even in situations of overwhelming numerical growth. From this case study I shall draw, in the third part, several relevant implications.

Church Growth as a Provisional Goal of Mission: A Biblical and Theological Perspective

In an article noted for its critical self-examination, Raymond Panikkar (noted phenomenologist of religion) suggests that the category of *growth* is essential to a correct understanding of all religious phenomena. Panikkar says: "Religion is essentially oriented toward the future. . . . In the life of a religion as in the life of a person, in the intellectual as well as other spheres, [if] there is no growth, there is deterioration: to stop means stagnation and death."[3]

This view of religion concurs with the dynamic character of Israel's religion. We see it in the Abrahamic Covenant, which at least in the canonical order presupposes the formal statutes of Israel's religion. Do we not find in the call of Abraham the response of love to the judgment of the nations, the promise of a new humanity that will begin with the "seed" of Abraham (Gen. 12:1–3, 10–11)? Is not the formation of Israel as a people dedicated to the religion of Yahweh (Sinai Covenant) a sign of Yahweh's universal kingdom and a call to proclaim that kingdom among the nations (Ex. 19:3–6)? Does not the Jesolimitanic liturgy, which confesses Yahweh as Lord and proclaims his salvation, affirm that the kingdom of Yahweh is above the kingdoms of this world and that his salvation extends to all the nations? (cf., e.g., Ps. 97; Isa. 40–55; Zech. 8:23). Does not the affirmation of God as creator of heaven and earth mean that God is the author of life who demands the obedience of all nations, having revealed himself to them (Ps. 19:1–7) and having included them in his plan of salvation (Ps. 86:9)? What is the meaning of the stories of Naaman, Ruth, and Jonah but that the God of Israel is also the God of the nations and desires to include them in the new humanity?[4]

This Old Testament vision of the dissemination and expansion of God's mission comes through many different channels and has a predominantly centripetal character. The vision, however, grows until it becomes the centrifugal force so clearly evident in the New Testament, where the emphasis is placed upon crossing sociocultural frontiers. The Old Testament clearly teaches that the God of Israel is no tribal deity, but, rather, the creator and sustainer of the world; that Israel is not an end but, rather, an instrument for mission; that the kingdom of God, which is a universal fact, is not recognized by all the nations; and that the hope of salvation has a universal scope. For this reason Israel's witness and proclamation before the nations is necessary (Isa. 42:6-7; 43:10-12; 49:6; 52:7-10; 61:1-2) and the future expansion of the knowledge of Yahweh, which knows no frontiers or limitations, is foreseen (cf., among others, Isa. 11:9; chaps. 40-55 and 60-66; Deut. 7:14).

This vision is clarified and concretized in the New Testament, which proclaims the presence of the kingdom in history (Lk. 17:20). The messianic hope of the salvific manifestation of God's lordship over the whole creation becomes a reality in Jesus of Nazareth. Jesus not only announces the nearness of the kingdom (Mk. 1:15) but also personifies that kingdom (Jn. 1; Lk. 7:22-27). Jesus proclaims the liberation of creation from its state of slavery and captivity and the restoration of humanity and the cosmos to its vocation: a new creation. He therefore links his mission to those who demonstrate most graphically the tragedy of sin: the poor—those who have nothing and no one to help them and to meet their needs; the captives—those whose liberty has been mutilated; the blind—those for whom it is physically impossible to contemplate and enjoy the good things of creation; the oppressed—those who have been enslaved and domesticated by other human beings. In word and sign, Jesus proclaims to all of these the Year of Jubilee, the liberation of history (cf. Lk. 4:18-19).

The kingdom that Jesus proclaims and personifies is therefore a new way of life, which breaks in upon the present.[5] The new community that takes form around Jesus—a community of love, freedom, justice, and peace—gives evidence of this. In at least three areas, the formation of this community overcomes Israel's deficiencies: (1) It is based upon a new covenant characterized by divine initiative in the forgiveness of sins and initiated by Christ's sacrifice upon the cross (cf., e.g., Mt. 26:28; 2 Cor. 3:6; Rom. 11:27; Heb. 8:6; 9:15ff.; 1 Jn. 5:20). (2) It is composed of both Jews and Gentiles; in other words, it is an intensively and extensively universal community (cf., e.g., Mt. 28:19ff.; Acts 1:8, 10; Gal. 3:28; Eph. 2:14ff.), in contrast to the universalism of Israel, which was implicit and intensive. (3) It is the result, sign, and instrument of a salvific movement that begins with the cross—of the crucified servant—and is spread abroad by the power of the risen Lord, made present by the Spirit in the proclamation of the forgiveness of sins (Lk. 24:46-49) to every corner of the world. For this reason the church is seen as a pilgrim community, called, in the words of the book of Hebrews, to its encounter with Jesus "outside the camp," "bearing abuse" and forming, as it were, a community in the desert (Heb. 13:13ff.). Its final goal is Jesus (Heb.

12:1-2) and the manifestation of his kingdom. In the course of its pilgrimage (Heb. 13:14), it must experience that process of growth and expansion that is both the result of its labor and the sign of the coming kingdom that it awaits. This growth constitutes a provisional goal of its mission.

While growth is certainly a gift from God (1 Cor. 3:7; Acts 2:47), it is a gift that should be expected as the firstfruits of the future and as evidence of the power of the Spirit. Throughout the New Testament are numerous references that directly or indirectly, implicitly or explicitly, transmit the image of growth (Mt. 5:16; 9:37-38; 10:1-40; 13:1-8, 18-23, 31, 47; Mk. 1:17; 4:1-8, 13-20; Lk. 8:5-8, 11-15; 10:2; Jn. 8:12; 9:5; 14:21-24; 15:5, 8; Rom. 8:15; 1 Cor. 3:9-11; Eph. 1:5; 2:22; 4:14ff.; 1 Pet. 2:2, 4ff.).[6] In addition to these images we also have the example of Jesus and the experience of the early church. It has already been stated that Jesus formed a community as both a sign and a fruit of a new order. The formation of this community is linked with his preaching (see, e.g., Mk. 1:14-20; 3:13ff.). Jesus devotes himself to training this community (Mk. 3:13-14; 4:10-12; Mt. 5:1; Lk. 6:12ff.; Jn. 6:3) and gives it power to preach and to cast out demons (cf., e.g., Mk. 3:14-15; Mt. 10:1ff.). He sends it to the ends of the earth to testify of his kingdom and to disciple the nations (Acts 1:8; Mt. 28:18).

The experience of the early church is clearly reflected in the book of Acts, the epistles, and Revelation (which pictures "a great multitude which no man could number, from every nation, from all tribes and peoples and tongues, standing before the throne and before the Lamb" [7:9; cf. 15:2-5]). The fact remains that by the end of the first century the gospel had spread throughout the Roman world, resulting in numerous congregations, a vigorous and exciting theological reflection, a quality of life sealed with the blood of those who remained faithful to Jesus Christ, even to the point of death, and an organic development which was so extraordinary that it still serves as a point of reference for our liturgical and ecclesiastical development and the process of ecclesial and missionary indigenization—all of this being motivated by the eschatological hope of the kingdom to come.

The idea of growth is therefore basic to the experience and missional expectancy of the first Christians and to the biblical theology of mission. Equally important is the multidimensional nature of that growth. The *numerical* is only one of the different dimensions among many in the process of missional expansion. It is without doubt an essential dimension, which may not be reduced in any way. The mission of God deals with the nations; the gospel is oriented toward the many. Christian faith has a universal projection; it is neither provincial nor "particularistic." It seeks to reach out to the ends of the earth because it proclaims a message of good news for all humanity. The Methodist church of Bolivia has expressed this idea aptly: "*every human being* who enters this world . . . [has] *the right* to know Jesus Christ and his liberating Gospel." The church has a debt toward every "man or woman . . . [toward] every child in existence" because the gospel "is not a property, but rather a stewardship."[7]

It is, however, precisely because the gospel is a "stewardship" that it cannot be reduced to evangelistic activism. The gospel demands reflection, internalization, and incarnation.

The church is called not only to proclaim the mystery of God in Christ (Eph. 3:9) but also to understand its "breadth and length and height and depth" (Eph. 3:18) until it attains "the unity of the faith and of the knowledge of the Son of God, to mature manhood, to the measure of the stature of the fullness of Christ" (Eph. 4:13). That this *reflective growth* is an intrinsic part of mission is clearly indicated in the command to disciple all nations, baptizing them and teaching them to observe all the commandments of Christ (Mt. 28:18-19); we also see it in Paul's missionary practice (cf. "the mystery [of] Christ . . . we proclaim, warning every man and *teaching* . . ." [Col. 1:27-28]) ; and we see it in the missionary experience of the early church in Jerusalem (Acts 2:42).[8] In other words, while it is impossible to underestimate the importance of the numerical, it is equally true that the role of reflective thought must not be relegated to a position of secondary importance in the life of the church, that is, whether by dissociating it from mission or by consigning it to a privileged few. The whole church is called to grow in its understanding of the faith. Its reflective thought is part and parcel of its obedience in mission.

Neither must we belittle the missionary character of the *organic* development of the community of faith. If there is one thing that the book of Acts and the New Testament epistles make clear it is that the kingdom takes shape in the system of relationships that is produced by the call to faith and repentance. The liturgical celebration, internal discipline, stewardship, leadership training—all of which are aspects of the internal life of the church—are an essential, indispensable part of the mission, not some extraneous imposition. The evidence and goal of growth in the faith is that the whole body should participate in mission. Also, the proclamation of the kingdom carries within it the invitation to participate in the life of the kingdom *now* in the community's experience of faith. Without a vibrant community, which stands behind the proclamation and receives those who are called, the numerical element becomes merely a consumer production.

This leads us to the vital importance of missional *incarnation*. Without lives that are completely committed to Christ and to the world, our participation in mission will lack authenticity. I'm not talking about merely going and proclaiming, or living and reflecting but, rather, about *being* with him in "the desert," "outside the camp," about "bearing abuse for him" (Heb. 13:13), that is, suffering the hopes and frustrations of the world. This demands a continual evaluation and questioning of the Christian presence in the world. When there is no growth in the *efficacy* of the church's involvement in structural and historical problems, in the personal and collective struggles of society, then its evangelistic work, its organic development and theological reflection lead to a reductionism of mission. As José Míguez-Bonino has aptly stated: "Mission . . . is not merely a set of actions but rather the manifestation of a new reality, the new life which is communicated and offered in Christ. . . ."[9]

Summing up my argument thus far: God's mission is fulfilled in a provisional sense in church growth, but not all growth responds to God's will or to the quality of life in the new order. Missiologically, one can only consider as legitimate and valid that growth which is characterized by the experience of forgiveness among the nations and their subsequent incorporation into the community of faith, by the organic and reflective development of the latter and its efficacious involvement in the world's afflictions.

Church Growth as a Mutilation of Mission:
The Case of Chilean Protestantism (1910–75)

I feel obliged almost immediately to dissociate the kind of church growth inherent in a biblical theology of mission from the kind of growth I see reflected in some circles of contemporary Protestantism. As a case in point I propose to examine the case of Chilean Protestantism in the years 1910–75, since its growth has attracted the attention of many scholars around the world. The validity of that growth, however, is questionable in the light of the life and work of Protestantism in Chilean society and of a biblical theology of mission.

It is common knowledge that the majority of Chilean Protestants are Pentecostal. The history of the church has, since the second decade of this century, revolved around the Pentecostal movement, taking its roots from the spiritual awakening of 1909–10 under the direction of Willis Hoover in Valparaiso and Santiago. To this we would have to add a latent underlying current of nationalism, which resulted in a structural clash between the emerging national leadership and the Mission Board of the Evangelical Methodist Church. Hoover himself had had to face the problem of nationalism within his own congregation ten years earlier, and this experience, in the opinion of J. B. A. Kessler, made him the only missionary capable of struggling with this problem during the crisis of 1909–10.[10] Hoover maintained this leadership for twenty years until the new indigenous leadership broke the last bonds of missionary control. It is interesting to observe that not until the 1930s (when the leadership passed into national hands) did the church begin to grow.

From 1930 to 1960 Chilean Protestantism experienced unprecedented numerical growth, doubling the number of adherents every ten years. From a total of 54,800 in 1920, the church grew to 425,700 in 1960. This growth is even more impressive when one observes the annual percentage of growth decade by decade:

1920–30	1.46 percent
1930–40	6.45 percent
1940–52	6.62 percent
1952–60	6.60 percent

This increase led Father Humberto Muñoz, a Chilean Catholic sociologist, to declare in 1956, "There is reason for alarm . . . for if the Protestants continue to grow at the same rate, 50 years from now the whole country will be Protestant . . ."[11]

This impressive picture characterized not only the numerical growth but also the organic growth. This is evident in the extraordinary development of an indigenous charismatic leadership, an autonomous financial structure, a contextualized liturgy, a dynamic communal life, and a vibrant evangelistic witness. It is also clearly seen in the social makeup of the parishes. "The Gospel," say the Chilean Pentecostals, "is for the broken and needy." Protestantism, for the first time in Latin America, made its presence felt among the urban proletariat, and popular culture entered into the life of the church. Chilean Protestantism represents, therefore, a true church of the masses, being the only sector of Protestantism that can be identified with the continental phenomenon known as "popular religiosity."[12]

This impressive growth of Chilean Protestantism (in its most representative variant) does not, however, tell the whole story. One must point to the paradox of stagnation in mission that accompanied this numerical and organic expansion. This phenomenon takes several forms.

The first, while it cannot be statistically documented, is readily evident to the eyes of an observer.[13] René Padilla has put his finger on a sore spot by calling church-growth students to study not only those who enter the church, but the "many who leave the church."[14] Insofar as I have been able to observe (and from what I have heard from others who have studied the subject more closely), there is not only a "wide-open door" at the front of every congregation, but also one at the back. This phenomenon is typical not only in the Chilean church but throughout Latin America. It has two variants: (1) the "spiritual" casualties who have abandoned the church; and (2) the "functional" casualties who, while remaining in the church physically, nevertheless receive their "spiritual nourishment" or do their theological reflection in para-church organizations. The number of the first is difficult to calculate, but it must be very high if we include all those persons who have been related to Protestant churches at one or another time in their lives. And the number is even higher in the university and professional sectors: there is a theological, ethical, and sociocultural frustration among those who either belong to that sector and are converted to the gospel, or are second- or third-generation evangelicals who experience an upward social mobility. In addition, pastors and the ecclesiastical hierarchy feel threatened by the presence of these persons in their congregations.

The second form that this stagnation of mission takes is in the area of interchurch relations, for it is widely known that Chilean Protestantism is in the midst of a profound ecumenical crisis. Sociologically speaking, its numerical growth (so greatly admired by persons all over the world) is the result not only of its psycho-sociocultural style (simple people preaching and witnessing out on the streets in the language of the people about what Christ has done for them), but also of its aggressive denominational competition, which could well be called "ecclesiastical capitalism." Pastor Míguer Gálvez refers to this competition in his evaluative report on the Evangelism-in-Depth project in Santiago: "For the past 20 or 25 years, the Chilean church has suffered from the satanic cancer of scandals, false leaders, economic interest, power struggles, etc., a tragic amalgam so strong that it has produced an indestructible sectarianism, tremendous suspicions and distrust."[15]

This brings us to the ethical problem. The phenomenon of missional stagnation appears, in the third place, in the moral deformation that characterizes the life and mission of Chilean Protestantism.

This church has created an extraordinary language of liberation. Lalive D'Epinay has commented that the church's liturgical experience and structure has provided a language for those who had no language.[16] Its evangelistic testimony has been the instrument of personal transformation for thousands of desperate, frustrated, and depersonalized Chileans. But when it comes to transferring this personal and spiritual liberation to the social and political level, there is a sharp break: the liberation process is truncated. This causes a radical difference between religious behavior and secular behavior.

This is all exceedingly strange because Chilean Protestantism is noted precisely for the manner in which it has been able to secularize and make authentically Chilean its worship and piety. This is a community that is concerned about the body (God wants to cure not only the soul, but also the body; sin has not only alienated humanity from God, but has also robbed it of its physical health). This community is neither ashamed of nor offended by the musical instruments, songs, and dances of its cultural setting, but rather, incorporates them into its worship and consecrates them to God. This is a missionary community, yet it suffers from a profound religious and missional alienation. God can save *individuals*, but not *society*. The world can be brought to the church, but the church cannot be in the world. The church, therefore, cannot and ought not to become incarnate in its social situation. It must always be at the service of mission (always preaching), but never at the expense of the church building.

The result of all of this was a most flagrant contradiction. This community, which for so many years exercised a prophetic role in Chilean society (not so much through its words and theology as in the way it offered the dispossessed of society a religious context in which they could express their protest to society), ended up, through its leaders, joining hands with a brutal, antisocial military dictatorship. On December 13, 1974, thirty-two Protestant church leaders signed in the presence of 2,500 lay men and women a declaration of support for the Chilean military junta.[17] Two days later General Augusto Pinochet, president of the junta, was present at the dedication of the new cathedral of the Methodist Pentecostal Church at Jotabeche Street.[18]

It has been said that government pressure was brought to bear on the signers.[19] It must be pointed out, however, that the declaration was made through the office of a Presbyterian pastor who was a staff member of the

General Secretariat of the junta, the same person who made the public presentation of the document, published it, wrote the preface, and directed the drafting committee of the introductory text.[20] It should also be borne in mind that there was at least one bishop and perhaps other leaders who refused to sign. The signing of the document reveals—at the very least—an uncritical and naïve attitude toward the current government, together with an ahistorical and privatistic missiology, and at the most, a betrayal of the prophetic mission of the church.

On September 14, 1975, another event took place, which throws additional light on the role of large sectors of Chilean Protestantism in the support (and justification) of the Chilean junta. On this occasion the "first Protestant 'Te Deum' on the Republic of Chile"[21] was held in honor of General Pinochet. The sermon was delivered by a distinguished and well-known Chilean Pentecostal leader. It was divided into three parts, each with a note of thanksgiving to God for the past, present, and future, respectively, of the Chilean people and of the Protestant community. The "Te Deum," commented the preacher, was a debut for the Protestant church of Chile, inasmuch as it marked "the first time" it had "officially received the highest authority of the nation."[22] Even so, he insisted that the moment was not a "protocol" performance, but a service of thanksgiving. Thus Protestants represented therein expressed solidarity with the military government, giving thanks to God for the presence of its president and legitimizing its functions as they conferred upon the junta the divine blessing for all its labor and interceded on behalf of its future work.

The content of the sermon and the act itself confirms my earlier affirmation: such public behavior either reflects a historically and politically naïve posture with an ethically inconsistent, spiritualistic, and privatistic missiology, or represents a morally and missiologically apostate gesture. Having refused for years to translate the liberating thrust of the gospel into the sociopolitical sphere, Chilean Protestantism had now decided to do so. But it had made this translation in terms that could only evoke memories of the Evangelical Church of Nazi Germany against whom the Confessing Church of the Barman Declaration was forced to turn.

Lastly, during the 1960s there was a stagnation in the area of numerical growth. In 1967 Read, Monterroso, and Johnson had numbered the Protestant population at 649,500 on the basis of an annual growth rate of 6.5 percent.[23] It was expected that, in addition, on the basis of the growth rate of other decades, the number of Protestants in 1970 would rise to 850,000 (from 475,700 in 1960). However, the 1970 census has shown that for the decade of the 1960s there was an increase of only 124,204, bringing the number to a total of 599,904. This represents an increase of only 20.70 percent for the decade, instead of the 100 percent increase that occurred in the years 1930-60. The annual growth rate decreased from 6.6 percent in the previous decade to 2.07 percent in the following decade.[24]

These facts are very interesting, since they show a decrease in the rhythm of numerical growth in the very decade when in Chile there was a widespread promotion of the interests of the masses. Can it be that Chilean Protestantism has the possibility for growth only in the midst of adverse social, economic, political, and psychological circumstances? This is the tragic possibility contemplated by Dutch social scientist J. Tennekes in the conclusion of his study of Chilean Pentecostalism in the early years of the 1970s. Referring to the situation in the country after the 1973 coup d'état, Tennekes says:

> Now that all legal opposition has been proscribed, the only avenue open is that of religious protest; now that there are no other organizations that may operate as communities, the search for religious community will be greater than ever. Pentecostalism, therefore, will be strengthened. Although we wish the best for this movement, we formulate this prediction in grief, because this expansion will be the fruit of a catastrophe which has moved the whole world. For the Chilean people, crushed in fire and blood by its own armed forces, religion will become the only legally accepted form of expressing its problems, doubts and hopes. And we are convinced that the Christian faith should not be the expression of man's impotence, but rather the instrument of liberation; it should enable the believer to discover a new life and to struggle to build the more just and human society which God in his love will one day give him.[25]

Lessons from Chile: Theses on Church Growth

What are the implications of this case study? Are there any lessons that we may draw from the Chilean situation in five decades of the twentieth century for our respective church-growth contexts? Allow me to respond through four theses.

First of all, *numerical* and *organic* growth in themselves do not necessarily mean that a church is indeed growing. It may be, in the words of Juan Carlos Ortiz, that the church is simply getting fat. The Chilean example illustrates the problem of "ecclesial obesity," an excessive fatness that may preclude (or at least cloud) the presence of the kingdom.

Second, without *reflection on the faith* and without an effective *incarnation* in the hopes and conflicts of the world, numerical and organic growth can be impeded or at least limited to infrahuman situations where the option of faith is more an escape mechanism, the result of social pressures, rather than a genuine call to participate in the new order of life that is proclaimed in the gospel. In such circumstances church growth becomes nothing more and nothing less than a mutilation of mission and an alienating opium.

Third, *church growth is a sign*, not an instrument, *of mission*. A sign is something that points beyond itself, in this case to the mission of God fulfilled in the proclamation and the presence of the kingdom. Multidimensional growth is a fundamental sign of the kingdom, which may open the way for the recognition of other signs. The church that is engaged in mission, that is proclaiming the gospel out of a situation of engagement and incarnation in concrete reality, a church in the midst of which people are coming to Jesus Christ and are responding to the call of the gospel, a church that is growing from within in indigenous leadership, worship, and stewardship, a church that is critically reflecting and growing in the understanding of its faith is much more capable, qualified, and prepared to recognize the other signs of the kingdom that are manifested in history.

An instrument, on the other hand, is "a means whereby something is achieved, performed, or furthered" (Webster). In God's mission, it is the church, not its growth, that is the instrument by which the mission is furthered and fulfilled. Multidimensional growth witnesses to the church's faithfulness in the execution of its task.

This distinction between growth as a sign and the church as an instrument of mission needs to be made in the face of those today who, getting their inspiration from "successful" church-growth situations like Chile, have taken the notion of growth and built it into a methodological category.[26] They thus propose church growth as a missional methodology; that is, as an instrument for the study and fulfillment of the church's mission. They bypass the church (its complex nature, composition, function, needs, and sociohistorical setting) and concentrate on its growth. Studying, inducing, planning, and cultivating *growth* is the means by which the mission is fulfilled. In so doing, however, they defeat their own cause because growth is meaningless without a subject. Therefore it cannot be an instrument, for it can subsist only in relation to a body. Growth is important as part of that body. It is an indicator of vitality, not the means by which the body functions. Mission is fulfilled through and by the church, not through and by church growth. Its fulfillment, however, is made evident and verified in and by the growth of the church.

This leads to my fourth thesis. There is *a fundamental difference* between *the growth of the church* and that of a *business*. The former is the result of the efficacious work of faith; the latter, of the efficiency of applied science, of technology.

The growth of a business is the result of sound marketing analysis, planning, promotion, effective controls, and supervision. It is influenced, to be sure, by certain ethical criteria. Nevertheless, it operates on the basis of economic principles, not of ethical standards. That is, sound investment can produce sound profit, provided there are favorable conditions and an appropriate climate.

But the church is something else. It is a community of faith. Its mission needs to be seen as the efficacious work of faith in the horizon of God's eschatological kingdom. It must be evaluated, therefore, not on the basis of its present institutional success, but on the basis of the future of God's kingdom.[27]

Someone may ask, however, "What happens when there are no results from the work of faith?" "What about unproductive mission?"

It seems to me that this question confronts us with two possible situations. Either there is not an efficacious actualization of faith or we are up against the problem of *the impatience of faith*. In both cases we are confronted with an anomaly. For a faithful church is always a believing church—that is, a church that *is*, not a church that *should*. The problem with many of us is that we think that we are *believing* when we say the church *should* be this and the church *should* be that. But believing is not recognizing responsibility. It is commitment translated into action.

A faith-filled church is a believing church because it actualizes its faith in its *action*. Therefore it is always a trusting, enduring, and steadfast church; trusting in the power of the Holy Spirit to transform persons, families, clans, tribes, and nations; steadfast in the promises of Christ to bless the witness of his people; enduring in the hope of God's coming kingdom; in short, always waiting upon the Lord.

A faith-filled church is always a working church. And therefore it is always testing the efficacy of its labor. It is always questioning and analyzing its missional performance in the light of God's Word, its complex nature, purpose, and sociohistorical setting, and the responses it gets from those who come under its care or are reached by its word and service. In all of this, it seeks to discover its strengths and weaknesses and develop more effective means of fulfilling its missionary vocation.

The issue seems to me to be not whether the church is growing, but whether it is authentically engaged in the mission of the triune God in its concrete sociohistorical situations. It is a matter of efficacious participation in the ongoing life-struggles of society in a total witnessing engagement, which, more than a program or a method, is a lifestyle. For when this happens, the church is turned upside-down. It becomes a living organism, a dynamic training and research center, and an effective team that is capable of leading multitudes to Jesus Christ. In such circumstances, the church is turned inside-out; its structures are put at the service of the kingdom and its missionary practice is transformed into a comprehensive endeavor, where the gospel is shared in depth and out of the depths of human life.

NOTES

1. See *El Reino de Dios y América Latina*, ed. René Padilla (El Paso, Tex.: Baptist Spanish Publishing House, 1974), especially the chapters by Emilio Antonio Nuñez (pp. 17ff.), Padilla (pp. 43ff.), and José Míguez Bonino (pp. 75ff.). On the interrelationship between anticipation (presence) and proclamation of the kingdom in the life and mission of the church, see chaps. 1 and 12 of my work, *Theology of the Crossroads in Contemporary Latin America* (Amsterdam: Editions Rodopi, 1976).

2. See, e.g., the positions taken by Donald McGavran and C. René Padilla.

McGavran insists that "a principle and irreplaceable purpose of mission is the [numerical] growth of the church" (*Understanding Church Growth* [Grand Rapids, Mich.: Wm. B. Eerdmans, 1969], p. 32). For Padilla "The numerical growth of the church is important, but only as an outgrowth of an action that goes far beyond the Church's concern for its own increase in numbers" ("El reino de Dios y la iglesia," *El reino de Dios*, p. 56). See also, Arthur Glasser, "Church Growth and Theology," *God, Man and Church Growth*, ed. A. R. Tippett (Grand Rapids, Mich.: Wm. B. Eerdmans, 1973), p. 52; John H. Yoder, "Church Growth Issues in Theological Perspective," *The Challenge of Church Growth: A Symposium*, ed. Wilbert R. Shenk (Elkhart, Ind.: Institute of Mennonite Studies, 1973), p. 44.

3. Raymond Panikkar, "The Category of Growth in Comparative Religion: A Critical Self-Examination," *Harvard Theological Review* 66 (1973): 135.

4. See Bengt Sundkler, *The World of Mission* (London: Lutterworth Press, 1965), pp. 11–17; Johannes Blauw, *The Missionary Nature of the Church* (London: Lutterworth Press, 1972), pp. 15–54; H. H. Rowley, *The Missionary Message of the Old Testament* (London: Carey Press, 1955); Orlando E. Costas, ed., *Hacia una teología de la evangelizacíon* (Buenos Aires: La Aurora, 1974), pp. 19–33.

5. See Wolfhart Pannenberg, *Theology and the Kingdom of God* (Philadelphia: Westminster Press, 1969), pp. 53–54.

6. For an exposition of this argument, see my work, *The Church and Its Mission* (Wheaton, Ill.: Tyndale House, 1974), pp. 91–97; and the work of Alan R. Tippett, *Church Growth and the Word of God* (Grand Rapids, Mich.: Wm. B. Eerdmans, 1970), pp. 9ff.

7. The Methodist church of Bolivia, "Evangelización hoy en América Latina: Tesis boliviana," *Boletín teológico*, no. 11 (July 1975); English ed. in *A Monthly Letter about Evangelism*, no. 2 (February 1975).

8. Donald McGavran's insistence upon dividing the Great Commission (or the process of Christianization) into two stages, one relating to evangelistic action (discipling) and the other relating to teaching (perfecting), lacks, in my opinion, a firm foundation. See Costas, *The Church*, pp. 142ff.; Yoder, "Church Growth Issues," pp. 41–43.

9. Míguez Bonino, "El Reino y la Historia," *El reino de Dios*, p. 85.

10. See J. B. A. Kessler, Jr., *A Study of the Older Protestant Missions and Churches in Peru and Chile* (Goes: Oesterbaan and le Cointre N.V., 1967), p. 109.

11. Humberto Muñoz, "Situación del protestantismo en Chile," *Mensaje* 5, p. 166, as cited in Christian Lalive D'Epinay, *El refugio de las masas* (Santiago: Editorial del Pacífico, 1968), p. 55. English trans.: *Haven of the Masses* (London: Lutterworth Press, 1969), p. 22.

12. See Juan Tennekes, *La nueva vida: el movimiento pentecostal en la sociedad chilean* (Amsterdam: published by the author, 1973), pp. 81ff.

13. The only study with which I am acquainted is that which was prepared by the Evangelism-in-Depth team in Santiago, "El descarriado," *Estudio socio-religioso*, no. 2 (Santiago: Instituto de Evangelización a Fondo, October 1974), pp. 18–25. It is based upon interviews with thirty-seven persons who have left Protestant churches: fourteen non-Pentecostal churches and twenty-three Pentecostal churches. The interest of the interviewers, nevertheless, was not in the number of dropouts throughout the given period but, rather, in discovering the reasons behind their abandoning the church. Perhaps the most interesting datum, in our opinion, is the fact that 40 percent of those interviewed responded that the reason they had left the church was "the

slander, the gossip, and problems with other members"; 29 percent responded that they left the church because it did not practice what it preached.

14. C. René Padilla, "La teología en latinoamérica," p. 5.

15. Míguer Gálvez, "Informe evaluativo sobre el proyecto Santiago"; circulated privately within the Council of Secretaries of the Institute of Evangelism-in-Depth, San José, Costa Rica, May 27, 1975 (carbon copy), p. 1.

16. Lalive D'Epinay, *El refugio de las masas*, p. 86.

17. See Ecumenical Press Service 42:2 (Jan. 23, 1975), 42:7 (Feb. 27, 1975), p. 6; "Chile: Church Tensions Increase," *One World*, no. 4 (March 1974), p. 4; "Declaración de la iglesia evangélica chilena," in *La iglesia y la junta militar de Chile* (Documentos), Coleccion Proceso 7 (Buenos Aires: Tierra Nueva, 1975), pp. 100–105.

18. Cf. "Situación de las iglesias evangélicas en Chile," in *La iglesia y la junta militar*, p. 109.

19. Ibid., p. 111.

20. Pedro Puente Oliva, ed. "Posición evangélica," in *La iglesia y la junta militar*, pp. 93–99.

21. Francisco Anabalon, "Mensaje pronunciado el 14 de septiembre [1975] en el templo catedral de la Iglesia Metodista Pentecostal con motivo del primer 'Te Deum' evangélico en la República de Chile," Santiago, Chile (photocopy), p. 1.

22. Ibid., p. 2.

23. W. R. Read, V. M. Monterroso, H. A. Johnson, *Latin American Church Growth* (Grand Rapids, Mich.: Wm. B. Eerdmans, 1969), p. 101.

24. Humberto Muñoz, "La fe de los Chilenos," *El Mercurio* (Oct. 27, 1974), p. 27.

25. Juan Tennekes, *La nueva vida*, p. 130.

26. C. Peter Wagner takes this position in his *Your Church Can Grow: Seven Vital Signs of a Healthy Church* (Glendale, Calif.: Regal Books, 1976). He defends it in *Church Growth and the Whole Gospel: A Biblical Mandate* (New York: Harper & Row, 1981), pp. 75–77. Though in the former his stated intention, as the subtitle indicates, is to describe seven signs of a "growing healthy church," one gets the impression that in the end he is not just describing but prescribing medicine for healthy church growth. This corresponds with his understanding of "church growth" as a science. He says that "Church growth science . . . tries to explain why some churches grow and others decline, why some Christians are able to bring their friends to Christ and into church membership and others are not or what are the symptoms of a terminal illness in a church" (p. 40). This analytical function, however, is not the only thing that "church growth science" does. It "helps us maximize the use of energy and other resources for God's greater glory. It enables us to detect errors and correct them before they do too much damage. It would be a mistake to claim too much, but some enthusiasts feel that with church growth insights we may even step as far ahead in God's task of world evangelization as medicine did when aseptic surgery was introduced" (p. 41).

It follows from the foregoing paragraph that when Wagner speaks of "church growth science" he is referring to a missional methodology (or a missiological method) rather than to a strictly scientific discipline. For he is concerned with the diagnosis of a particular problem (growth) in a given phenomenon (the church) and the development of a proper therapy for the correction of that problem, rather than with the systematic study of the phenomenon of which it is part. It should be added, moreover, that in missiology the object of study is neither the problem of growth nor of the church as such (this is the function of ecclesiology), but rather, the mission of

God. As a missiological method, the church-growth school is weakest at this precise point: it does not offer means comprehensive enough for the systemic study of the phenomenon of God's mission in the world.

27. Wagner, in discussing the question of faithfulness and success, points to the parable of the talents (Mt. 25:14–30) as evidence that success is a correlate of faithfulness. He asks, Why were the two servants who put their talents to work faithful and the one who did not unfaithful? "Very simply," he says, "because they were successful" (*Gospel*, p. 81). The point of the parable, however, is not the money they made but, rather, the fact that they did not hide it away. They were faithful not because they were successful (made money), but rather, because they *faithfully* put to work the resources the Master had entrusted to them. Wagner gets so enthused with the premise that "in the commercial world the task is to use capital to make more money" that he misses the point of the parable. He thus makes an eschatological warning (the true disciple will be found having been occupied in the work of the kingdom "when the Son of man comes in his glory. . . ," Mt. 25:31) into a case study on capital investment!

4

Captivity and Liberation in the Modern Missionary Movement

Is the modern missionary movement an entrepreneurial force? That is, is it a "business enterprise," a religious counterpart of the capitalist movement? Is this the reason so many churches and Christians historically related to the modern missionary movement have divorced themselves from their respective cultures, have embraced an ethic of neutrality, and have been more comfortable with structures of oppression than with movements of liberation? Could it be a mere coincidence that Christian mission has experienced its greatest expansion during the colonial era? Is it a matter of simple semantics that missionary activity has been called an "enterprise"? Could not this designation logically arise because missionary activity is possible both thanks to the prosperity of those countries that have enthusiastically sent missionaries to distant lands and because such activity accompanies—or at least prepares the way for, or follows in the steps of—commercial, military, or political activities of such countries? Should we not see behind this the reason why the modern missionary movement has assumed the corporation model as its organizational structure?

These are no frivolous questions. They arise out of concrete historical situations. Therefore, they cannot be brushed aside with simplistic defensive answers.

The fact of the matter is that during the last five centuries Christian mission has shown features of a large entrepreneurial network. The agents of this network have been mission societies, with their stockholders (individual and collective supporters), boards of directors, administrators, and employees (missionaries). This system has succeeded not only in subjugating Christian mission, but also has turned it into a tool of domestication, thereby stripping it of its liberating content.

In this chapter we shall try to demonstrate why Christian mission has been joined to the world of free enterprise. This will allow us to explain the why and the wherefore of such a union, and will help us to distinguish between the effect of that process (the subjugation of the church insofar as it is the People of God as well as of those whom the church has been called to serve) and the basic purpose of Christian mission (to be a channel of wholeness and liberation).

Mission as Enterprise: The Missionary Societies

For Latin Americans this issue dates back to the discovery of their continent. It is well known that the people who came to those shores from Spain were not only looking for gold and glory, but were also deeply motivated by religious concerns. Hence a representative of the church accompanied Columbus as early as his second voyage. Thus it was that conquest and colonization followed evangelization. (In fact, one pretext of the *encomiendas—* grants of slaves to the colonists—was to evangelize the Indians.)

If it is well known that the Iberian expansion was motivated by a genuine missionary zeal, it is no less well known that those missions also most effectively extended Spanish and Portuguese culture and rule. In 14   P   e Alexander VI granted to the Spanish kings political and religious   over all the territory already discovered or yet to be discovered that la   han "one hundred leagues" west of the Azores in the western part of the Atlantic, provided that those territories did not already belong to a Christian monarch. One year later this privilege was amended to include Portugal, to whose lot fell the territory of Brazil. The papal bulls of Alexander VI do not represent merely political privilege, but also a missionary duty: ". . . for the popes of the Renaissance who were more interested in the arts than religion, this was the easiest way to unload their responsibilities onto the kings of Spain and Portugal."[1] In this way these monarchs became the pope's vicars in the New World.

From 1516 on, all vessels heading to the New World were required to carry at least one missionary. Traditional mendicant orders such as the Franciscans and the Dominicans dedicated themselves to this task. To these were added the work of the Jesuits and the Mercedarians, in addition to some secular priests. In this way the chief Catholic missionaries early became part of the Ibero-American colonial process. Centuries later their Protestant counterparts were to be absorbed into a new colonial process: North Atlantic neo-colonialism.

For us who come from the Protestant tradition, the issue dates back to the Reformers. Both Melanchthon and Zwingli, Calvin and Bucer held that mission work was the responsibility of the civil authorities. Therefore it does not surprise us that Protestant mission work began with the political and economic expansion of such Protestant countries as Holland, England, and Denmark.

After becoming independent from Spain (1581), the Dutch set out to develop a naval empire. In 1602 they founded the East India Company. In addition to its obvious commercial goal, that company's objective was to propagate the Christian faith in the East Indies. Hence the company, and not the (Reformed) church, contracted missionaries, even going so far as to establish a seminary for their training. This also explains the commercial stimulus that was part of the beginnings of Dutch mission work: "Missionaries were paid for every baptism they performed."[2]

The corporation model as a means of commercial expansion had already been used by the English since the last decades of the sixteenth century. The idea of companies with limited liability, in which the owners were liable only for the actual stocks of the company and not for other economic interests they might have, produced an extraordinary incentive for English merchants and enormous dividends for the crown. All the same, the deep religious feelings of the English made Parliament charge the mercantile companies with the duty to evangelize such pagan peoples with whom they might come into contact. Thus a missionary goal was added to the economic and political goals in the constitutional charter granted to Humphrey Gilbert in 1583 for the colonization of North America. The Virginia and Massachusetts Bay companies had the same responsibility written into their charters. In this way the English mission work, like that of Holland, was in its beginnings part of its mercantile expansion. When in 1648 Parliament decided to take care of mission work separately, it created a mission corporation, a company with limited liability, the Society for the Propagation of the Gospel in New England. This was the model that would characterize most modern mission work.

Denmark accompanied Holland and England in their mercantile and mission efforts. In 1622 this Lutheran nation founded an East Indian Company (like England in 1600 and Holland in 1622), though it did not include mission work among its duties. This company established two colonies in India: Tanquebar in the south and Serampore in the north. In 1706 King Frederick IV felt compelled to add the missionary dimension to Tranquebar. Since he was not able to find candidates in his own country, he turned to the University of Halle in Germany, which since the time of its founder, Jacob Spener, had become the center of German Pietism. Thus the first missionaries of the famous Tranquebar mission set out from Halle. Later the Danes supported missionary efforts in Greenland and Labrador, with everything under the auspices of the crown.

Interestingly, this Danish initiative, with its Pietist link in Halle, greatly influenced the missionary work that the Moravians undertook in 1732 under Count Ludwig von Zinzendorf. I say that this is interesting because the Moravians were the first Protestants who put into practice the idea that missionary work was the responsibility of the *church,* and not of a corporation or a government. Besides this, the missionaries of the Unitas Fratrum, as the Moravians called themselves, used the experience of the Herrnhut community and developed a radically different mission focus. They would immigrate to their place of service, support themselves by manual labor, live in communities, and minister from them.[3] Beginning with the Danish colony of

Saint Thomas in the Caribbean, the Moravian missionaries, most of whom were simple workers with little formal education but filled with love and evangelistic courage, soon spread to all parts of the world.

Because of the breadth of their work, however, the Moravians found it hard to pay passages and to start work in different mission fields. In the middle of this situation was founded a "mercantile enterprise to make profits for the Lord's work."[4] At first Zinzendorf opposed the idea (partly due to his aristocratic background and partly for theological reasons), but he later agreed to the idea, provided that the profits were exclusively used for mission work. Under the leadership of Abraham Durninger, who has been called a "mercantile genius," the Moravians developed "a complex international business in textiles, especially linen, tobacco, and wholesale and retail sales."[5] Thus the Moravians added the principle "profit for the Lord" to their missionary "communalism" and thereby unconsciously helped develop an entrepreneurial identity for the missionary cause.[6]

Undoubtedly the Moravians' experience was a great inspiration for William Carey, who has been called the "father of modern missions." Carey, a self-taught person who earned his living as a cobbler, challenged himself and his English brothers and sisters to "expect great things from God" and to "undertake great things for God." He set out for India hoping to support himself by his trade, but that noble goal could not happen except through the formation of a missionary structure. So, the Particular Baptist Society for the Propagation of the Gospel among the Heathen was founded.[7] The English East India Company did not allow Carey, on his arrival in Calcutta, to enter as a missionary because it feared the subversive effect that his work could have among the Bengali people. The only way he could remain in India was to work in North Bengal as an administrator of an indigo plantation. When new missionaries arrived five years later, Carey was able to move with them to Serampore, fifty kilometers from Calcutta, thanks to the manager of the Danish East India Company.

Once settled in Serampore, the missionaries established a genuine commune in which they shared the little that they earned with their manual labor. Later in their free time they carried out impressive work: they founded churches and schools; developed botanical projects; undertook linguistic and cultural investigations; and established the first newspapers in the region. In 1818 they founded the first university in North India: Serampore College. Despite their English Baptist links, Carey and his colleagues attempted to develop a work with indigenous foundations. Perhaps this explains the many tensions between the Mission Society and the Serampore College and Mission. Finally the society refused to give Serampore financial support and dismissed Carey as one of its missionaries. In England false rumors flitted about regarding the lives and work of Carey and his colleagues. The work was seriously affected because of the struggle between the society and the local leaders—especially the missionaries—for the control of the mission and the college. Shortly after Carey's death the Serampore College and Mission had to submit to the control of the British Baptist Mission Society in order to survive.[8]

This account of William Carey and his colleagues clearly shows the sad experience of mission work throughout the last three centuries. Mission work is so dependent on the world of free enterprise that it is practically impossible for it to exist without that support. Despite the progress of his work within the local reality and despite his profound commitment to the Bengali people (Carey never returned to England), this pioneer of modern mission work found himself forced time and again to depend on the prevailing economic system—from the banking system (which enabled the transfer of funds from England by the use of letters of credit) to the mercantile companies. On the other hand, because modern missions have been built along the lines of the corporation model, they have made Christian mission part and parcel of the colonial or neo-colonial system. As a North American missionary colleague has aptly stated in an unpublished paper:

> The majority of missionary societies [have been] organized following the pattern of business corporations, operating in a given country or in their colonial extensions to make a profit through manufacture, sales, finance or whatever. The structure consists of a Board of Directors, administrative officers, and employees. The efficiency of this system depends on the fact that those who are involved are working within the same laws and economic conditions. The golden era of this type of mission was during the colonial system of the last century, and Marxists continue to remind us of the dependence of missions on the colonial powers. Even today, North American missionary societies work by and large in countries that have diplomatic relations with the USA and Canada.[9]

The trouble with all of this is that it has branded the churches and Christian institutions of the third world that have arisen from mission work. Meanwhile the majority of these churches, institutions, and believers depend on the mother country, if not economically, at least in theology, ecclesiology, missiology, and political ideology. Educational agencies such as the Theological Education Fund, whose initial capital was donated by John D. Rockefeller, Jr.; organizations such as the World Council of Churches; ecumenical social programs such as Church World Service, Christian Aid, and Bread for the World; Catholic agencies such as Caritas, Adveniat, and Miserior; and Evangelical agencies like World Vision, Tear Fund, World Relief, and World Concern are all made possible thanks to the economic power of the North American, Western European, and Australasian countries.

This reality is reinforced by the extraordinary missionary presence today in third world countries. In 1979 it was estimated that there was a worldwide Protestant missionary force of 81,500 and a Catholic force of 138,000.[10] Nearly two-thirds of Protestant missionaries came from North America—the United States and Canada—and, of these, 33.2 percent were working in

Latin America and the Caribbean respectively. (Of the 9,958 North American Catholic missionaries serving overseas, 47 percent were concentrated in Latin America.) Although we do not have the data as to the approximate number of agencies through which this impressive number of missionaries carries on its work throughout the world, we do know that in regard to North America there are no fewer than 714 Protestant mission societies[11] with a total annual income of $1,148,169,321.[12] These figures show, on the one hand, the uneven concentration of missionary personnel from the continent with one of the largest concentrations of missionaries in Latin America, which is both one of the least populated (with less than 10 percent of the total world population) and one of the most economically exploited parcels of the third world. They suggest, on the other hand, that missions are expressions of a definite entrepreneurial network, which, though not occupying a very high place among large corporations, is nevertheless alarming when we take into account the impact that such a presence is bound to have on their self-understanding, reflection on the faith, and social, political, and cultural attitudes of those churches and Christians that are related in one way or another with missionary and para-missionary agencies from the first world.

Enterprise as Mission: The Liberal Project

The incorporation of the modern missionary movement into the world of free enterprise did not occur by accident; it fits into the great liberal project of Europe and North America. Although the modern missionary movement dates back to the sixteenth and seventeenth centuries for Catholics and Protestants respectively, this project did not begin to stand out until the end of the seventeenth century. All the same, liberalism's roots go back to the Renaissance, which is both economically and sociologically connected to mercantilism. The modern missionary movement, as we have noted, is a product of mercantile expansion. That is, it has obvious links with the platform that was used to launch the liberal project. For that reason we should not be surprised to find very early in modern missionary work key postulates of liberalism such as progress, liberty, and individualism.

Thus it was not by accident that mission work took an entrepreneurial shape. It occurred because the modern missionary movement is the child of the world of free enterprises. This is not to deny the fact that missions developed from theological influences, much less that the Holy Spirit's sovereign initiative, presence, and activity guided the motives of the missionary movement. However, it is an established sociological fact that religious movements always sprout in relation to concrete historical situations. In theological terms the work of God does not exist outside of history; instead it occurs amid history's tensions and conflicts. Hence there are relationships between faith and culture, theology and ideology, church and society. In the case of the modern missionary movement, Christian mission was not only made to depend on the model of the colonial-mercantile-imperial or neo-colonial-liberal-capitalist enterprise, but also on its goal to reorganize society in terms of an economy free from state control, of a governmental structure based on voting rights, and of a universal vision founded on the idea of progress. From this perspective, the missionary movement was called to various tasks.

First, it had to legitimate the liberal project with symbols, doctrinal statements, and ecclesial practices. In order to do this, missionary societies organized churches with a representative or congregational form of government wherein liberal democracy could be exercised. They founded schools and religious-education programs based on personal honesty, dedication to work, temperance, and moderation, respect for civil authorities, self-control, and avoidance of vices and worldly pleasures. They established seminaries, institutes, or theological faculties where pastors, teachers, and administrators could be trained in accordance with liberal ideology. Finally there was the task of interpreting the faith in symbols and categories that corresponded to the liberal project through translated literary works and original publications.

In the second place, the missionary movement has sometimes been called to prepare the way for agents of liberal economics or politics. This was the task that the Wesleyan movement performed in the eighteenth century and David Livingstone in the nineteenth. The Wesleyan movement first set out to evangelize the English proletariat and then moved to evangelize the heathen. Thus it provided a religious alternative to the French Revolution's "Liberty, Equality, and Fraternity" in the form of what Bernard Semmel has called the "Methodist Synthesis." This synthesis combined the old and the new: a passion for liberty and respect for order, and the internal renewal of England along with its outward expansion. In addition it established the ideology of the Victorian era. In this way the Wesleyan movement's home-mission project preceded its worldwide mission work and also prepared the way for England's national mission, namely, the British empire.[13] We can talk in similar terms of the great explorer-missionary David Livingstone. Not only did Livingstone open up the routes into the heart of Africa for English business; he also set the foundation for Britain's colonization of Africa.[14]

Third, and most recently, mission societies and other related agencies have enabled the church (both at home and abroad) and the nations they serve to adapt to the entrepreneurial system's new strategies. It is well known that since the mid-1950s the entrepreneurial world has been undergoing a profound change. Panamanian economist Xabier Gorostiaga has divided this process into two parts: the internalization of production (1955–65) and the internalization of capital (1965–75), which has resulted in the development of multinational companies and transnational financial centers.[15]

Curiously enough, the world missionary movement has been experiencing similar changes. In 1963 the 7th World Missionary Conference, meeting in Mexico and sponsored by the World Council of Churches, developed the idea of "witness in six continents." Since then the idea of an internationalized mission has become popular in Protestant mission circles.

Among Catholics the impetus of Vatican II gave birth to the idea of "mutuality in mission"; that is, all of the church is to be involved in mission and not simply the church located in so-called mission lands. Thus many Catholic missionary societies have a multinational missionary staff serving in many lands and cultures.

In Evangelical Protestantism a series of missionary and evangelistic congresses has created an ever greater international awareness of mission work. This series began in 1966 with the Wheaton Congress on World Evangelization. It continued with the First and Second Latin American Congresses of Evangelization (Bogota, 1969; Lima, 1979) and other similar congresses in Asia, Africa, North America, and Europe, and culminated in the International Congress of World Evangelization held in Lausanne in 1974, which was followed by the Consultation on World Evangelization held in June 1980, in Pattaya, Thailand, and the Congress on Frontier Missions held in Edinburgh, Scotland, in October 1980.[16]

At Lausanne there was a discussion about a new missionary era (an expression that was also used in the 8th World Missionary Conference sponsored by the World Council of Churches in Bangkok, Thailand, in 1973). The meeting in Lausanne concluded that "the dominant role of Western missions is fast disappearing. God is raising up from the young churches a great new resource for world evangelization."[17] The emerging mission societies of the third world are this new resource.[18]

During this time mission societies such as the Latin American Mission (nondenominational), the Paris Mission (Reformed), the World Mission Council (Congregational), and service agencies such as World Vision were turning into "multinational" organizations. The Latin American Mission (LAM) became part of the Community of Latin American Evangelical Ministries (CLAME), the Paris Mission became the Evangelical Community for Apostolic Action (CEVAA), and the Council for World Mission, successor to the London Missionary Society, went through a reorganization that has brought into its fellowship congregational churches in the United Kingdom, Australia, and New Zealand plus all of the other churches with which the old London Missionary Society was related. World Vision, an organization which for some time has had its financial base in the United States, Canada, Australia, and New Zealand, has developed a separate international corporation with a board of directors and an executive and program staff from the first and third worlds.[19]

One of the most interesting examples of this process is the United States Center for World Mission, founded in 1977 and located in Pasadena, California. This center includes a consortium of new mission societies that function within historical churches as alternatives (shock troops) to the work of mission boards or official denominational departments. Furthermore it has stimulated the organization of a national committee that brings together mission committees of local churches throughout the United States and offers, among other things, advice for the financial support of mission work. It also sponsors William Carey University, which offers opportunities to young university students who hope to serve either as career missionaries or (more preferably) as missionary volunteers through secular employment abroad. The university attempts to be a link with several centers of missiological research and missionary activity that are located in strategic parts of the world. This mission complex focuses its attention in areas of the world where there are the greatest numbers of peoples as yet untouched by the gospel, such as China, animist groups, and the Muslim, Hindu, and Buddhist worlds. Its strategy is to spread the gospel to these places via the most workable method. In some instances this may involve business executives or members of the diplomatic corps. Its organizational principles are a combination of the old voluntary association (connected to missionary societies), computer technology (e.g., the use of computers to gather statistics and form a network of contacts with the financial bases of the churches), and the construction of a network of multinational operations.

It should be said at the outset that relationships of this sort are unconscious and indirect. They are not concocted by specific groups of people. We must avoid what Gorostiaga calls a " 'detective view of history' that suspects Machiavellian plots whenever one mentions power elites that try to institute a structurally functioning system."[20] Christians who participate in the modern missionary movement do so, by and large, out of a sincere commitment to Jesus Christ and the Christian missionary mandate. Nevertheless they are part of a worldwide system that often uses people, movements, and institutions for purposes other than the communication of the gospel and its liberating power.

Given the traditional alliance between the world of free enterprise and the missionary movement, it appears that whatever change occurs in the former would sooner or later affect the latter. The simple fact is that the missionary movement has been supported economically by women, men, and agencies committed to the so-called free-enterprise system and its liberal capitalist ideology. Since many mission benefactors are people whose lives are involved directly or indirectly with multinational enterprises, it is natural that mission organizations not only develop work methods, organizational structures, and administrative techniques from the capitalist system, but also that they are part of that economic system. (Many missionary agencies as well as other religious institutions of the North Atlantic have invested substantially in large corporations.) Furthermore, the hope is that just as missions supported the ideological system in its early stages, so they will do it again in this new phase. For this reason it is deemed necessary to adapt the mission system to the new shape of the commercial system.

The evidence submitted thus far seems to indicate, at least, that one of the contemporary functions of the missionary movement is that of facilitating the process of adaptation of significant regions of the third world to the new mode of international capitalism. Such adaptation takes both negative and positive forms. Negatively it involves the rejection of any attempts to break with the system of international capitalism. Positively it involves the spreading and strengthening of ethical values, of doctrinal positions, of ecclesial practices, and of lifestyles that conform to that system.

This may partly explain the fantastic support that has been given in recent years by many missionary-minded churches and individuals to large evangelistic campaigns, social-assistance projects, activities that overemphasize numerical church growth and de-emphasize other dimensions of the church's life, the promotion of popular religious literature that tends toward spiritual sensationalism, and the development of church administration techniques. This may also partly explain the great opposition one notices in such circles to educational and theological-pastoral programs that attempt to be critically contextual; to literature of the same kind; to evangelistic efforts that do not conform to traditional patterns or contents; to social programs dedicated to macro-structural issues, and church activities that are based on a contextualized and liberating Christian ethic. By the same token it may explain why many mission societies and para-mission service agencies support (sometimes implicitly, sometimes explicitly) fascist governments in some parts of Asia, Africa, and Latin America. Finally it may explain their displeasure with liberation movements (such as the Popular Coalition in Chile).

Enterprise as Domestication, Mission as Liberation

Earlier we stated that the issue of the missionary movement as an instrument of domestication is not frivolous but is based in concrete experiences that raise serious and penetrating questions. In the first section of this chapter we have pointed out the links between the modern missionary movement and the world of free enterprise. In the second section we have sought to understand the domesticating role that the Christian world mission—insofar as it is an entrepreneurial force—has played in the last five hundred years. But is this all that we can say about Christian mission? By no means!

We must bear in mind that Christian mission is grounded on the mission of God as revealed in the history of Israel and incarnated in the person and work of Jesus Christ. The Old Testament discloses a God who is opposed to any attempts to subjugate; a God who is on the side of the widow and the orphan, the poor and the stranger; a God who raises the humble and casts down the oppressor; who frees from slavery, demands justice, freedom, and peace. The New Testament witnesses to the incarnation of this mission in the person and work of Jesus Christ. Thus Jesus identified with the poor, proclaimed wholeness for the sick, liberty for the captives, and restoration for the marginated and deprived. It is in this perspective that the missionary mandate has been given. Jesus commands his disciples to continue his work under guidance through the power of the Holy Spirit.

Christian mission is therefore a liberation movement. To be sure, it is a liberation from the power of sin and death. As I have noted elsewhere in this book, in the Scriptures sin and death are understood in social and personal terms, cosmically and historically; that is, as opposition to God's work, as deformation and corruption of the way of life that God gives. They are understood as alienation and enmity among people and between humanity and creation. Therefore forgiveness from sin means, on the one hand, liberation from all sorts of enmity, and, on the other, reconciliation with God, neighbor, and creation. Such an experience gains validity in concrete practice. It is verified in life. This is the message that the church has been sent to proclaim and to teach to the nations. The church should bear witness to the liberating God of the Bible; it should anticipate the shalom of God's kingdom; it should practice his justice; it should be a "free" servant community that celebrates God's love in daily life.

We must also remember that from its beginning the Christian world mission has had to struggle against the threat of subjugation. We find groups in the New Testament such as the Zealots, the Judaizers, and the Gnostics, which attempted to subdue the liberating cause of Jesus Christ. The Zealots tried to combine the liberating project of Jesus with their national chauvinism, but Jesus refused to allow that. The Judaizers wished to convert the early church into a Judeo-Pharisaic sect, but the disciples, especially Paul, turned back that attempt, emphasizing the interracial, international, anticlassist, and antisexist nature of Christian faith. The Gnostics intended to turn the gospel into an ahistorical and privatistic message, but leaders such as John the apostle vigorously attacked that by declaring the historicity of the gospel (the incarnation) and its apostolic and communal character.

We can point to similar attempts at domestication in later times.[21] Despite the cooptation of the gospel that followed the Edict of Milan (A.D. 313), Christian mission was able to resist complete perversion in the Constantinian era by means of prophetic groups as disparate as the heretical Nestorians and the mendicant orders. Despite the intrusion of mercantile and imperialistic elements in the modern mission era, we can find many landmarks of liberation. Thus we find in sixteenth-century colonial Spanish America missionaries such as Bartolomé de las Casas and Luis de Montesino; or such moving gestures as that of the Moravians in Saint Thomas, who were willing to become slaves in order to minister to the slave population; or William Carey in the beginning of the nineteenth century, who planted the seed that was to encourage the Bengali people to fight for Indian independence from the British colonial yoke; or Johannes Verkuyl in the twentieth century, who took the risks of excommunication from his own church in Holland, of expulsion from his mission society, and of being considered a traitor by his fellow citizens when he sided with Sukarno and his freedom fighters in the struggle for Indonesia's liberation.

Nowadays the vanguard of the missionary enterprise must contend with a minority of Christians who are committed to the liberating project of Jesus Christ. These Christians are not merely resisting the domesticating role that has been ascribed to the Christian world mission by the missionary movement. They are also developing a new missionary presence in the world. This minority is present on practically every level of the Christian church as well as in many mission circles. Those who identify with this stream need not be intimidated by the power structures of the missionary enterprise. There is no reason to worry or feel inferior when facing the missionary apostasy that we see in many parts of the Christian church today. On the contrary, such prophetic missionary minorities should join forces and with courage and commitment continue to unmask the secret alliance between the world missionary movement and the internationalist capitalist enterprise, repossessing the liberating character of mission by building new plans of action and missionary organizations, by changing the direction of those missionary, paramissionary, and ecclesiastical organizations that want to be renewed and are opening themselves to the winds of the Holy Spirit, and by letting the transforming power of the gospel work in their personal lives and ministries.

NOTES

1. Justo L. González, *Historia de las misiones* (Buenos Aires: La Aurora, 1970), pp. 142–43. Trans. from Spanish to English by O.E.C.

2. Ibid., p. 190.

3. An excellent example of such missional communalism is the economic system set up at the Moravian settlement in Bethlehem, Pa. (founded in 1742). According to J. Taylor Hamilton and Kenneth G. Hamilton, the system, which became known as the Economy, was "adopted . . . so as to develop the resources of the new settlement as quickly as possible and thus free the latent power of the community for the work of the Savior." They add that "Basic to the Economy was a community of labor rather than property. . . . Any member who owned property was permitted to retain it if he chose, but all were required to place their time, talents, and labor at the disposal of the Church. No private enterprises existed in the community; every form of business and manufacture belonged to the Church, as did all real estate. All branches of the common Economy came under the supervision of committees. . . . With all its defects . . . the Economy served its purpose remarkably well in its day. . . . The Economy supported about fifty evangelists and pastors and maintained some fifteen schools and provided the traveling expenses for missionaries to the West Indies and Surinam" (*History of the Moravian Church: The Renewed* Unitas Fratrum *1722-1957* [Bethlehem, Pa.; Winston-Salem, N.C.: Interprovincial Board of Christian Education, Moravian Church in America, 1967], p. 137).

4. William J. Danker, *Profit for the Lord* (Grand Rapids, Mich.: Wm. B. Eerdmans, 1971), p. 21. Cf. Hamilton and Hamilton, *History,* p. 113.

5. Danker, *Profit,* p. 23.

6. Ibid., pp.31ff.

7. "Particular Baptists" were those who held to Calvinist theology as against "General Baptists" who were Arminian. Interestingly enough, it was Calvinist Baptists who championed the missionary cause among Baptists rather than the "free-will" Arminians.

8. William S. Stewart, ed., *The Story of Serampore and Its College* (Serampore: The Council of Serampore College, n.d.), pp. 20ff.

9. Charles Troutman, "On Missions as Corporations," unpublished paper, San José, Costa Rica (1976), p. 4.

10. Cf. Samuel Wilson, ed., *Mission Handbook: North American Protestant Ministries Overseas,* 12th ed. (Monrovia, Calif.: MARC, 1980), pp. 20–21.

11. Ibid., pp. 20–22. There are approximately three hundred Catholic missionary societies in the United States but their total-income figure is unavailable.

12. In 1976 Richie Hogg compared the income of the American Protestant overseas missionary enterprise to the "Fortune 500" list of the largest industrial corporations in the United States and found it stood only at 410th place. See Richie Hogg, "The Role of American Protestantism in World Mission," *American Missions in Bicentennial Perspective,* ed. R. Pierce Beaver (Pasadena, Calif.: William Carey Library, 1977), p. 370.

13. Cf. Bernard Semmel, *The Methodist Revolution* (New York: Basic Books, 1973), pp. vii, 20, 170ff.

14. Cf. Judith Listowel, *The Other Livingstone* (Sussex, England: Julien F. Friedman Publishers, 1974), pp. 232–46; Tim Jeal, *Livingstone* (London: Heinemann, 1973), pp. 370–74.

15. Cf. Xabier Gorostiaga, "Notas sobre metodología para un diagnóstico económico del capitalismo latinoamericano," in *Capitalismo: violencia y antivida*, vol. 1, ed. Elsa Tamez and Saúl Trinidad, Colección DEI (San José, Costa Rica: EDUCA, 1978), pp. 40–48; idem, *Los banqueros del imperio: Los centros financieros en los países sub-desarrollados*, Colección DEI (San José, Costa Rica: EDUCA, 1977), passim.

16. For a report on Edinburgh 1980, see William Cook, "A Church for Every People by the Year 2,000," in *Occasional Essays* 8 nos. 1–2 (December 1981), 18–19.

17. "The Lausanne Covenant," article 8, in *Let the Earth Hear His Voice,* ed. J. D. Douglas (Minneapolis, Minn.: Worldwide Publications, 1975).

18. While no exact figures on the number of third world Protestant missionaries exist, there are some limited studies that have been able to identify several hundred. Third world missionary societies could include well over 5,000 missionaries. For outdated yet helpful statistical evidence, see James Wong, Peter Larson, and Edward Pentecost, *Missions from the Third World: A World Survey of Non-Western Missions in Asia, Africa and Latin America* (Singapore: Church Growth Study Center, 1972). For a discussion on issues related to the work of Protestant third world missions, see Theodore Williams, ed., *World Missions: Building Bridges or Barriers* (Bangalore, India: World Evangelical Fellowship Missions Commission, 1979).

19. I have been referring specifically to the Protestant missionary movement, although the work of Catholic missions has similar links in countries like the Federal Republic of Germany, the Netherlands, the United States, and Canada. It is interesting to note that the Catholic churches of Holland, Germany, France, Italy, the United States, and Canada also began to form missionary societies in the nineteenth century.

20. Gorostiaga, "Notas," p. 40.

21. See, e.g., the historical analyses of Max Warren, *I Believe in the Great Commission* (Grand Rapids, Mich.: Wm. B. Eerdmans, 1976), pp. 56–127; and González, *Historia*, pp. 41–132.

5

A New Macedonia:
The United States as a Mission Field
for Third World Christians

Can the nation with the greatest missionary presence[1] in the world be regarded as "a mission field"? If so, can that sector of the world which represents the habitat of the have-nots and the oppressed of the earth have anything to contribute to the missionary situation of the United States?

The first question raises the issue of what constitutes "a mission field." According to Alfred Krass, a mission field is a place "where many people still need to hear the gospel for the first time . . . [and] where people follow heathen customs and worship heathen 'gods.' " A mission field would thus be "any situation where [people] do not know to whom they belong." In such a place "we can find heathendom."[2]

But, as I have argued elsewhere, mission has not only to do with the specific communication of the gospel.[3] A mission field, therefore, cannot be defined solely in terms of the personal relation of people to the gospel and "heathendom." There are at least two reasons why this cannot be done.

The first is the simple fact that life is a contextual reality. There are numerous factors that in one way or another affect or are affected by the sharing of the gospel with those who "do not know to whom they belong." These so-called nontheological factors (ideologies, political and economic systems, social classes and movements, cultural distinctives, and psychological phenomena) must also be taken into account in designating a place as "a mission field."

Second, insofar as God's mission (at whose service are the missions of the churches) deals with the unfolding of his redemptive purpose for the world, it has not only a personal but also a political-ecumenical dimension. As J. Verkuyl has said: "There is such a thing as a *missio politica oecumenica,* a vocation to work together in world-wide cooperation toward development and . . . liberation from economic exploitation and political and racial oppression."[4]

The United States qualifies as "a mission field" because many of its people are alienated from God and neighbor. In spite of the millions who profess to be Christians by virtue of baptism, church membership, or conventionality, an overwhelming number of Americans have not really heard[5] the gospel or had a reasonable opportunity to consider it as a personal option. They go through life without a personal awareness of the God who in creation and redemption has staked a claim upon their lives and invites them to experience, by the power of his Spirit, freedom, community, and hope. The dominant symptoms of this situation of alienation are fear, anxiety, and distrust at the personal level, and racism, classism, and sexism at the social level.

The United States also qualifies as a mission field because the witness of American Christians is intrinsically related to their life and thought as a church and as an indissoluble part of their culture and society. Whatever they do affects their missionary activity at home and abroad. Whatever happens in the American sociocultural milieu affects the life and thought of the American church. This in turn affects the life and thought of churches abroad, especially their own missionary witness, and the fulfillment of the *missio politica oecumenica* noted above. To see the relevance of the United States as "a mission field" today is not missiologically urgent only for American Christians. It is just as crucial for third world Christians.

In referring to the missionary challenge of the United States for third world Christians, we must distinguish between the general and the specific. The United States should be seen *generally* as a mission field by *all* third world Christians, whether in or out of the United States, because of the existing correspondence between their social, economic, cultural, and political situation and that of mainstream American culture and society. A similar correspondence exists between church and theology in the third world and in mainstream American culture and society, and between church and theology in the third world and in mainstream American church life and theology. The United States also represents a *particular* missionary challenge for third world Christians because it confronts them with the challenge of crossing new frontiers.

Several major missionary challenges may be identified. The remainder of this chapter will offer an analysis of each and the delineation of several possible ways by which third world Christians can respond. We begin with the most particular one.

A New Ethno-Cultural Panorama

That the United States is a nation of immigrants is well known. Very few nations of the world can boast such a complex ethnic composition. Today, however, this nation faces a new ethno-cultural panorama. This reality poses a unique missionary challenge.

Besides the traditional European groups, which have "melted" into the main "pot" of North American society, there are said to be over 120 ethnic groups communicating in more than 100 languages and dialects. They represent roughly one-third of the total population. But, as Eduardo Seda Bonilla has reminded us (among other social scientists), in dealing with United States ethnic minorities it is necessary to distinguish between (1) the immigrants of different nationalities, and (2) the racial minorities.[6]

The latter can be grouped into four categories: Blacks, Hispanics, Native Americans, and Asians. All of them are classified by the mainstream culture and society as "non-White." This is another way of saying that they are not of European stock. Hispanics, though having among them many Whites, represent, as a group, the halfbreed offspring of Europeans and Amerindians; consequently they are not *pure* White. As a matter of fact, when grouped together these minorities represent the regions that have suffered the greatest impact of Western civilization (Africa, the Middle East, Asia, the Pacific, Latin America, and the Caribbean). They are the offspring of the worst social rape in the history of humankind. Forced or induced to migrate or relocate for economic, social, military, or political reasons, they have settled mainly in the large urban centers of the country and the rural areas of the southwest and midwest. Not only have they been marginated socially and culturally, but economically and politically. Their plight is therefore relatively identical with their African, Middle Eastern, Asian, Pacific, Latin American, and Caribbean counterparts.

For many years these "non-White" contingents were forced to deny their cultural heritage. Their children were forced to acculturate into the mainstream culture. They were prohibited from speaking their languages, were looked down on because of their diets, criticized for grouping together and, above all, ridiculed for their physical characteristics. The process of forced acculturation, however, was resisted both internally and externally: internally because, though each of these minorities adapted to the new environment, they created institutions of their own which enabled their traditions, languages, and values to survive; externally because, even when they tried to adhere to the rules of the mainstream, they would find it extremely difficult to integrate culturally and socially on account of the mainstream's blatant racism. Dutch, Germans, Swedes, Norwegians, Italians, Jews, and Poles were able to assimilate because they had basically similar characteristics. The fact that they were white and came from a continent with a history of cultural and political fertilization made it possible for them to become integral parts of the "American way of life." This was not the case with the Asians, Hispanics, Native Americans, and Blacks. Though forced to acculturate, they were kept in the fringes of society as the "non-White" contingent.

This situation remained relatively the same for many years until the Blacks unleashed a "fascinating process of reverse acculturation . . . to an African cultural identity."[7] Native Americans, Chicanos, Puerto Ricans, Chinese, and other Asian groups began to follow in their footsteps. Today the United States presents a radically new ethno-cultural panorama, which has even affected other oppressed sectors of society (e.g., youth and women).

Two missionary possibilities seem to be opened to third world Christians vis-à-vis the ethno-cultural panorama of the United States. The first is the need for solidarity. For far too long "mainline" third worlders have tended to associate their American brothers and sisters much too quickly with the mainstream culture. Yet they have not hesitated to link their own colonial and neo-colonial masters with European societies. Many Africans have been seen wanting to maintain a distance from North American Blacks, little realizing the extraordinary parallels between the racial situation in southern Africa and the United States. Many Latin Americans have treated despicably Chicanos and Puerto Ricans, failing to recognize the parallels between their plight and that of oppressed minorities in Latin America, such as Indian and Afro-Caribbean groups. The mainstream American establishment has, of course, welcomed this distancing, since it has always insisted, especially in socioscientific and political circles, that the differences between what I have called "mainline" third worlders, and especially between them and their American counterparts, are simply too great to merit any collective-entity status. As in the colonial period, so in the age of neo-colonialism, the Euro-North American mainstream, and particularly that of the United States, has sought to break and divide the natural ties that bind the peoples of the third world together, bonds that stem from the common social, economic, cultural, and political situations of marginalization and oppression, to which they have been and are still submitted.[8] But, if Christians are called to be the conscience of society, if they are to be prophetic witnesses of justice and liberation, if they are called to identify themselves with the poor and oppressed mainline third world Christians, who have experienced in the flesh the global reality of oppression and have been given (along with other Christians) the gift of discernment, they cannot remain neutral or passive in the face of the concrete oppressed situation of non-White American minorities. Indeed the seriousness of their commitment and solidarity with their own particular societies is tested in their planetary solidarity with all oppressed peoples, including those in a nation like the United States. If, as it shall be noted later on, American Christians must be called to accountability for their responsibility toward the third world, then third world Christians must also be called to accountability as the "keepers" of their oppressed American brethren and sisters.

The other missionary opportunity for third world Christians vis-à-vis American minorities is in the sharing of suitable personnel to minister effectively the Word of God. Note that I say "sharing" and "suitable." There have been many third world Christians who have come to the United States and are currently engaged in ministry among ethnic minorities, but have been neither trained for the task nor carefully and prayerfully selected and sent. They have come as any other migrant in search of a better way of life, or as foreign students, or as clergy called by a local congregation or a denomination to fulfill a professional task. While many of the latter have turned out to be effective leaders, it has not been without a long, painful process of adaptation, which has drawn much of their energy and resources. Moreover, the abandonment of their national-ecclesial context has left many resentments, interpreting it in the same way as the so-called brain drain that third world countries suffer from the migration of their professional and highly skilled personnel to more advanced and prosperous countries.

The time has come, however, for third world churches and missionary organizations to enter into partnership with their American counterparts for the sharing of suitable personnel to help meet the challenge of American minorities. I know of a few cases where such a partnership has begun to take place. In this connection it is ironic that, while the World Council of Churches has an Ecumenical Sharing of Personnel Program, practically all of the exchanges it has sponsored (so far as I know) have been between third world countries as such. It is also ironic that while there are numerous American training centers for missionary work outside the United States into which, in fact, many foreign students are encouraged to enter, hardly any of them are engaged in the preparation of personnel from overseas for missionary service in the United States.

An Emerging Pluralistic Religious Frontier

As the ethno-cultural panorama has changed, so has the religious situation. It used to be that—apart from Native American religions, New England Transcendentalism, and other rather small "harmonious" religious movements—the overwhelming majority of the religious frontiers that United States Christians had to cross in the evangelization of their fellow Americans were rooted in the Western tradition. In the last few years, however, the United States, along with other Western nations, has seen the emergence of non-Western, non-Christian religious frontiers.[9] The Eastern Missionary Advance—as the activities of the various movements, older Eastern religions, and occultist sects may be labeled—is not only attracting numerous Americans but is also forcing a new religious pluralism in the United States.[10] It is revealing, at the same time, how missiologically stagnant have been North American Christian churches and believers *at home* and how spiritually empty are, especially, Middle Americans.

How to cross this relatively new religious frontier? How to create the necessary space to live in a religiously plural society, working toward greater community with other religious groupings while affirming the Christian missionary commitment? How to witness positively and effectively to the adherents of non-Christian religions and movements? And above all, how to fill the obvious lacunae which make possible the loss of personal identity and social frustration and set the stage for a flight from the social world into an inner, private self through the medium of Eastern sects and religions? These are questions that many third world Christians have had to contend with. Their much closer and firsthand knowledge of the Eastern religious world could, and should, enable them to assist American Christians as they wrestle with the challenge of the Eastern advance.

Here is one area where missionary service abroad could turn out to be a profitable training ground for service in the United States. Instead of limiting themselves to what they can do *for* people in the foreign field, missionaries should also see their presence there as an opportunity to learn *from* them in order to help their own home churches to respond more effectively to their own missionary frontiers. Likewise, home mission strategies could profit from an on-the-job training experience in the Eastern and Southern worlds, and home mission boards and evangelization committees could benefit from the consultative services of third world Christian leaders, especially those who are in the front lines of mission.

A Critical Politico-Ideological Consciousness

A third reality may be witnessed among certain sectors of American society. Sydney Ahlstrom has called it the end of "the Puritan era." Wesley Michaelson has referred to it in terms of "the gradual disintegration of a dominant, traditional culture."[11] James Wallis has described it as the growing awareness of "what two centuries of doctrines of racial and national superiority, of Manifest Destiny, of violence have done to the American spirit." Wallis goes on to state: "The traditional American civil religion which blesses the social order rather than calling it into question is now under serious attack, and for many quarters that civil religion is being named for what it is—misplaced allegiance which usually degenerates into outright idolatry."[12]

Such critical consciousness has called into question traditional parameters of American political existence. It has unmasked the ideological postulates that lie beneath "the American way of life." It has demythologized the religious myth of American politics and the political myth of its religious life. Indeed, no longer is it intellectually tenable to hold to the notion of "a nation under God," just as it is no longer possible to speak of a politically neutral American religious life. Or to put it in other terms: the god of the American Constitution ("the deists' God, the religiously distant Ground of things as they are"[13]) has been at last dissociated from the God of biblical faith (the God of love and justice who calls to accountability persons and institutions). Likewise the "public space" traditionally (though latently) assigned to American religion ("embracing every aspect of public life except" that of making actual decisions as to the future of the nation[14]) has been increasingly exhausting itself in the sphere of a privatistic religious practice. Thus comments Robert Jenson:

> . . . Unable either to guide or condemn what we do in the polity or the economy, our religion's only relation to these arenas is now that it bucks us up for what we would do in them anyway; just so evangelical religion becomes in truth the comfort of the oppressors and opiate of the oppressed. In this setting, the Bible is, of course, a stumbling block. We could get rid of it by generally adopting authentically privatist Eastern religions, or religions invented specially for the purpose; and that is actually what many are doing.[15]

The consciousness just described has received strong support from—and in many instances can be said to have been provoked by—the third world. One need not go very far in contemporary intellectual circles to be confronted with prophetic voices from the "non-White" and oppressed world. This is especially the case in the field of religion and theology. Whether Catholic or Protestant, numerous third world religionists and theologians have addressed themselves in recent years to issues related to American political reality.[16] One of the most potent contributions of the last decade was "An Open Letter to North American Christians" from a group of Latin American Protestant church leaders. Sent on the eve of the 1976 national elections, this letter sought not only to explain the predicament of Latin Americans vis-à-vis the United States ("We are trapped in the same system . . . , and we all move within one economic-political-military complex, in which one finds committed fabulous interests of financial groups which dominate the life of your country and the creole oligarchies of our Latin American nations"[17]), but to challenge American Christians to respond faithfully to their missionary responsibility in the political arena of the United States:

> If in the past you felt it to be your apostolic duty to send us missionaries and economic resources, today the frontier of your witness and Christian solidarity is within your own country. . . We, between tears and groans, are interceding for you, in order that you may respond with faithfulness to the historic responsibility which, as citizens of one of the great contemporary powers and as disciples of Jesus Christ, it falls on you to assume.[18]

A Global Economic-Technological Reality

Closely related with the foregoing is the new economic-technological reality that can now be witnessed around the globe. While Western technology (of which the United States is a senior partner) has induced certain economic growth around the world, thereby contributing to the transformation of global society, it has also created numerous problems for itself and others. For one thing, it has severely damaged its own environment. For another, it has become the means through which Western societies (and particularly the United States) have been able to dominate, domesticate, and oppress less-developed societies. This has given way to a twofold reaction from the third world: on the one hand, a global rebellion against Western models of "development" with a concomitant critique of what Rubem Alves has called the ideology of "technologism"[19]; on the other, an increasing recognition on the part of Western societies of the much healthier attitude of less-advanced third world societies toward their environment. Indeed, the absence of the dichotomy between humankind and nature and the mistreatment of the latter by the former, so characteristic of Western technological society, has become a fundamental point of reference in the Western quest for a "theology of nature."[20]

The global economic-technological reality becomes more acute the moment we consider such world problems as hunger, energy, and economic order. Can the most affluent nation on earth be morally indifferent to the starving millions around the world? Is it not ironic that for years decisions that were made in Washington and on Wall Street determined the fates of the people in the third world, and that in a matter of a few years decisions made in OPEC-member countries (all of them being from the third world) are affecting the destiny of the United States, among other advanced technological societies? Can the United States go it alone in relation to energy and other essential raw materials? Can it afford to be indifferent to the economic situation of the third world? Yet the United States has given that impression. For example, when in May 1974 the General Assembly of the United Nations approved a resolution calling for a New International Economic Order, the United States opposed it. Instead it embarked on a counteroffensive against the third world by calling together several "economic summits" of North Atlantic nations. How long can the United States "continue to ignore the gross inequities between the have's and the have not's of this world?"[21]

The witness to planetary interdependence in North American society is a crucial missional challenge that third world Christians cannot ignore. The scandalous "prosperity at the expense of the Third World"[22] is a matter that cannot be foregone either by Christians in the stricken lands or by their brothers and sisters in the United States. The cry of the "Open Letter to North American Christians" mentioned above becomes, therefore, profoundly relevant and penetrating: ". . . you must ask yourselves if you will or will not be 'your brother's keeper' in these lands of America (and, for that matter, in the entire Third World), from which the blood of millions of Abels are clamoring to heaven."[23]

A Crisis of Church and Theology

The fact is, however, that American Christians seem almost paralyzed by the crisis of the institutional church and its theology. This crisis has many facets.

A Culturally Bound Church and an Ideologically Captive Theology

The cultural boundness of the church and the ideological captivity of its theology are one aspect of this crisis. Michaelson is right in stating that "the distinct problem with mission to America is that the Christian church finds itself deeply identified already with the dominant but disintegrating culture" of the United States.[24] One need not go far to see this uncritical acculturation to the "American way of life." From the corporation-type pattern of church organization to the types of ministerial training, worship, and evangelization, patterns of church administration and lifestyles, the majority of American churches reveal an uncritical commitment to their sociocultural milieu. This being so, the affirmation that American theology has been and still is ideologically captive to the "American way of life" should not come as a surprise. As James Cone said:

> . . . American theology from Cotton Mather and Jonathan Edwards to Reinhold Niebuhr and Schubert Ogden, including radicals and conservatives, has interpreted the gospel according to the cultural and political interests of white people. . . . White theologians, because of their identity with the dominant power structure, are largely buoyed within their own cultural history.[25]

A Clergy-dominated Church and a Laity-dominated Clergy

Another facet of this crisis is the clergy-dominated character of the American church and the laity-dominated situation of its clergy. In the North American Interchurch Study conducted by the National Council of Churches in the early 1970s, the role of pastors as intermediaries of church life was strongly underscored. They not only controlled the flow of denominational information in their respective congregations, but projected their own fears and feelings on the information which their congregations rendered to the denomination.[26]

Because of their professional training and the prestige carried from the colonial and frontier periods, clergy dominate local church and denominational church programs and priorities. This dominating role may be witnessed even in the realm of theology. As Martin Marty has pointed out: "Almost all church theology is clerical; almost always ordained ministers in seminaries or in congregations are called upon to depict the meaning of the Christian life in any profound way." In consequence, the laity have been generally absent from "the circles out of which theological interpretation of life occurs."[27]

Conversely, American laity exercise an extraordinary control over clergy. The fact that the clergy are considered employees of the church speaks for itself. Many clergy are conscious and fearful of the fact that their job depends upon the "happiness" of their respective boards and/or congregations. If they control the flow of information to and from their congregations and if their denominational colleagues are eager to get their messages through to the laity, it is because they suspect (indeed know) that their respective vocations depend upon the laity itself. To quote Marty once again: The laity "expect ministers to speak in hushed and hollow tones, not to reveal the true range of human emotions, to be soft and compromising or unprincipled adapters to what their congregations want them to be."[28]

A Gospel without Demands and Demands without the Gospel

The crisis of American church and theology becomes even more intensive when one reflects on two opposite patterns that can be witnessed in churches throughout the United States. The first pattern offers *a gospel without de-*

mands. The content of this gospel is a conscience-soothing Jesus, with an unscandalous cross, an otherworldly kingdom, a private, inwardly limited spirit, a pocket God, a spiritualized Bible, and an escapist church. Its goal is a happy, comfortable, and successful life, obtainable through the forgiveness of an abstract sinfulness by faith in an unhistorical Christ. Such a gospel makes possible the "conversion" of men and women without having to make any drastic changes in their lifestyles and value-systems. It guarantees, moreover, the preservation of the status quo and the immobility of the People of God.

The second pattern lies at the other end of the spectrum: *demands without the gospel.* Whether it be the individual legalism characteristic of some Holiness church groups or the collective legalism of the Moral Majority or some radical Christian groups, the accent is the same: judgment without grace, with similar results—moral exhaustion, discouragement, and frustration. The first pattern robs the gospel of its ethical thrust; the second, of its soteriological depth. The first reduces the church to a social club and theology to an ideology of the status quo; the second enslaves the church and buries the gospel.

A Mission in Crisis and a Crisis of Mission

This leads to the fourth aspect of the crisis. With such a truncated view of the gospel and the prophetic task of the church, the fact of a mission in crisis and a crisis of mission becomes obvious. This double missionary crisis represents two sides of the same coin. The world mission of the American church is in crisis because of the burden of what Carl Braaten has rightly called the *impedimenta Americana,* that is, the interplay between the American missionary movement and American imperialism.[29] This interplay, which Ruben Lores, among others, has linked with the ideology of "manifest destiny," has made the American missionary movement the carrier of Anglo-Saxon Christianity and "the American way of life" rather than the gospel of Jesus Christ.[30] A credibility gap can be thus witnessed between "a faith that proclaims a living, loving Lord," and the participation of its "adherents . . . in inhuman ventures, exploitation, hate and death."[31]

In the face of this credibility gap, the American church seems to be turning inward, spending "more and more of its energy analyzing itself, financing costly studies of its functions and structures and affirmations." This would not be such a dangerous path if it were not for the fact that "such studies keep the church in motion through revolving doors, and do not drive it to the frontiers of world history." Instead of calling the church to accountability, they seem to be driving it "to retreat from world history and to enter into a new religious isolationism."[32]

The crisis of the American world mission calls not for a new religious isolationism with an inward kick that hides itself behind a mission to the backyard, but rather, for the removal of the scandal of the American missionary movement. This implies a radical break with the ideology of "manifest destiny" and thus American cultural, economic, and political imperialism. It implies the "maintenance of a low profile by Americans within international structures of world mission."[33] This is necessary if the imperialistic image attached to the modern missionary movement is to be effaced. Such a restructuring demands that American Christians do away with the notion of a mission to the world and replace it with the concept of *participation* in a global mission to, from, and within all six continents, a mission that will involve all the resources of the world church, and that will be based on Christian solidarity, respect, and trust, and not on the multinational-corporation mentality criticized in the previous chapter. This may mean, that, for the present, American mainstream Christians "may have to play a more passive role abroad and a more active role at home." For how can they "expect to cross the racial, cultural and economic barriers abroad when their experience at home proves that their white, affluent, middle-to-upper class status creates a gap they have not yet effectively bridged?"[34]

Toward a Third World Contribution
to American Church and Theology

Such a perspective imposes a strong dose of responsibility upon third world Christians in relation to the United States. For how can there be a truly global mission if a partner fails to come to the aid of the other when a situation of crisis arises? The issue here—as was pointed out at the beginning of this chapter—is not just that it is to the missionary interests of third world Christians that the American church and theology experience a radical conversion. It also has to do with the fact that third world Christians *are* the keepers of their American brothers and sisters!

What then can third world Christians do on behalf of church and theology in the United States? How can they respond to this crisis? Following are some concrete ways by which third world Christians can participate in this ecclesiotheological dimension of the American missionary situation.

First, third world Christians can serve as a mirror for the critical self-understanding of American Christians. The writings, lectures, and leadership of theologians and church leaders from the third world have already played a significant role along this line. They have given American Christians a vision of themselves from outside their cultural milieu. This vision has been greatly enriched by the work of American Black Christians. Indeed their critical insight into White-dominated church and theology has become one of the most significant moments in the history of Christianity in the United States. Moreover it has stimulated Christians from other ethnic minorities to offer their own insights and has made possible a meeting point with mainline third world Christian leaders. These leaders, being the representatives of those peoples who have suffered the consequences of the Pax Americana in their respective continents, have engaged in critical prophetic exposures of American behavior abroad while offering, at the same time, interpretations of their own of church and theology in the United States.

Second, third world Christians can offer models of authentic contextualization. To be sure, after almost two hundred years of Anglo-Saxon-culture Christianity, the American church and theology need desperately a process of deculturation. Michaelson's assertion that mission in America "must begin by de-Americanizing the Gospel"[35] cannot be treated lightly. Yet the process of de-Americanization must go along with an inverse process of incarnation in the present American reality. Otherwise the Christian faith in the United States will succumb further to an otherworldly, escapist faith, which in the end will be no more and no less than a silent supporter of the same system. If it is true that American-culture Christianity is the fruit of many years of contextualizing the gospel *a la Americana,* it is equally true that not all contextualization is good or desirable. What is needed in the United States is not a spurious form of uncritical contextualization, but an authentic process that will make church and theology critically responsible to the gut issues of American society—and the place to witness such a process today is the world of the poor and the disfranchised. Third world Christians may not be able to provide money or an overwhelming amount of missionary personnel, but they can provide models of a critical insertion in their culture and society that have given prophetic depth to their life and witness. To see and hear what is happening in the churches of Africa, the Middle East, Asia, Latin America the Caribbean, Oceania, and in the Asian, Black, Hispanic, and Native American communities of the United States should be a top priority of mainstream American Christianity.

Third, they can provide meaningful paradigms of dynamic, liberating church leadership. In contrast with the highly clericalized American church life and theology, third world Christians form, by and large, churches with strong lay leadership, drawn from among themselves. They begin their training in the heat and sweat of everyday-life Christian service. This being so, their patterns of ministerial training and leadership formation are not bound by the formal, heavy-laden, sterile structures of American (and for that matter Canadian, European, and Australasian) theological education. This is why the third world has produced such movements as Theological Education by Extension, Basic Ecclesial Communities, and Liberation Theology. These movements have not only stimulated a wave of dynamic indigenous leadership, but have initiated third world churches into a process of liberation from the clergy-laity dualism so common in American Christianity.

Fourth, third world Christians can offer a partnership for radical discipleship. For, as has been noted in the course of this chapter, there are significant sectors in the American church that are rediscovering what it means to be a disciple of Christ in its concrete historical reality. They have thus embarked on a radical course even to the very root of biblical faith and to the philosophical foundations of their cultural milieu. In this pilgrimage their faith and commitment have become ever more profound and their prophetic energies ever more intensive vis-à-vis the American religious establishment. They have thus come to where significant sectors of the third world church are. Little wonder then that at the International Congress on World Evangelization held in Switzerland in 1974 and at the Consultation on World Evangelization held in Pattaya, Thailand, in 1980 these two currents produced a "Response to the Lausanne Covenant" and a "Statement of Concern," which have caught the attention of many church leaders around the world. Indeed this partnership in radical discipleship has already begun, and only the Lord can tell what it may mean for the future of Christianity around the world, but especially in the United States.

The United States today is one of the most challenging mission fields on the globe. Not only does it have millions who find themselves outside the frontier of the gospel, but its own culture and society, its churches and their theologies have become inescapable missionary frontiers. Walbert Bühlmann is certainly right in stating, "We are not at the end of the missions but rather at the beginning of a new and extraordinary missionary era."[36] In this new era the clarion call comes particularly to the offspring of the former missionary era to go to the land whence came many of their missionary forebears and witness there to the liberating Word of God. For third world Christians the United States has become truly a "new Macedonia."

NOTES

1. Cf., e.g., Samuel Wilson, ed., *Mission Handbook,* 12th ed. (Monrovia, Calif.: MARC, 1980), pp. 20ff.; R. Pierce Beaver, ed., *American Missions in Bicentennial Perspective* (Pasadena, Calif.: William Carey Library, 1977), passim.

2. Alfred Krass, *Beyond the Either/Or Church: Notes Towards the Recovery of the Wholeness of Evangelism* (Nashville, Tenn.: Tidings, 1973), p. 58.

3. Orlando E. Costas, *Theology of the Crossroads in Contemporary Latin America* (Amsterdam: Editions Rodopi, 1976), pp. 9, 328.

4. J. Verkuyl, "The Mission of God and the Missions of the Churches," *Occasional Essays* 4, nos. 1-2 (January 1977): 39. Cf. also by the same author, *Contemporary Missiology: An Introduction,* trans. from the Dutch and ed. Dale Cooper (Grand Rapids, Mich.: Wm. B. Eerdmans, 1978), pp. 394ff.

5. That is, "the millions who are geographically near, but live on distant socio-cultural frontiers. To say, for example, the de-Christianized masses of the West have had ample opportunity to reasonably consider the option of the Christian faith is to oversimplify the complex reality of western society, with its fantastic input from the mass media, the socio-cultural roadblocks in the clusters of men and women that make up the western mosaic and the psychological distance which syncretistic religious tradition has brought about between them and the faith of the New Testament" (Orlando E. Costas, "Churches in Evangelistic Partnership," *The New Face of Evangelicalism,* ed. C. René Padilla [London: Hodder and Stoughton, 1976], p. 149).

6. Eduardo Seda Bonilla, "Ethnic Studies and Cultural Pluralism," reprint from *The Rican,* n.d., p. 1.

7. Ibid., p. 2.

8. See, e.g., Peter Berger, Brigitte Berger, and Hansfried Kellner, *The Homeless Mind: Modernization and Consciousness* (New York: Vintage Books, 1974), pp. 105ff.

9. Sydney Ahlstrom, *A Religious History of the American People* (New Haven, Conn.: Yale University Press, 1972), pp. 1037ff.; Harvey Cox, *Turning East: The Promise and Peril of the New Orientalism* (New York: Simon and Schuster, 1977); Howard A. Wilson, *Invasion from the East* (Minneapolis, Minn.: Augsburg Publishing House, 1978).

10. Ahlstrom, *Religious History,* p. 1079.

11. Wesley Michaelson, "De-Americanizing the Gospel," *The Future of the Missionary Enterprise,* no. 17: *Mission in America in World Context* (Rome: IDOC, 1976), p. 57.

12. James Wallis, "Evangelism: Toward New Styles of Life and Action," *Mission in America in World Context,* p. 67.

13. Robert W. Jenson, "The Kingdom of America's God," *Religion and the Dilemmas of Nationhood,* ed. Sydney E. Ahlstrom (Minneapolis, Minn.: Lutheran Church in America, 1976), p. 13.

14. Ibid.

15. Ibid.

16. See, e.g., in addition to the better-known American third world authors, the contributions of Odhiambo Okite, "Guest Editorial," *International Review of Mission,* April 1974, pp. 153–60; Okite, "A Talk with Chief John Snow," ibid., pp. 180–82; U Kyaw Than, "A Third World Critique of American Civil Religion," *The Future of the Missionary Enterprise,* no. 17: *Mission in America in World Context* (Rome: IDOC, 1976); Raul S. Manglapus, "Global Justice and the American Dream," ibid.; Samuel Escobar, "Mission in the Age of the Righteous Empire," ibid.; Sergio Arce, Plutarco Bonilla, et al., "An Open Letter to North American Christians," reprinted by the National Council of Churches of Christ in the USA, October 1976 (mimeographed), 3 pp.

17. "An Open Letter," ibid., p. 1.

18. Ibid., pp. 2–3.

19. Rubem Alves, *A Theology of Human Hope* (Washington, D.C.: Corpus Books, 1969), pp. 21–22.

20. Cf. E. C. O. Ilogu, *Christian Ethics in an African Background* (Leiden: E. J. Brill, 1974), p. 178. For further discussion on the question of technology and the third world, see Rubem Alves, *Tomorrow's Child: Imagination, Creativity and the Rebirth of Culture* (New York: Harper & Row, 1972), passim; Rubem Alves, *O Enigma da Religão* (Petropolis: Editora Vozes, 1975), pp. 150–66; Rubem Alves, "Identity and Communication," *WACC Journal* 22, no. 4 (1975), passim; Berger, et al., *Modernization,* passim; and Stephen C. Knapp, "Mission and Modernization: A Preliminary Critical Analysis of Contemporary Understanding of Mission from a 'Radical Evangelical' Perspective," *American Missions,* pp. 146–209.

21. Arce, et al., "Letter," p. 3.

22. Ibid.

23. Ibid., p. 2.

24. Michaelson, "De-Americanizing the Gospel," p. 52.

25. James H. Cone, *God of the Oppressed* (New York: Seabury Press, 1975), p. 47.

26. Douglas W. Johnson and George Cornell, *Punctured Preconceptions* (New York: Friendship Press, 1972), pp. 24–25.

27. Martin Marty, *The Pro and Con Book of Religious America: A Bicentennial Argument* (Waco, Tex.: Word Books, 1975), p. 84.

28. Ibid., p. 85.

29. Carl Braaten, "The Christian Mission and American Imperialism," *Religion and the Dilemmas of Nationhood,* ed. Sydney E. Ahlstrom (Minneapolis, Minn.: Lutheran Church in America, 1976), p. 72.

30. Ruben Lores, "Manifest Destiny and the Missionary Enterprise," *Study Encounter* 11, no. 1 (1975): 15.

31. Arce, et al., "Letter," p. 2.

32. Braaten, "Imperialism," p. 71.

33. Ibid., p. 72.

34. Ibid.

35. Michaelson, "De-Americanizing the Gospel," p. 57.

36. Walbert Bühlmann, *The Coming of the Third Church* (Maryknoll, N.Y.: Orbis Books, 1978), p. 166.

6

Christian Mission in the Americas

Is a joint Christian mission possible in the Americas? That question should not surprise those of us who represent the peoples south of the Rio Bravo, the Caribbean islands, or the oppressed minorities of North America, for we have been able to observe at close range the great contradictions within the mission work that Christians and their respective churches experience in all the vast American territory. It may come as a surprise to those Christians from both sides who, due to their dedication to the missionary mandate, have been able to see only the strong points and not the weak; the triumphs but not the failures of Christian mission in the Americas. But for those of us who have identified with the realities of these closely related continents and with the missionary practice carried on by Christians and their churches within their respective countries, the issue is eminently relevant and practical.

The Americas

Let us clarify the question that we want to consider in this chapter. What is it about the Americas that presents a mutual challenge for Christians and their churches? And, further, as followers of Jesus Christ how are we to understand our mission within that reality?

To discuss the Americas is to be concerned with a region of great contrasts. These contrasts are not merely geographical, cultural, linguistic, religious, or ethical, but are also sociological, economic, and political in nature.

Latin America and the Caribbean

Latin America and the Caribbean have been stratified into an exploitable region.[1] Its countries are for the most part ruled by unpopular repressive governments. The majority of the people do not have access to the goods their countries produce; they lack adequate food and housing; public health and educational services are only minimally available; and their whole culture is at the mercy of the culture of the affluent groups that control the means of social communication. These minority groups enjoy good food, housing, and education. On the whole, it can be said that, with few exceptions, the entire region has been incorporated into the structure of international capitalism as the provider of raw material and cheap labor. Accordingly it finds itself not only in a situation of dependence, but worse yet, of misery, since it gets poorer and poorer as the years go by.

Northern America

In Northern America (the United States and Canada) with its predominantly Anglo-Saxon culture (though Canada has a strong Francophone minority), the situation is the other way around. Most parts of the society live in relative comfort, with employment that provides high wages, modern schools, hospitals and medical facilities, modern means of transportation, and time for rest and recreation. These groups have a strong economic position combined with political power: they choose—and remove—public leaders; they make the rules of the (political) game and organize society life. Therefore the means of social communication respond to their interests, and North American culture advertises their *modus vivendi*: the "American Way of Life." (Canadian lifestyle differs only in degree from that of the United States.)

To be sure, these sectors of North American society have their problems. They have fallen victim to "consumerism"; they suffer serious psychophysical disturbances and live in a chaotic process of sociocultural disintegration. In short, they are victims of the "technical-managerial dinosaur."[2] But, in contrast with the rest of the world and especially with the oppressed minority ethnic groups, their situation is extremely affluent.

What the majority of people in Latin America and the Caribbean suffer is what certain minorities suffer in North America: in the United States, Blacks, Native Americans, Hispanics, and Asians; in Canada, the Francophones and Native Canadians; in both countries, women and handicapped persons. All of these sectors have been stratified (in various degrees) into exploitable nuclei. Their social, economic, and political marginality responds to the interests of dominant groups, the institutions they control, and the ideology that guides their behavior. Racism, sexism, and the indifference that often characterizes both public and private sectors of society toward the handicapped are mechanisms created by order to preserve the economic advantages that go along with the domination of the weak by the strong—to mention some of the most obvious: cheap labor, the expropriation of property without fair compensation, menial jobs in subhuman working conditions, the submission of women to men in all spheres of human production, and the lack of adequate care for the plight of the handicapped.

The reality of this internal conflict helps us to understand, in part, the tremendous military complex and the extensive investigative machinery ("the intelligence community") that exists in the Anglo-Saxon countries of

Northern America. One does not need much imagination to understand the great threat to society represented by an oppressed minority whose counterpart in the other America is the majority. "National Security" is the catchphrase that nourishes both militarism and the "intelligence" complex (in the United States this embraces about ten federal agencies, from the Central Intelligence Agency [CIA] to the Federal Bureau of Investigation [FBI]). "National Security" rises like a war cry in order to protect the economic and political interests of the majority of North Americans ffom the (potential) revolutionary threat posed by the "wretched" of the Americas, the minority from the North and the majority from the Caribbean and Central and South America. This explains why in the last decades most aid of United States origin to Latin America and to the Caribbean nations has been military aid.[3]

The Mission of God

In these circumstances of contrasts and conflicts within these two continents, what can we say about Christian mission?

We must look for the answer to this question in the mission of God. This proceeds from the fact that the mission of Christians can be understood only in the light of the mission of Jesus Christ, which is grounded in the missions of the Father and the Holy Spirit. A basic presupposition of Christian mission is thus the missional dynamic of the Father, the Son, and the Spirit, in and for history. To understand the mission of Christians in any situation we need first and foremost to understand God's mission as it is revealed in his trinitarian history.

A Trinitarian Mission

In referring to the trinitarian history of God, I am dissociating myself from those who conceive of the trinitarian God in metaphysical categories and apart from reality. God's mission is not grounded on metaphysical speculation and theoretical abstractions inspired by classical Greek philosophy, but rather on historical *deeds*. I wish to understand the God of Christian faith in his missionary activity in history, in his relation with the world, and in his plan for humanity. I wish thus to understand God because the faith that Christians profess is derived from the Old and New Testaments, which speak of God as Father, Son, and Holy Spirit, and describe his work in the world historically, as the trinitarian history of God.[4] This is also the reason why I am motivated not by a theoretical but by a practical and pastoral concern. Ultimately I am interested in understanding the implications of God's trinitarian activity for the church's task in the Americas today.

What is therefore the biblical witness about the mission of the triune God in the world? How is that mission related to our situation in the Americas? What are the pastoral implications?

The Bible states that "God is love" (1 Jn. 4:8). God's relationships with the world are based on this affirmation. The psalms especially tell us of love as the foundation of creation (cf. Pss. 33; 74:12–17; 104). Israel is created in love (Deut. 7:7–8), is a priestly people (i.e., a mediator of God's love) in the presence of the nations (Ex. 19:4–6) because of God's love for it (Isa. 42:5–7). If the predominant Old Testament traditions present Yahweh in relationship with Israel, it is because at bottom Yahweh is interested in the well-being of all nations. Surely Yahweh is the shepherd of Israel (Ps. 23:1ff.; Isa. 40:11; Ezek. 34:12), the father and mother of the nation (Ps. 103:13; Isa. 49:15; 66:13), its progenitor, provider, and protector (Isa. 43:1ff.; 44:2ff.). Nevertheless the background of this parenthood is creation (in which Yahweh is revealed as creator of all humanity) and the sovereignty that Yahweh exercises over all peoples. Israel is a prototype of the new humanity that God wants to create. Hence Hosea refers to Israel as both Yahweh's wife (2:1–23) and son (11:1ff.). Israel is the partner whom Yahweh chooses in order to procreate a new race and is also the first offspring of this union.[5]

In the New Testament we notice a correspondence between Israel and Jesus of Nazareth. Jesus is the authentic Israelite (Mt. 2:15), the only one who fulfills the mission entrusted to Israel (Mk. 1:8–11; Jn. 1:49ff.; Lk. 1:31–33, 76–77; Heb. 1:1–4) because he is the man in whom God's Eternal Word became flesh (Jn. 1:14). Jesus Christ, Son of God, is the firstborn of the new humanity (Eph. 2:14–18), the head of the new body (Eph. 1:23), the cornerstone of a new temple and leader of a new people (1 Pet. 2:6–8). As a result, those who follow him are born to a new life (Jn. 1:12), are incorporated into the People of God, and are made to be his body. In this way, the Son, because of his death on the cross, finds a wife who, as in the case of the first Adam, is taken from his side, but who, in contrast with the first Eve, must await his return (Mt. 25:1–13), developing (in the fullest sense of the word), and preparing herself for the marriage that will take place in the consummation of the kingdom of God. By his resurrection he has also opened the way for a new people, the emerging new humanity already prefigured and announced in the history of Israel.

At the heart of this great mystery is the Father's love manifested by the Spirit. We are dealing here with the same Spirit that "moved over the face of the waters" at creation (Gen. 1:2); the breath that gave life to Adam's body (Gen. 2:7); the power that rested on Israel and its leaders in times of national crisis and that fertilized the womb of the humble virgin (Lk. 1:35) so that she could be the bearer of the Son of God; that enabled Jesus to offer himself to the Father as a perfect sacrifice for the sins of the world (Heb. 9:14) and by whose power Jesus was raised from the dead (Rom. 1:4). The Spirit spreads God's love to men and women everywhere, shaping them into the body of Christ, comforting, guiding, and teaching them "all the truth" (Jn. 16:7, 13); "convincing" the world of its sin, of justice and righteousness (Jn. 16:8); and nourishing the hope of all creation for its future liberation (Rom. 8:20–23). The Spirit is the agent of love that the Father has revealed in the Son. The focus of the Spirit's work in the world finds its goal precisely in the reconciliation of all created things under the lordship of the Son and for the glory of the Father (Eph. 1:14).

An Eschatological Mission

It goes without saying that the Holy Spirit's special function within the mission of God is eminently eschatological. The Gospels introduce us to Jesus as he begins his ministry in the power of the Spirit (Lk. 4:14ff.; Mk. 1:8, 12, 14–15; Mt. 3:16–17). The content of that ministry is the proclamation of the good news of the kingdom of God. This proclamation is not a mere reminder of God's sovereignty over all creation.[6] On the contrary, something totally new is happening here: the eruption of a new era, a new order of life, the new creation. This messianic "newness" is made possible by the death and resurrection of Jesus. Men and women appropriate this messianic reality by faith in Christ. Thus they are freed from the power of sin, experience a new life with messianic values, become part of the messianic community (which is committed to the cause of freedom, justice, and peace), and share in the hope of new heavens and a new earth. Conversely, faith in Christ is verified in the development of a messianic lifestyle, active involvement in the messianic community, and participation in the struggle for a just and peaceful world in anticipation of the promised new heavens and new earth.

As a messianic community, the church is that fellowship of men and women, both liberated and in the process of liberation, which appears in Acts and in the epistles as the firstfruits of Pentecost (Acts 2:1ff.) brought into being by the power of the Spirit. The Spirit is the earnest of the kingdom, that messianic reality, the new creation and order of life that the Father offers to humanity in Jesus Christ the Son (Eph. 1:14). The Spirit makes possible the acceptance of the promise of the kingdom as ultimate, sure, and genuine. The Spirit creates *faith* where there is no faith, making believers participants in God's *love* and heirs to the *hope* for a new world. This activity turns believers into truly spiritual persons, who are nonconformists within history. They are happy only in the new life they have begun to enjoy and are not satisfied with anything that obscures or eclipses the hope for the final appearance of God's kingdom of freedom, justice, and peace.

A Historical Mission

Hence the mission of God is not only eschatological but also historical. The fact that it has as its goal the final consummation of the kingdom and that it is transcendentalized in the hope of new heavens and a new earth does not mean that this mission is either atemporal or beyond history. On the contrary, it is a mission whose stage is history. The hope that infuses it is nothing less than the hope to transform history: a redeemed creation; the definitive overcoming of hatred, chaos, and corruption; and the burgeoning of a world of love, justice, freedom, and peace. This hope is adumbrated in the crossroads of life, amid the tensions of history where ideologies and political, economic, social, and religious systems clash. Because of this the New Testament adds the kingdom's present reality to the hope for the future (Lk. 17:20–37). Furthermore the future hope of the poor (of whom it is said that they are privileged recipients of the good news) is nourished by concrete signs: "the blind see, the lame walk, the lepers are cleansed, the deaf hear, the dead are raised . . ." (Lk. 7:22). Those who own nothing in the world need not await the consummation of the kingdom to recover their rights as creatures of God. Instead they can begin now to anticipate (and appropriate by faith) the kingdom's transforming power. Because of its eschatological nature, the mission of God is historical.

The new order of life is seen most concretely in the small and large transformations that occur within history. To be sure, these historical signs are not easy to discern. Just as wheat and chaff grow together, so signs of the new order appear in the middle of contradictory situations and thus make it very difficult at times to distinguish clearly between a real signal and a short circuit. Nevertheless it is possible to discern the "signs of the times" through the Holy Spirit's guidance and by the orientation of the Word of God. The church, as the community nourished by the Spirit and the Word, has the privilege and the responsibility to interpret history, distinguishing the signs of the kingdom of God from the antisigns produced by the kingdoms of this world. Thus not every historical change may be identified with the kingdom, but only those that conform to kingdom principles: love, justice, freedom, and messianic peace.

The Frame of Reference: The Kingdom of God

The kingdom serves as the frame of reference for the mission of God. His working in history, as we have noted, is made known by the conclusive revelation of his liberating purpose and by the consistent denial of all tendencies that counter his will. The participation of the People of God in his mission will have to be directed, therefore, by the message of the kingdom.[7]

Proclaiming the Kingdom

To participate in the mission of God is to announce the good news of the kingdom. This is an all-embracing and dynamic activity that is not limited to a predetermined set of verbal propositions, be they doctrinal or homiletical. Surely, proclaiming the kingdom implies an affirmation of faith that is frequently expressed in doctrinal formulations. Thus we have the church's great creeds and "evangelistic sermons." Such sermons and doctrinal affirmations, however, must be part of what I should like to call a "kerygmatic climate." Because of its transcendence and its constant newness, announcing the kingdom is considered a part of the new life and not an isolated occurrence divorced from reality. The proclamation is always contextual, presented in new Spirit-filled words and by means of a dynamic transforming witness.

This becomes clear in Jesus' own life and ministry, where the announcement of the kingdom appears in these impressive words: "And all spoke well of him and wondered at the gracious words which proceeded out of his mouth" (Lk. 4:22; cf. Mk. 1:22). The words are accompanied by prodigious acts. "What is this? A new teaching?" asked the people. "With authority he commands even the unclean spirits, and they obey him" (Mk. 1:27). The apostle Paul continues in the same vein when he testifies to the Romans: "For I will not venture to speak of anything except what Christ has wrought through me to win obedience from the Gentiles, by word and deed, by the power of signs and wonders, by the power of the Holy Spirit, so that from Jerusalem and as far round as Illyricum I have fully preached the gospel of Christ" (Rom. 15:18–19). The proclamation of the kingdom is not a matter of words or deeds, but of words and deeds *empowered* by the liberating presence of the Spirit.

The Demands of the Kingdom

The kingdom of God is not simply good news but also exigencies. The new order of life demands a radical change. There can be no reconciliation without conversion, just as there can be no resurrection without the cross, much less new life without birthpangs. Hence Jesus came not only announcing the kingdom, but calling for repentance and faith (Mk. 1:15).

On a personal level this implies a change of attitudes and values, the appropriation of a new relationship with God and neighbors, and a new commitment to the messianic cause. The kingdom demands a transfer from "self" to "other," from an individualistic and egocentric consciousness to one communally and fraternally oriented. Zacchaeus is exemplary: "Behold, Lord, the half of my goods I give to the poor, and if I have defrauded anyone of anything, I restore it fourfold" (Lk. 19:8). We are not talking of salvation by works; rather, of works that authenticate salvation by grace. "Today salvation has come to this house" (Lk. 19:9), for Zacchaeus demonstrated what he believed. His works were evidence of a profound change of values and attitudes.

The demands of the kingdom are not limited to personal attitudes or a single historical incident. They are permanent: "If anyone would come after me," Jesus said, "let him deny himself and take up his cross daily and follow me" (Lk. 9:23). The kingdom's demands affect all areas of life: "You are the salt of the earth; but if the salt has lost its taste, how shall its saltiness be restored? . . . You are the light of the world. A city set on a hill cannot be hid. . . . For I tell you, unless your righteousness exceeds that of the scribes and Pharisees, you will never enter the kingdom of heaven" (Mt. 5:13–14, 20).

It is this situation of "permanent change" to which Paul refers when he speaks of the transformation that the Spirit effects in those whose faces are turned to Christ (2 Cor. 3:18). Similarly Paul has this in mind when exhorting the Romans to present their bodies to God "as a living sacrifice, holy and acceptable to God," to live not conformed to the old order and to be renewed in their understanding in order to confirm God's will (Rom. 12:1-2).

The demands of the kingdom do not encompass only personal and ecclesial affairs, but also social and institutional issues. This new order is not limited to the community of faith. Instead it embraces all of history and the universe, and it is the task of the ecclesial community to witness to that all-encompassing reality. As Revelation 11:15 tells us, "The kingdoms of the world have become the kingdom of our Lord and of his Christ, and he shall reign forever and ever." Paul adds in Colossians 2:15 that on the cross Christ "disarmed the principalities and made a public example of them, triumphing over them . . .";[8] at the very least, this implies that the kingdom of God is to be present among the kingdoms of this world. But how?

The Gospels tell us that the kingdom works in history like yeast, leavening all the dough (Lk. 13:21). Paul tells us that the kingdom manifests itself by limiting evil via political institutions (the "governing authorities") whom God has appointed in order to guarantee order and the commonwealth (Rom. 13:1-5). This authority can, however—in agreement with Revelation—become corrupted and turn into a demonic beast (cf. Rev. 13:1ff.). Above all, the kingdom makes itself felt in the hopeful groanings of creation (Rom. 8:22).

The kingdom makes demands in every one of these instances. For example, for dough to rise there must be yeast. The church is God's yeast; therefore it needs to be present in the world to help and transform it. So that political institutions may be agents of good, their citizens must cooperate. Christians are called to set examples by respecting all public institutions that work for the common good (that is, for the well-being of all, especially the poor and the oppressed). But they are also called to unmask and resist those institutions when they become possessed of the devil and turn into enemies of justice. The children of God are bearers of the hope for universal liberation. They are called to await patiently not only for their own final liberation, but also for the liberation of all creation, by suffering the birthpangs of the world that is about to be delivered. Their own hope is directly related to the hope for the creation to be freed "from bondage to decay" (Rom. 8:21).

Christians bear a double eschatological burden: their own and that of the rest of creation. It is this to which Paul refers when he says: "Likewise the Spirit helps us in our weakness, for we do not know how to pray as we ought, but the Spirit himself intercedes for us with sighs too deep for words" (Rom. 8:26). In other words, the Spirit helps us suffer the birthpangs of that new world that God has promised in the Son, perfecting our intercession until the day of total redemption. That intercession assumes a vicarious form. It is manifested when Christians are willing to bear the suffering of creation, a suffering that we can describe today as hunger and poverty, as persecution and loneliness, environmental pollution, the constant threat of war, racism, exploitation (economic, social, and sexual), political imperialism, and hegemonism that besiege our planet. But it is also evident in a hopeful enthusiasm when we discern and interpret the signs of the kingdom in the middle of this suffering.

Priorities of the Kingdom

The kingdom's demands go hand in hand with its priorities. I am not referring to priorities arranged in order of importance, since all of the kingdom's demands are important. Accepting the kingdom as a point of reference for mission implies acceptance of *all* its demands in the missionary mandate of God's people. Moreover, these priorities are historical, they correspond to the context of mission. Since situations change, particular *emphases* of the kingdom's message also change. This explains, for example, the varying emphases of the New Testament documents, the different kinds of churches that arose very early in Christian missions, and the changes in theme (hermeneutic keys) that we notice throughout the history of Christian theology. The setting of priorities does not mean, however, that other issues are put in "storage." The church is not only called to *accept* all the demands of the kingdom but to *communicate* them. It should do so, however, in order of need and opportunity, a responsibility that requires pastoral wisdom and courage.

The Pastoral Challenge: Kingdom Priorities in the Americas

The question before us now is this: What are the kingdom's priorities in the Americas today? To answer this question we need to turn to the sociohistorical analysis with which we began because it gives us a pastoral focus. Indeed the question is none other than the challenge that the kingdom sets before Christians in the Americas today. This challenge is pastoral, since it assigns us concrete tasks. (By pastoral is meant all those actions whereby God's People announce the good news of the kingdom and make its demands clear.) Our problem, therefore, is to find our bearings in order to direct God's People in general and our respective churches in particular so that all of us may carry out the mission that God has entrusted to us. In other words, we must define the historical priorities for the kingdom in the Americas today.

Affirming Life and Denouncing Violence

During the last decade a dark cloud has surrounded the peoples of the hemisphere. Life has been denied and death has been exalted through the violent machinery of oppression and repression in the name of law and order, in defense of the Christian tradition, and under the pretext of benevolence and humanitarianism. The first priority of the day is to snatch the kingdom from the agents of death by affirming life and denouncing violence. This affirmation is, of course, with implications.

The first implication is, *the poor's right to life must be defended and the machinery of socioeconomic oppression and repression that contributes to poverty must be fought.* During the Carter administration much attention was paid to the matter of human rights. Interestingly, however, very little was said in the Americas about the rights of the poor. While we should not take lightly the positive impact of President Jimmy Carter on human rights in many repressive Latin American countries, we should not forget that the greatest and severest violations took place against the poor people of the hemisphere and that this policy suffered at times from the old ambiguity of American foreign policy.

In 1976 and 1978 respectively we saw such an institution as the International Monetary Fund (IMF), under the pressure of the Carter administration, force Jamaica and Peru into inhuman, cruel, and repressive austerity programs that increased the basic cost of living and led to widespread unrest and deaths. In 1977 this same agency, again under the pressure of the United States, helped Argentina, a country with one of the most cruel, repressive records of the 1970s in all Latin America, to borrow $1.1 billion in Eurocurrency and United States markets. Then, in May 1979, with United States support, the IMF granted Somoza a $66 million loan so that he could continue to bomb innocent Nicaraguans.[9]

As Christians we ought strongly to criticize such contradictory behavior. We ought to oppose the inter-American socioeconomic oppression and repression.

In the same way we ought to defend the rights of the poor to enjoy the basic amenities of life by championing more communal structures of social organization, such as an economy that offers genuine possibilities of socialized production and consumption, and a political structure that allows greater participation and guarantees personal rights and public safety. In my opinion this can only be achieved in a socialistically organized society, though, admittedly, there are several models of socialism, none of which could be applied to any one situation without some kind of modification.

In the second place, affirming life and denouncing violence mean *condemning torture and championing fair legal procedures.* In less than fifteen years we have made a nearly 180-degree turn in the Americas, regressing hundreds of years in history with the reintroduction of cruel methods of punishment, such as torture, that had been replaced by more humanitarian, civilized procedures. Torture has been employed as a normal repressive method in order to put down any form of opposition and as a police method to obtain information. Its reappearance in the Americas is directly related to the disappearance of constitutional rights, with all their implications, including the right of habeas corpus. But more than anything, it has arisen as a fundamental part of the ideology of "national security" spread by the Pentagon and current regimes. (Where did the repressive governments of Latin America learn to use torture as a political tool, if not in the courses for training in nonconventional warfare that United States military agencies have offered to Latin American police and military?)

The complicity is worldwide or at least nearly so. Certain parts of the

Christian church have spoken up in response to this situation whereas others have kept quiet. Those that have kept silent have done so either because of their radical historical isolation or their uncritical acceptance of the idea that this happens only to subversives, propaganda that the torturers themselves spread. Moreover the majority of the churches that have spoken out against torture have done so only when their members have become victims.

In the third place, to affirm life and denounce violence implies *that human freedoms must be defended and that the arms complex that permits their repression must be attacked.* We Christians in the Americas may not sit by twiddling our thumbs in the face of systematic violation of voting rights that occurs with shameless and impudent prohibition of free elections, with fraudulent elections, or with legal conditions that hinder popular participation in electing officials. We Christians may accept neither the systematic persecution of those whose opinions differ from the majority nor the denial of the right of free association. At all costs these and many other freedoms must be defended on every level of society.

At the same time we Christians of the Americas ought to attack the arms race that the developed countries are carrying on. Not only has the entire planet's well-being been jeopardized by their nuclear arsenals; the doors have also been opened for such poor nations as Brazil to start on the same road. Furthermore the arms race allows the military-related industries of the United States and Europe to grow wealthy on the sweat and blood of the underdeveloped peoples of the hemisphere. The sales of arms to these peoples enables the systematic violation of the freedoms listed above. (Curiously that same industry nourishes the national violence that convulses the countries of the North, since the arms industry strongly opposes arms control. Add to this the film industry's support and you have an atmosphere of terror, especially in the streets of major cities in the United States.)

The challenge to denounce this panorama of violence and to affirm life becomes unavoidable for Christians and churches in the Americas. The kingdom of which we are part and whose message we have been called to proclaim demands that we side with love, not with hate; with justice, not with inequality; with peace, not with aggression. Since this is the case, we have no alternative but to marshal our forces to denounce institutionalized violence, to affirm the right of the poor and oppressed to life, and to commit ourselves to programs that place the human being above the state and its institutions. To do anything different would be to turn coward and to deny our duties as firstfruits of God's new order of life.

Human Solidarity and Christian Unity

That responsibility demands human solidarity, since it is not possible to affirm life without making a commitment of solidarity with all humanity in its struggle for life. The division of peoples into economic classes, ideological blocs, racial groups, religious movements, and sexual chauvinisms reflects the threat of death that besieges the human race. This is especially evident in the western hemisphere where we see such a long history of fratricidal wars; of economic blocs; of antagonism among classes, races, and sexes; of religious conflicts; and of ideological prejudices. At present the American hemisphere is, both internally and externally, one of the most divided and broken parts of planet earth. In order to affirm life, it is necessary to overcome these frictions and to form a united human front.

These hemispheric divisions find their counterpart in the extraordinary divisions among Christians. The conflict among Christians is not simply the traditional Catholic-Protestant controversy. On the contrary, we are speaking here of divisions between Catholics and Catholics; between Protestants and Protestants; between laity and hierarchy; between local organizations and national bodies; between church structures and para-church groups; between differing theological positions and various pastoral positions. In short, we are dealing here with a compound fracture. Because of this, Christians in the hemisphere find themselves unable to serve as agents of reconciliation among the peoples of the Americas, unable to be the firstfruits of the new humanity.

As Christians of the Americas we cannot evade the ecumenical challenge. It is urgent that we develop an ecumenical pastoral strategy, a combined effort to benefit cooperative Christian programs that aim for a more fraternal life of solidarity among the peoples of our continents. Such programs will have to be of various kinds and degrees—from interconfessional theological meetings to interchurch activities of common witness and socioreligious coalitions in favor of human dignity and the social well-being of all peoples.

Commitment to Evangelization and Church Growth

In order for this to occur we need a deep commitment to an integral evangelization and a healthy church growth. I understand by "commitment to an integral evangelization" a total devotion to the cause of communicating the good news of God's kingdom in word and deed, "in season and out of season," with all available means at our disposal. In my opinion such a dedication is possible only when a deep conversion experience occurs. (Here we see one of the basic problems of the Christian mission in the Americas: an amorphous community with very shallow rootage in the gospel of Christ.) By "healthy growth" I understand a process of holistic development in which the community of faith is fed by new *members*, expands the participation of its members within its *organic* life, deepens its *understanding* of the faith, and becomes an *incarnated* servant in its social situation.[10]

Such evangelization and growth are imperative among the churches of both continents, because presently these churches have been stagnant (and thus subject to obvious deterioration) or getting fatter by the day (thus running the risk of a fatal aneurysm). No wonder the fruits of the kingdom have been so little evidenced in the Americas! Its proclamation has been distorted;

its demands have been cheapened! The Americas *still* need to be evangelized.[11]

Therefore a prophetic mobilization of the People of God for a profound and effective evangelization is urgently needed. This would bring about a new wave of Christians deeply rooted in the gospel, dedicated to proclaiming the kingdom and its demands in all areas of society, and supported by vibrant and healthy churches. Without a mobilization of such magnitude the churches will remain stagnant and will become more impotent every day. For their part Christians will lose the opportunity to contribute significantly to the transformation of their history by denying their missionary vocation and by allowing themselves to be absorbed by the kingdoms of this world. If we wish to be faithful to the kingdom of God, we ought, therefore, to pool our resources to develop programs that foster a radical commitment to the gospel and that stimulate healthy growth in our respective churches.

We began this chapter by asking if it were possible for Christians of both American continents to develop a united mission. We can conclude that not only is it possible, it is imperative. Such a mission will have to be grounded in the mission of God and will have to be steered by the message of the kingdom. Seen from this perspective, our mission priorities would be, first, to create and take part in programs that affirm life and denounce violence; second, to promote human solidarity and to encourage unity among Christians by using all means within our reach and at all levels; and, third, to cooperate in evangelistic efforts that foster holistic church growth and a deep historical commitment to the gospel. Thus we shall be helping to pour out our churches' energies toward the transformation of the space we occupy on our planet.

NOTES

1. For a historico-anthropological explanation of this process, see Darcy Ribeiro, *The Americas and Civilization*, trans. from Portuguese by Linton Lomas Barrett and Marie McDavid Barrett (New York: E. P. Dutton, 1973). For a historico-economic analysis, see Eduardo Galeano, *Las venas abiertas de América Latina* (Mexico City: Siglo XXI Editores, 1971); English trans.: *Open Veins of Latin America: Five Centuries of the Pillage of a Continent* (New York: Monthly Review Press, 1973). For additional material on the precarious economic history of Latin America, see further Celso Furtado, *La economía latinoamericana: Formación histórica y problemas contemporáneos* (Mexico City: Siglo XXI Editores, 1971); and Agustín Cueva, *El desarrollo del capitalismo en América Latina* (Mexico City: Siglo XXI Editores, 1977).

2. Cf. Rubem Alves, *Tomorrow's Child* (New York: Harper & Row, 1972), pp. 1ff.

3. Cf. José Comblin, *The Church and the National Security State* (Maryknoll, N.Y.: Orbis Books, 1980), pp. 64–120; Penny Lernoux, *Cry of the People* (Garden City, N.Y.: Doubleday, 1980), pp. 155ff.

4. Cf. Jürgen Moltmann, *The Church in the Power of the Spirit: A Contribution to Messianic Ecclesiology*, trans. from German by Margaret Kohl (New York: Harper

& Row, 1977), pp. 50ff. See also Lesslie Newbigin, *The Open Secret* (Grand Rapids, Mich.: Wm. B. Eerdmans, 1978), pp. 20ff.; David J. Bosch, *Witness to the World* (London: Marshall, Morgan and Scott; Atlanta: John Knox Press, 1980), pp. 239ff.

5. Cf. H. Berkhof's concept of the history of salvation as God's quest for a faithful covenant partner. *Christian Faith*, trans. from Dutch by Sierd Woudstra (Grand Rapids, Mich.: Wm. B. Eerdmans, 1979), pp. 225ff.

6. For a further elaboration of the proclamation of the kingdom, see my *The Integrity of Mission* (New York: Harper & Row, 1979), pp. 1ff.

7. Cf. J. Verkuyl, *Contemporary Missiology* (Grand Rapids, Mich.: Wm. B. Eerdmans, 1978), pp. 197ff.; Carl E. Braaten, *The Flaming Center: A Theology of the Christian Mission* (Philadelphia: Fortress Press, 1977), pp. 39ff.

8. On the theme of principalities and powers, see chap. 10.

9. Cf. Washington Office on Latin America, *Update Latin America*, (September/October 1979), p.2.

10. On this perspective of church growth, see chap. 3 and my book *Integrity*, pp. 37ff.

11. This is one reality that is readily admitted by Catholics and Protestants alike. Cf. John Eagleson and Philip Scharper, eds., *Puebla and Beyond* (Maryknoll, N.Y.: Orbis Books, 1980), pp. 123ff.; Fraternidad Teológica Latinoamericana, *América Latina y la evangelización en los años 80* (Mexico City: FTL, 1980), passim; Comité Editorial del CLAI, *Oaxtepec 1978: Unidad y misión en América Latina* (San José, Costa Rica: CLAI, 1980), pp. 205ff.

Part II

**FROM THE PERIPHERY
OF THE AMERICAN METROPOLIS**

7

Response to the Cry of Latin America

During 1980–81 Protestant denominations in the United States focused their mission-study programs on Latin America.[1] By Latin America is meant, of course, the Spanish and Portuguese-speaking nations south of the border plus the Spanish-speaking countries of the Caribbean (Cuba, Dominican Republic, and Puerto Rico). But with over 23 million Hispanics in the continental United States, Latin America cannot be defined in mere geographical terms. It is true that in the Hispanic community there are many who were born and reared in the United States. In fact, some come from families that have been in the United States longer than many Anglos, especially in the Southwest. ("Anglo" is a term coined by Mexican-Americans to describe the dominant white North American population. Blacks are not "Anglos." Nor are Asians or Native Americans. It is the Hispanic counterpart to the "White" in Black parlance.)

The reality of many United States-born Hispanics notwithstanding, the fact remains that the overwhelming majority of them have cultural roots in the Hispanic countries of the Caribbean and Central and South America. Hence, in reflecting on Latin America, North American denominations cannot bypass or exclude those who represent the Latin American world inside the United States, because when one looks at the Spanish-speaking populations around the world they represent the fourth largest Spanish-speaking population pocket in the world.

When we look at the contemporary Latin American world, we see an oppressed people bearing an affliction as painful as the Hebrew slaves in Egypt. We hear them raising a cry against their oppressors that is as loud as the cry of the children of Israel against their slave masters. Now we know that the God and Father of our Lord Jesus Christ hears their cry and sees their affliction. We know that the crucified Jesus is present in their midst through the Holy Spirit, bearing their abuse, liberating them from fear, and filling them with hope. We know that God has raised many prophets and prophetesses among them who have dared to denounce the evil of their oppression and have announced the coming of a more equitable, fraternal, and peaceloving society.

103

We know that at certain points of their history these prophets and prophetesses have been catalytic agents in the mobilization of various sectors, which in turn has led to the accomplishment of intermediate goals in the direction of that new society envisioned deep in the souls of Latin Americans.

But what about those who live next door? Do they not see their affliction and do they not hear their cry? Of course they see and hear it! Not often, but they do see and hear it. The mass media, our cultural institutions, the government of the land make sure that they do not see and hear it too often. All one needs to do is read any major newspaper over a month to see how stingy the print media in the United States are with Latin American news.[2] Once in a while one of the networks will have a documentary on Latin America, especially if a revolution has taken place. Once in a while Latin America makes the headlines of a major daily newspaper or the 6:30 P.M. national newscast, as was the case during the first months of 1981 with the campaign of the Reagan administration in relation to the so-called communist infiltration of El Salvador. Churches, mission boards, and ecumenical organizations do their best (sometimes) to interpret the situation. And so in one way or another the news gets through; the cry is heard; the affliction is seen.

The question remains: What are they going to do about that affliction? What are they going to do about that cry? How shall they respond? Let me offer four concrete suggestions.

Understanding the Content of the Cry

First, Christians in the United States can, indeed should, respond by seeking to understand the content of their neighbor's cry. People do not always understand what they hear and see. In fact they are often conditioned to hear and see without probing deeply into content. The media work in such ways that one can hear the sound and see the picture of affliction without understanding what it means. Hence the starting point of a responsible response must be an attempt to understand the nature of the cry.

The Latin American neighbor's cry is, above all things, for *justice* and *liberation*. For the last 150 years Latin America has been controlled by economic oligarchies and military forces. Externally it has been at the mercy of international capitalism, having been made an economically dependent region with an industry, a labor force, and an agriculture developed in function of the North American and (to a less extent) the Western European metropolis. It has been dominated culturally by consumerism. Its language, literature, music, visual arts, educational institutions, and mass media are, with a few noble exceptions, either a reflex of the American consumer society or a protest against it and its local economic and political subsidiaries. Therefore the cry of Latin America is for liberation from cultural domination, economic exploitation, military repression, social marginalization, and political imperialism; it is a cry for fairness in international trade and the establishment of a social order that promotes human dignity, respects democratic institutions, and guarantees an equitable distribution of wealth.

The cry of Latin America is also for *truth:* social, personal, and theological. The facts of Latin America's social reality have been by and large hidden from the eyes of the world by sophisticated, dominant (Western) social sciences. The social science departments of the major universities in North America and Europe have failed, with few exceptions, to reveal the truth behind the social, economic, and political statistics. Hence the cry for an understanding of the concrete Latin American reality.

The affliction of our neighbors is both social and personal. In the religious world of Europe and North America it has been largely assumed that Latin America has been already evangelized and that its men and women do not have personal religious needs. The fact of the matter is that the majority of Latin Americans today do not have a personal knowledge of Jesus Christ. They have not had the opportunity to consider the gospel as a personal option. This is why the evangelization of Latin America is still to be completed, and the first to recognize this is the Catholic church.[3] At the most 20 percent of Latin Americans are true practicing Roman Catholics. Latin America is a continent of mission. Its people find themselves in a quest for personal meaning, a quest that in the perspective of the Christian faith can be solved only with a personal knowledge of Jesus Christ.

In addition to sociological and personal truth, there is in Latin America a cry for theological truth. Not only have the social reality and the inner needs of people been covered up, but also the Word of God; it has been hidden in the barrels of imported theologies from Europe and North America. These theologies have given the churches little opportunity to develop their own theological reflection—until recently. But their incipient indigenous reflections have brought about an avalanche of reactions from the halls of North American and European academia. The cry is precisely a demand for the rights of Latin American Christians to think through the faith in the light of their own situation, to set their own theological agenda, and work out their own responses to the real questions of the region.

Acknowledging Responsibility

Second, Christians in the United States should respond by acknowledging their share of responsibility. They need to recognize that the affliction of their neighbors has been created in part by the United States.

The United States is responsible *economically* for the poverty of Latin America. Soon after the wars of independence, the economy of Latin America began to be shaped in function of its northern neighbor. The Monroe Doctrine (1823) was the mechanism created to protect United States interests in the region. As a result Latin America was shaped to be the provider of raw materials and cheap labor and to utilize in return the technology and capital of the northern neighbor; it became "a dollar area."

As has been indicated elsewhere in this volume, in the last two decades parts of Latin America and the Caribbean have become new financial zones. Panama and Puerto Rico, in addition to the Bahamas and Grand Cayman, have become new banking centers (tax havens). United States bank investments in the region have been absolutely extraordinary. By 1975, 61 percent of United States bank subsidiaries were concentrated in Latin America. By 1976 approximately 75 percent of the utilities of United States banks were originated in operations abroad.[4] While banks inside the United States could pay dividends of only 5.75 percent and up to 10 or 11 percent on long-term savings, their subsidiaries in Latin America have been paying 20, 25 and, in some places, as much as 35 percent interest.

Latin America has become the most profitable market for the United States. For every dollar that United States companies invest in the region, three dollars come back in profit.[5] Miami has become the region's new financial capital.[6] Thanks to a high inflationary rate and the commercial genius of Cuban exiles, Miami is now getting the business of the Latin American middle classes.

United States-controlled agencies, like the International Monetary Fund, set the financial policy, which must be strictly adhered to by those countries that wish to receive their low-interest loans. The overnight 80 percent hike on prices forced on Peru a few years ago inflicted a tremendous social wound on an already impoverished land, including the alarming spread of tuberculosis. According to unofficial estimates in the last several years a growing number of Peruvians has become afflicted with tuberculosis.

Jamaica was destabilized as a result of IMF policies. In consequence its Socialist-Democratic government was out of office following elections. Today Jamaica has a conservative government that is developing a fiscal policy that corresponds to the demands of the IMF. Most likely, however, the social cost of such a policy will be enormous.

The United States government is also *politically* responsible for the cry of our neighbors. United States foreign policy has been influenced by corporations that have a history of intervening directly in the political processes of Latin America. In 1954 the United Fruit (Brands) Company managed to enlist the collaboration of the then secretary of state, John Foster Dulles, and his brother, Allen Dulles, then chief of the CIA, to mastermind a plot to overthrow President Jacobo Arbenz in Guatemala. (The Dulles brothers had been company lawyers of United Fruit.) The same company has intervened in Honduras. ITT is known for its intervention in Chile, and Gulf + Western in the Dominican Republic. The list of United States interventions in Latin America, in response to and in collaboration with North American corporations, goes on and on.

This explains why United States economic aid has been used to boost United States business interests in Latin America. Hence the economic aid that came with the Alliance for Progress was conditional upon the purchasing of United States goods. As Penny Lernoux has noted: "When the Alliance for Progress was finally buried at the end of the 1960s, about the only thing that the Latin American countries had to show for it was an enormous foreign debt: 19.3 billion dollars compared to 8.8 billion in 1961 when the program was launched."[7]

Just as financial aid has been used as a leverage for securing more business for United States corporations, so the withdrawal of that aid has been a weapon against countries whose politics do not respond to United States interests. This is what happened in Chile during the period of Allende, in Guatemala during the time of Arbenz, and in Nicaragua more recently.

United States policy toward Latin America has by and large fluctuated between open support of dictatorships and hostility toward movements of liberation, and advocacy of a "restricted democracy," where a limited amount of political space is allowed if it does not rock the economic and political boat, internally and in the hemisphere. This was the model proposed for Nicaragua in the last days of Somoza (which did not succeed) and the rationale behind the support of the military-civilian junta in El Salvador.

The United States is *militarily* responsible for the cry of Latin America.[8] Not only is there a history of American economic and political interventions in the region, but also of direct and indirect military involvement in its internal affairs. Puerto Rico, Cuba, the Dominican Republic, Haiti, Panama, Nicaragua, and Mexico are witnesses to direct armed interventions. The entire region bears witness to more subtle forms of indirect interventions. Since 1947, when the nations of the Americas signed the Inter-American Treaty of Reciprocal Assistance, the United States has had a Military Assistance Program (MAP), which has had as a fundamental objective the influence of the region's future military leaders in order to control and maintain a favorable climate for the United States-dominated free-market economy. The concrete result of this program is a sophisticated network of United States-oriented military officers, who in recent years have become the political bosses of Latin America. As Lernoux has noted: "Between 1950 and 1975 the United States trained 71,651 Latin American military personnel including eight of the region's current dictators and in addition supplied 2.5 billion dollars' worth of armaments."[9] These officers were trained at the Inter-American Defense College in Washington's Fort McNair and the School of the Americas in the Panama Canal Zone.

The problem is also *cultural*. Latin American culture has become the victim of United States consumerism. The majority of television stations are controlled by the major networks in North America.[10] The print news media, especially Associated Press and United Press International, control the level of information of many newspapers. To obtain a wider view of reality, one has to discover the not too easily accessible independent news centers scattered here and there. The story is repeated when it comes to books, especially textbooks, and many of the educational institutions.

Iberian-rooted culture has been a victim of Anglo-Saxon messianism. Spanish and Portuguese have been looked down upon by the largely monolingual English-speaking world. One of the goals of "manifest destiny" (which more than an American ideology belongs to Anglo-Saxon culture as a whole) was the demonstration of the superiority of English over Spanish, Portuguese, and French in the Americas and the establishment of its dominance in the hemisphere.

In reference to Spanish, different tactics have been used to achieve this end. For example, during the first three decades of the twentieth century, English was imposed in the Puerto Rican school system.[11] This tactic backfired; Puerto Rico remained a strongly Spanish-speaking island. Since the 1950s, a more subtle approach has been followed through the mass media and business.

In the Southwest, Spanish was legally rejected in the educational system and openly scorned in other public and cultural areas. In Dade County, Florida, Spanish, which several years ago was officially recognized as a second language—a factor that is generally agreed to have brought enormous economic advantages—has lost its legal status as a result of an Anglo backlash.

But the most influential offensive against Hispanic languages and culture in the hemisphere is the Anglo-Saxon (in its American variant) penetration of Latin America by way of consumerism. United States products, from hotdogs to movies, have managed to penetrate deep inside the territory of the Latin American world, effecting fundamental changes in the language and mode of being of its people.

With such cultural aggression it is ironic to see the dominant Anglo sectors in the United States so indignant when Hispanics argue for Spanish as a second language. It not only reflects an unwillingness to recognize the obvious fact that Spanish (and Portuguese) share with English a legitimate partnership in the Americas, but even worse, demonstrates a cultural intolerance that militates against peaceful coexistence inside the United States. As White racism has created a state of hostility between the dominant Caucasian population and the color minorities, so English monolingualism and Anglo-Saxon cultural chauvinism are threatening further to impair relations between the growing Hispanic minority and the Anglo majority.

Christians in the United States should also acknowledge their share of responsibility in the *religious* field. As I have already shown in chapter 4, Latin America has been a market for American religious movements. Approximately 50 percent of the missionary force of the Roman Catholic church in the United States and Canada is concentrated in Latin America. One-third of the missionary force of the Protestant churches in the United States and Canada is also concentrated in Latin America, which has less than 10 percent of the world's population.

Two factors may account for this phenomenon. There is the fact that Latin America has been able to absorb a lot of the troubled missionary "market" in other parts of the world. For example, after China closed its doors to foreign missionaries, a great number of them were redeployed to Latin America. Beyond this, Latin America has attracted missionaries because it offers instant numerical success. Anything grows in Latin America: Mormons, Jehovah's Witnesses, Eastern religions, independent Protestant groups. It is much easier to be a missionary in a region where people are open to religious change than to serve in areas where people are resistant. Hence Latin America has become the most popular mission field of the second half of the twentieth century. While I am grateful for the missionaries who have made a significant, sacrificial contribution to the gospel during this period, the fact that Latin America has become a market of missionary consumerism is missiologically upsetting. Indeed it represents a blatant denial of the Christian mission insofar as it makes the desire to be "successful" the central missional motivation. Moreover such a phenomenon represents an escape from the tough challenges of a religiously plural world and further increases the spiral of domination of a weak neighbor.

Something similar has occurred in theology. As stated above, Latin American theological reflection was, until recently, largely dependent on European and North American theological thought, a fact that is still true of the majority of Protestants. In the latter case there have been two main instruments of theological penetration: publishing houses and theological schools.

Protestant publishing houses have done a remarkable job in disseminating and popularizing American theology, especially and overwhelmingly so in its various conservative brands. As for the schools, they have been shaped in the image and likeness of Bible institutes, colleges, and theological seminaries in the United States. To the extent that they remain faithful to the theologies of their American supporters and their Latin American constituency (which unfortunately has been theologically conditioned by their northern mentors), these publishing houses and theological institutions have their continued existence guaranteed. But let one of them depart from "the script" and begin to theologize, write, and publish in terms that respond to the issues and questions of the concrete Latin American reality, and the pressures, criticisms, and open opposition mount. Latin American Protestant seminaries, theologians, and publishing houses have a relatively limited space wherein to move, work, and think, and one (though not the only one) of the reasons for this is the financial and ideological pressures of American Christian churches, mission boards, and societies.

The problem is not simply one of educational institutions, publishing houses, and individual theologians. It is also one of academic arrogance on the part of American and European theology. As has been shown, in the last fifteen years Latin America has given the world church a creative theological thought. After an initial success for some of the better-known expressions of this thought, an avalanche of reactions followed in American and European professional circles, mostly in the form of a snobbish dismissal of its content on the ground that it is faddish and not academically serious. With a few notable exceptions, American publishers are showing little interest in the avalanche of theological literature that has been produced in Latin America, because it has a limited market. Mainstream theologians have failed to take seriously the various types of Latin American theologies because in their opinion they do not fit the standard criteria of theological inquiry. Accordingly, few rank and file American/European academic theologians dialogue with their Latin American colleagues.

Paying Old and New Debts

Third, to respond with integrity to the cry of Latin America, Christians in the United States need to acknowledge their share of responsibility in its suffering and oppression. If they understand and are prepared to acknowledge their share of responsibility, then the next step is to begin to pay their debts. By this I do not mean that they should now start paying reparations for all the damage done to Latin America during the last 150 years. That would be politically and economically unrealistic. Indeed, such a move could only take place in a context of total economic, political, and social transformation of the two Americas, something I can see happening only at the consummation of the kingdom of God!

The New Testament, however, speaks of an "evangelical" debt. The apostle Paul considered himself under obligation to Greeks and barbarians, the wise and the foolish (Rom. 1:14). He considered himself their debtor for the sake of the gospel. Hence he was "eager to preach the gospel" in Rome (Rom. 1:15). The gospel was for Paul "the power of God to salvation" (Rom. 1:16): the revelation of the justice of God (Rom. 1:17). That is why he carried out his gospel ministry in words and deeds. "For I will not venture to speak of anything except what Christ has wrought through me to win obedience from the Gentiles, by word and deed, by the power of signs and wonders, by the power of the Holy Spirit . . ." (Rom. 15:18–19).

As Christians, North Americans owe Latin America the gospel: the good news of liberation from the power of sin and death, a message that has meaning only in the context of justice. To proclaim the gospel is to declare in words *and* deeds, "by the power of signs and wonders," that in Jesus Christ God is declared forever to be on the side of the destitute of the earth, setting women and men free from selfishness and greed, and calling them to the obedience of faith. To believe in the gospel is, above all things, to commit oneself to do justice, love mercy, and walk humbly before God (Mic. 6:8) in the power of the Spirit of the risen Christ.

To say then that Christians to the north of the Río Bravo owe Latin America the gospel is to affirm their responsibility to work for the integral liberation of this region of poverty and oppression. Concretely it means responding with actions that are commensurate with the content of their neighbor's cry and their share of responsibility for that cry.

Economically, North American Christians owe Latin America an advocacy for fair trade. Latin America does not need favors; it needs a just treatment toward its products. That means, at least, support of the quest for a New International Economic Order and willingness to share generously the tremendous profit the United States has been getting out of the region, through substantial financial aid for public works, food, education, and housing projects.

Politically, Christians in the United States owe Latin America an advocacy for the rights of its people to organize their society in whatever way they consider correct. Relations with Latin America should not be based on what is politically expedient for the United States. North American Christians should lobby for international and public morality. The Carter administration came into office with high moral standards in foreign relations. In Latin America it became a strong advocate for human rights. But in difficult situations, like those in Nicaragua and El Salvador, it assumed a contradictory stance, falling into the temptation of political expediency for fear that to do what was right might contribute to a form of political organization that does not conform to United States standards. The Reagan administration has now begun to back any government so long as it protects United States interests. It does not matter whether a government represents a brutal dictatorship that stands diametrically opposed to American political and judicial principles and constitutes a flagrant violation of the United Nations Declaration of Human Rights and an offense against human life. What matters, in the thinking of the Reagan administration, seems to be the protection of United States business and political interests. Hence the renewed friendship with brutal and repressive governments, like that of Chile, the blanket endorsement of the unpopular former military-civilian junta of El Salvador, and the cutting of all economic aid to Nicaragua. North American Christians should challenge such immoral and contradictory policy by every democratic means at their disposal.

In the *military* field they need to become an advocate for the demilitarization of Latin America. Armaments, and the business deals that go along with them, are responsible for the murder and destruction of the people of the region rather than their protection from "the menace of international communism."

Christians need to work for peace by demanding justice, not by increasing military repression.

Furthermore, Christians owe Latin America an advocacy for *cultural* pluralism in the Americas. This implies a close scrutiny of North American cultural networks and endeavors. It demands the empowerment of ethnic minorities (like the aborigines), the promotion of Spanish and Portuguese as major hemispheric languages, and the support of institutions that are dedicated to the stimulation and defense of Latin American cultural values. It means supporting international agencies (like UNESCO) in their efforts to promote more equitable cultural development.

On the *religious* side North American Christians owe Latin America an advocacy for ecclesial indigeneity, partnership in mission, and a contextual evangelization. By ecclesial indigeneity I mean letting the church become itself and not forcing it to be a carbon copy of something else, as has been the case with far too many churches that are the direct product of Protestant mission work. Partnership in mission implies a willingness to *collaborate* with Latin American churches and denominations in the fulfillment of the mission God has given them rather than doing things *for* them, as is too often the case with many Protestant mission boards. As for contextual evangelization, it means letting the evangelistic approach be decided in the light of the concrete reality and not simply in terms of the perceptions that United States Christians and churches may have of that reality, or worse yet, from the perspective of the North American situation, as is too often the case with some mission boards and para-church evangelistic organizations.

Starting with the Nearest Neighbor

Fourth, in order for their actions to be credible, Christians in the United States need to *start with their nearest neighbor.* It is usually easier to respond to the farthest than to the nearest. Concretely that means Puerto Rico and the Hispanic community in the United States mainland.

The small Caribbean island of Puerto Rico has been a United States territory since the Spanish-American War and is one of the last colonial vestiges in the entire hemisphere. After almost ten years of American maneuvering, the United Nations Committee on Decolonization declared the island a colonial territory (over the protest, of course, of the United States and a representative sector of the island population, who argued that in 1953, when Puerto Rico became a so-called commonwealth as a result of a popular election, it ceased to be a colony, becoming instead a "free associated state"). There is no question that Puerto Rico today is a political "hot potato." Not only are its people polarized more than ever over the status question (whether to become a sovereign nation, a state of the federal union, or stay as is), but it is the most impoverished American territory, with an unemployment rate of over 20 percent, 65 percent of the population on federal foodstamps, and 38 percent with an income below the poverty line. A process of industrialization launched more than thirty years ago (where mainland corporations were offered numerous economic incentives to establish textile industries and oil refineries) has backfired with tremendous air and water pollution, the almost total destruction of the island's agriculture, and a host of social ills (crime and drug addiction being the two most notable)—typical of most industrial societies. In Vieques, an adjacent island-municipality, which is practically in the hands of the United States armed forces, the fishing industry, which is the sole livelihood of the majority of the population, has been practically driven out of existence by the U.S. Navy.

It is a fact, nevertheless, that most Americans seem to know about Puerto Rico only what the media tell them: that it is the place from which many Hispanics in the northeast come and that it is a beautiful winter paradise, easily accessible by air, with wonderful beaches and luxury hotels. Most of the mainline Protestant churches, with the exception of the Puerto Rican

Episcopal church, which recently became an autonomous church, are institutionally attached to their parent bodies, functioning as if Puerto Rico were *already a state.*[12]

United States Christians and churches should reflect critically on the current situation of Puerto Rico. They should become aware of its enormous political, economic, and social problems. They should critically inquire into the ideological role that churches and mission boards have played in the Americanization of the island. They should reflect on the correspondence between the latter process and the enormous sociopolitical problems afflicting its people. Above all, churches, denominational agencies, and individual Christians should demand the immediate withdrawal of the U.S. Navy from Vieques and carefully monitor the way dissenting Puerto Ricans are being treated by the Department of Justice and the federal court system.

Responding to the nearest neighbor, however, also implies dealing with those who live inside the continental United States: the Hispanic community. There are those who express concern for Latin America while callously neglecting the Hispanic minority in their own country. They follow the examples of those who express concern for Africa and the Afro-Caribbean community, but fail to demonstrate a similar concern for their Black brothers and sisters in the United States. That can no longer be tolerated. The credibility of the response to the cry of Latin America must be measured by the way the North American Hispanic community is dealt with, just as the credibility of the effectiveness in dealing with Africa and the English and French Caribbean must depend upon the capacity to relate effectively with the North American Black community.

Hispanics are the fastest-growing minority in the continental United States. Their official numbers have increased, nationwide, by 61 percent in the last decade, and their unofficial numbers probably by twice that amount. It is projected that by 1985 Hispanics will be the largest minority in the country.

But Hispanics are not just numerically significant. They are also one of the most depressed minorities in the nation. A "windshield" survey of such areas as New York City; Jersey City and Camden, New Jersey; Chester and northeast Philadelphia, Pennsylvania; Chicago; Detroit; East Los Angeles; New Mexico; or South Texas immediately reveals a socially marginated and economically oppressed people.[13] Indeed the overwhelming majority of Hispanics have been condemned, along with the majority of Blacks, to be the permanent underclass of North American society. In the case of Hispanics the harsh social and economic reality is further aggravated by their lack of communication skills in the dominant English language and the illegal status of an impressive number of them.

Hispanics, like Blacks, are a very religious people. Indeed their churches constitute one of the few institutions in society where they can be persons. It is a fact, nevertheless, that the Hispanic church in the United States remains the absentee of American religious consciousness. Be they Catholic or Pentecostal, mainline Protestant or conservative-evangelical, the fact of the matter is that they do not seem to count much when it comes to the interpretation of the American religious experience, church attendance, theological education, and missionary commitment.[14]

If the dominant American Christian community is really interested in responding to the cry of Latin America, it should take notice of its brothers and sisters in the ghettos of the cities and the *ranchos* of the rural communities. Indeed American Christians should begin to lobby strongly for the legalization of the more than 9 million undocumented migrants, the majority of whom are Hispanics. They should become advocates for educational programs that will enable Hispanics to study in the language that they know best and strengthen their access to professions heretofore closed to Hispanics. They should work for social programs that will improve Hispanic housing conditions and participation in industry, labor, and the arts. Above all, they should cry for justice, on behalf of Hispanics, in religious institutions that continue to ignore their existence: denominational and ecumenical agencies that shine with the absence of Hispanics; theological institutions that *refuse* to hire Hispanic professors (and even discourage theological students from doing their doctorates); religious journals and magazines that fail to publish materials dealing with the life and faith of Hispanic churches; and mainline churches that refuse to make an all-out commitment to a ministry among Hispanics, even though Hispanics constitute one of the most religiously receptive sectors in the United States today.

The cry of the oppressed Latin American neighbors is loud and clear, and if North American Christians but look around them they can easily detect ways and means available to them for a committed and responsible response. I have offered several specific suggestions. The question is whether American churches, agencies, and individual Christians are prepared to respond *in deed*. Only through their concerted leadership can there be a credible response.

One thing should be made clear, however: the response to the neighbor's cry is not a take-it-or-leave-it affair. As Christians they do not have a choice. They are indebted to their neighbors! Therefore the cry of the Latin American world puts at stake the *integrity* of the Christian profession of faith in the United States. They can take all the time they want, but only at the expense of their Christian integrity.

NOTES

1. Cf. Esther and Mortimer Arias, *The Cry of My People* (New York: Friendship Press, 1980), which has been designated as the official textbook by the National Council of Churches.

2. E.g., in November 1980 the first four issues of the Sunday *New York Times* carried only five news items on Spanish- and Portuguese-speaking Latin America,

and three on the English Caribbean (cf. *New York Times,* Nov. 2, 9, 16, 23, 1980). In January 1981, however, news coverage of Latin America tripled. Armed conflicts do catch the attention of the press, especially when they affect United States interests.

3. Cf. John Eagleson and Philip Scharper, eds., *Puebla and Beyond* (Maryknoll, N.Y.: Orbis Books, 1979).

4. Xabier Gorostiaga, *Los banqueros del imperio* (San José, Costa Rica: EDUCA, 1978), p. 29.

5. Penny Lernoux, *Cry of the People* (Garden City, N.Y.: Doubleday, 1980), p. 58.

6. See, e.g., "The Latinization of Miami," *New York Times Magazine,* Sept. 21, 1980.

7. Lernoux, *Cry,* p. 211.

8. For a documented analysis of the role of the United States in the political, economic, and military situation of Latin America, see Lernoux, *Cry,* pp. 137ff.

9. Lernoux, *Cry,* p. 56.

10. For an informative study of North American TV networks in Latin America prior to 1971, see Alan Wells, *Picture Tube Imperialism* (Maryknoll, N.Y.: Orbis Books, 1972).

11. Cf. Aida Negrón Montilla, *Americanization in Puerto Rico and the Public School System: 1900–1930* (Río Piedras, P.R.: Editorial Universitaria de Puerto Rico, 1975).

12. E.g., the Iglesia Evangélica Unida de Puerto Rico is a regional conference of the United Church of Christ, and the Iglesias Bautistas de Puerto Rico are a regional administrative unit of the American Baptist Churches U.S.A. Puerto Rican Presbyterians are a synod of the United Presbyterian Church and Puerto Rican Methodists constitute a conference of the United Methodist Church under the bishop of Eastern Pennsylvania.

13. In 1978 Hispanics had a median annual family income of $12,600, compared with $17,600 for the nation as a whole. The worst off among them were Puerto Ricans, with a median family income of only $8,300 and 38.9 percent living in poverty. They were followed by Mexican-Americans, with a median family income of $12,800 and 18.9 percent in poverty. All in all, 21.4 percent of Hispanic families had incomes below the poverty line, compared with 9.3 percent for the country as a whole (Source: United States Department of Commerce, March 1978).

Such economic plight is understandable if one bears in mind that Hispanics constitute one of the least-educated social groupings in the United States. Hispanic children are "two to three grade levels behind other students. A mere 30 percent manage to complete high school. In urban ghetto areas, the school drop-out rate for Hispanics reaches as high as 85 percent. Less than 7 percent have completed college. In 1975–76, Hispanics received only 2.8 percent of the B.A. degrees awarded, 2 percent of the master's degrees, 2.6 percent of the law degrees, 2.3 percent of the medical degrees, and 1.2 of all doctorates" (Alan Pifer, "Bilingual Education and the Hispanic Challenge," *Foundation News,* January/February 1981, pp. 23–24).

14. A case in point is the statement by members of the Hispanic community at the Conference on the City sponsored by Riverside Church in New York City, March 12–14, 1981. They listed the following five complaints against "mainline Protestant, conservative fundamentalist, and establishment evangelicals":

1. The social issues relevant to the Hispanic community are not included in a significant manner in the conferences, T.V., and radio programs funded and staffed by the above. Social issues which are of particular interest to Hispanics are: the

undocumented aliens, U.S. foreign policy in Latin America, the impact of multinational corporations in Latin America, bilingual education in America, and the adverse impact of Reagan's economics on the Hispanic people.

2. The contributions of Hispanic people in the life and ministry of the church in the city are systematically and categorically ignored. National and regional conferences (such as the Riverside Church Conference on the City, Washington 80, and the American Festival on Evangelism) exclude significant participation of indigenous Hispanics in the planning and implementation stages. The absence of Hispanic speakers in regional and national events deprives the Christian community of the vital Hispanic perspectives.

3. The American religious establishment must assume its share of the responsibility for the decay of urban areas and the deplorable conditions under which Hispanics must live in the American cities. The church's policy in Hispanic communities has been to neglect, desert or undermine the resources of the Hispanic people. The only churches that have remained to service the spiritual needs of Hispanic people in the inner cities of our country are the indigenous and independent Hispanic churches.

4. Hispanic liturgy and theology have been denied their rightful place in the American religious community. Our music, theology, literature, and language, have been rejected. The church has served as an instrument of assimilation instead of human liberation and fulfillment. The church has perpetuated paternalism, division and oppression which have mitigated against the development and has deprived the American religious establishment of the contributions of the Hispanic religious experience.

5. Theological seminaries and graduate schools of religion have discriminated against Hispanics by refusing to hire indigenous Hispanic faculty, provide supportive services, allocate financial resources. The educational establishment has rejected the legitimacy of bi-lingual theological education as a viable and indispensable ingredient for men and women for ministry. There has always been plenty of rhetoric but little action or financial support.

The list of complaints concluded with a general demand for "immediate concrete responses to these serious complaints and indictments" and a specific summons to churches, denominational agencies, and individual Christians to fund "a conference that will bring together the Hispanic leadership of the church in North America and Puerto Rico" (Coalition of Hispanic Leaders, "Complaints against Mainline Protestant, Conservative Fundamentalist, and Establishment Evangelicals," presented to the participants at the Conference on the City, Riverside Church, New York, N.Y., March 12-14, 1981 [photocopy]).

8

Prophetic Significance of Third World Liberation Theologies

The last decades have seen a dramatic change in Christian theological circles. After centuries of Western dominance, theology has been confronted with a growing number of voices from the third world. This is not to say that prior to the theological boom of the 1960s and 1970s there were no theologians in the third world. Indeed the first half of the twentieth century saw the rise of an impressive list of theologians, especially in Asia and Latin America.[1] And we must not forget that Western theology has a great debt to Africa, which gave it theologians like Origen, Cyprian, and Augustine. Nor should we take lightly the case of the Angolan prophetess Béatrice, who, around the year 1700, set forth a basic claim of African and Black theologies (that Jesus Christ is black), dying for it at the stake.[2] But not until the 1960s did third world theological thought begin to make its presence felt in Western circles. Several factors may account for this.

First, there is the fact that the ecumenical movement has forced Western churches to become aware of ecclesial developments in the third world. Prior to the founding of the World Council of Churches and the convocation of Vatican Council II, knowledge of the churches outside the first world was confined to missionaries and their sponsoring bodies. With the rise of the ecumenical movement, Western Christians and their churches have been forced to come out of their isolation and meet, see, and hear their brothers and sisters from the traditional mission lands. The experience has been both enlightening and shocking.

Second, the post-World War II period has witnessed the emergence of a new religious pluralism in the West. Until World War II, religion in the West was basically a Protestant, Catholic, and Jewish issue. After the war not only did the question of Christian-Jewish relations intensify, but an influx of people from Asia, Africa, and the Caribbean into Western Europe, Australasia, and North America opened the door for established Eastern religions, Islam, and several newer religious movements. The traditional hegemony of Christianity was challenged. Faced with a religious pluralism never before experienced, many Christian theologians have been forced to look outside their cultural and theological tradition for an understanding of, and a relevant response to, the new religious situation in the West. This has naturally made necessary a dialogue with their Christian colleagues in those lands where the question of other religions is the crucial theological issue.

Third, there is the fact that the post-World War II period has seen the dismantling of the colonial project, the coming into being of new nations, and the spread of Marxian revolutionary theory and praxis. An initial Christian-Marxist dialogue in Europe proved to be too theoretical to shape the life and thought of the church, even though it did contribute to the rise of a critical political theology which not only has affected the course of theology in the West but has made a significant impact in the third world. It was in the latter, however, where the process of decolonization on the one hand, and the rise of Marxist-inspired revolutions on the other, gave way to a series of theologies focused on the theme of liberation. Thanks to several progressive publishing houses, ecumenical organizations like the World Council of Churches, and several sensitive Western theologians and missiologists, these emerging theologies have begun to make an impact in traditional theological circles, even though, it must be admitted, there are still far too many theologians and institutions that persist in their Western provincialism and chauvinism, refusing to acknowledge the novelty and creativity of their third world colleagues, or the liberating perspective of third world theological thought and its prophetic significance for theology in general and the church's mission in particular.

Locating the Third World

"Third world" is a controversial term, much debated in sociopolitical circles. It was first used in 1955 at the Bandung Conference of nonaligned nations. At that time it meant basically Asian and African nations. Most recently, it has been used in reference to countries outside the industrialized, capitalist countries of Europe and North America, as well as Japan, Australia, New Zealand, and South Africa (first world), and the socialist, Eastern European countries, including the USSR (second world).[3] Thus understood, the third world is distinguishable from the first and second worlds by the fact that it is neither industrialized nor capitalized and lies outside the socialist countries of Eastern Europe.

Others, however, among whom I would include myself, prefer to define the third world not so much in terms of geographical and ideological boundaries as socioeconomic conditions. Seen from this perspective the third world is the world of the sociological impoverished, oppressed, and marginated. By this definition the third world is also present in the first and second worlds. In the latter there are significant minorities who find themselves in oppressed and marginalized situations (though, granted, more for political, cultural, and/

or religious reasons than for socioeconomic ones). There is a historical and cultural correspondence between the oppressed and marginated in the first and third worlds: Blacks, Hispanics, Asians, and aboriginal minorities in the first world are the victims of the colonial and neo-colonial projects of the industrialized, capitalist nations. The only difference between the third world *in* and *outside* the first is that whereas in Africa, Asia, the Caribbean, Latin America, and the Pacific, the oppressed and marginated are in the majority, in the first world they are a minority. Be that as it may, when put together they constitute more than two-thirds of humankind. It is this human mass that the Peruvian theologian Gustavo Gutiérrez has aptly described as "the underside of history"[4]: those who have suffered the last five hundred years of human history but have not been able to shape it. They are the victims of global injustice and exploitation, condemned to a history of poverty and marginalization. In spite of its historic humiliation and exploitation, its technological backwardness and dependence, the third world is nevertheless a place of struggle, patience, courage, and hope.

This is the social context that shapes the emerging theologies under consideration. They can thus be described as theologies "from the underside of history."[5] It should be borne in mind, nevertheless, that the third world represents not only a socioeconomically impoverished and exploited sector of humankind. It is also a vast, culturally rich mosaic with a deeply rooted religiosity. This religio-cultural dimension is as complex as it is geographically extensive. It encompasses cosmic, primordial religions, such as those found throughout Africa and Oceania, and in pockets of Asia, North America, Australasia, Latin America, and the Caribbean. But it is metacosmic religions like Hinduism and Buddhism,[6] and biblical religions like Islam and Christianity, that claim the loyalty of the largest number of third world peoples. Hence third world theologies have both a sociopolitical and a religio-cultural focus.

Issues in Third World Theologies

This double focus is reflective of the tensions experienced by Christians in the third world. Two of them, indeed the most acute, are the tensions between religious discontinuity and cultural continuity, and historical engagement and eschatological distance. These tensions constitute, in my opinion, the leading issues in third world theologies. It is in order, therefore, for us to outline them briefly.

Religious Discontinuity vs. Cultural Continuity

The first issue arises out of the missionary roots of Christianity in the third world. Christians in this part of the world are the product of the modern missionary movement. Conversion to the Christian faith has involved, among other things, acceptance of a foreign religious tradition. This is understandable, since Christianity is the offspring of Judaism. In this respect the Christian missionary movement can be said to be a carrier of Jewish values and world-view to peoples of other religions and cultures. Nevertheless the Christian faith did not remain Jewish. It also became Greek. In fact, so much did it come under Hellenistic influence that in a few centuries it forgot its Jewish heritage and became the carrier par excellence of Greek culture in all its complexity and diversity. This accounts for the intrinsic connection between Christianity and Western civilization. Hence, even though it was hardly possible to name the name of Jesus Christ without recollecting his Jewish roots, this problem was solved once he began to be conceived of as a Western-God-human. In time this image was refined even more to be conformed with the technological dominance of Western Christians. Since the greatest expansion that the Christian faith has ever known has taken place in the last two centuries, the period when the West set its technological imprint on the entire globe, it should not surprise us to discover that this expansion—stimulated, supported, and shaped by Christians in this part of the world—not only has portrayed a Western Christ but also has extended all over the third world the religious tradition that produced this Christology.

Today we find a growing number of Christians in the third world who are rapidly becoming aware that the religious discontinuity that they have had to suffer on account of their Christian faith has also implied an uprootedness from their culture, since religion is a fundamental component of culture. In past decades the brightest theological voices from the first and third worlds avoided the problem by simply dereligionizing the Christian faith, affirming its revelatory nature, and dissociating it from the religions.[7] This argument, however, has become increasingly difficult to sustain, given the growing awareness of the cultural boundness of the language of faith. Accordingly, while we can assert with all biblical and theological certainty that the Christian faith is grounded on the self-disclosure of God in the special and unique redemptive event of Jesus Christ, the moment we start explicating the meaning of this self-disclosure and the uniqueness of Jesus Christ, we find ourselves immersed in a cultural and religious discourse. All human discourses are mediated by cultural symbols, signs, and codes. Since religion is that aspect of culture that enables us to express our experience of transcendence, it is as basic to life as culture itself. It is not possible, therefore, to talk about God, revelation, and Christ in a noncultural framework. This means that the Christian faith can only be expressed in religious language.

A fundamental question facing Christians in the third world today is that of affirming faith in Christ without breaking their religio-cultural ties. This implies a renunciation of their Western-inspired state of antagonism with their indigenous religious roots. Consequently, just as there are those in the West who claim to be Christian Jews, so there are those in the third world who are entertaining the possibility of being Christian Hindus, Christian Muslims, or Christian Buddhists. Indeed, some will go as far as to say that only as third world Christians are prepared to participate in the religious traditions of their respective cultures can the Christian faith ever cease to be foreign and become rooted in their soil.

To be sure, this entire issue carries several potentially explosive problems. There is the problem of the distinctiveness of Christ and the refusal of biblical faith to reduce him to one among many lords (Acts 4:12). There is also the critical and liberating dynamic of the Christian faith, namely, the fact that it questions all absolutistic (totalitarian) systems and seeks to free life from the captivity of selfishness, injustice, and exploitation for community, justice, and well-being. It is not possible, therefore, to be a Christian without experiencing change or transformation into something new.

These potential problems are, however, part of the risk of the Christian faith. The danger facing Christians in the third world who are trying to understand and serve Jesus Christ in the light of their own religious and cultural traditions is no different from that which Christians in the West have faced, continue to confront, and shall have increasingly to grope with in the days to come.

Furthermore, no Christian has a franchise on the mystery of God's salvation. In the words of Gerald H. Anderson, as Christians "we cannot determine—or even adequately discuss—the limits and means of Christ's redemptive activity."[8] Our task is simply to bear witness to Jesus Christ by sharing in his saving action from within our respective religio-cultural realities.

Historical Engagement vs. Eschatological Distance

Another issue in third world theologies is that of historical engagement and eschatological distance. Christian faith is not a privatistic gnosis. It is faith in the Lord of history. It demands therefore a public or political witness (i.e., a redemptive engagement in the affairs of this world). This is hardly possible without some form of political ideology. A political ideology involves a vision of the future, a coherent interpretation of reality, and a programmatic line of action conducive to the reorganization of society.

At the heart of the Christian participation in the struggles of the world lies, consciously or unconsciously, an ideological stance. To be sure, the confession of the lordship of Christ is not an ideological affirmation. Faith in Christ is not an ideology; it is acceptance of God's free gift of forgiveness, obedience to Christ's will through the help of the Holy Spirit, and hope in the future revelation of God's kingdom. But just as it is impossible to talk about our God-experiences without religious language, so there cannot be a public confession of Christ without an ideological mediation.

On the one hand, Christians are not islands unto themselves. They both affect and are affected by their social environment. Their behavior is in many ways conditioned by their sociohistoric reality. They thus envision society, interpret history, and program their lives in accordance with the interests of the social groups to which they belong. In other words, all Christians, regardless of their station in life or geographic location, carry with them ideological baggage.

On the other hand, faith in Christ involves commitment to certain ethical imperatives. Christians are expected to love their neighbors, to practice justice, and to work for peace as a consequence and verification of their love of God, their forgiveness and justification by the work of Christ, and their hope in God's kingdom. To fulfill these demands, they need a coherent scheme whereby they can understand the concrete meaning of love, justice, and peace in their respective contexts. At this point ideologies become basic mediations for the work of faith. They fulfill a positive function because they give faith a historical rationality.

Ideologies, however, can be potentially explosive for Christians, since they tend toward absolutism when they demand complete loyalty from their adherents to a coherent (and inflexible) system of political thought and action. Insofar as Christians are motivated by the vision of God's eschatological kingdom, they will always find themselves uneasy with any ideology, even with those that come close to their ethical concerns. Accordingly Christian eschatology will always demand a certain distance in the redemptive engagement of believers in the struggle of history.

Third world theologians have to cope with the challenge of ideologies. They are well aware of the fact that to be engaged in one's social context as a testimony to Jesus Christ demands the assumption of a historical rationality (an ideology). Such an awareness has not come overnight. It is the direct result of the long process of political awakening that the peoples of the third world have been experiencing during the second half of the twentieth century. In this process old colonial powers have been forced to give up control of conquered lands, oligarchical and dictatorial regimes are being overthrown by rebellious forces, and neo-colonial powers are being challenged at all levels by the oppressed and exploited majorities of the third world. In Cuba, Nicaragua, Southeast Asia, and Portuguese Africa, Christians are having to learn to live under Marxist socioeconomic systems. The Central American countries of Guatemala and El Salvador, Asian lands like South Korea and the Philippines, and the entire region of southern Africa are all areas where Christians are faced with having to choose between a supposedly supra-ideological neutrality, which in the end becomes an implicit support of the status quo, or to take a stance against the existing regime and in favor of a just social order. Thus third world theologies reveal the ideological struggles in which many Christians find themselves inescapably caught, and attempt to offer them spiritual discernment and prophetic courage.

This has, understandably, created new divisions inside the third world church. It has also broadened the gap between Christians in these poverty-stricken continents and in the affluent countries of the West. For one thing, third world Christians have become much too aware of the ideological ties between the modern missionary movement and the colonization and exploitation of their countries. For another, they have uncovered the historic economic and ideological ties between Western missionary expansion and the economic interests and military aggression of the United States and its European allies. This has led to a growing suspicion not only of the hidden motives behind a lot of present-day foreign missionary activity and development projects, but especially of the ideological presuppositions in Western theological thought. This being the case, it is understandable why most third world theologies would tend to be theologies of liberation.[9]

The Latin American Model

Liberation theologies constitute both a protest against oppression and injustice as well as a struggle for emancipation and justice. Justo and Catherine Gonzalez have rightly observed that liberation theologies emerge from a context of "powerlessness in society and voicelessness in the church."[10] They are theologies of a liberating engagement, grounded on *theo-praxis*. As such they are not divorced from the fundamental source of knowledge of the Christian faith: the Scriptures. On the contrary, they are characterized by a critical dialogue with biblical faith, bringing to the Scriptures the questions that arise out of reality.

One of the better-known liberation theologies in the third world is that which has been developed in Latin America. The influential role that the latter has played throughout the oppressed world[11] is justification enough for highlighting it as a representative model of third world theologies.[12] In the remaining part of this chapter, I want to summarize the basic characteristics of Latin American liberation theology, considering its context, method, and program, as well as some of the leading questions it raises and the challenge it poses.

The Context

Latin American liberation theology emerges out of a complex socioecclesiastical context that can only be understood and appreciated in the light of the continental history of poverty and oppression, colonialism and imperialism. Though it began to take shape in the 1960s, its roots can be traced back to the days of Bartolomé de las Casas in the sixteenth century.

During this period we find the first attempt to reflect on the Christian faith in the light of the oppressed.[13] Las Casas denounced the conquest and oppression that the aboriginal population had been subjected to in the name of Christ and the gospel. He called for a just treatment of indigenous people, an evangelization that respected their personhood, and a contextualization of the gospel in their cultures.

The process initiated by Las Casas was gradually stopped in the next three centuries. It was revived somewhat in the second half of the nineteenth century, when Protestants began to arrive under the protection of liberal politicians. Protestants challenged Catholic Christendom in its alliance with local oligarchies, corrupt and conservative politicians, and the army. They defended the cause of justice and liberty, established schools, organizations, and hospitals, and founded "free" churches where people could develop as persons under a democratic system.

In the 1930s there was a massive exodus from the country to the city, produced by the world economic crisis, which changed the physiognomy of Latin America. The concentration of poor masses around the urban areas accentuated the economic gap between the local oligarchies and the displaced (poor) majorities. The urban experience shook the traditional categories and thus the conceptual and psychological grip on the masses of a conservative Catholic clergy. A political awakening began to take place through a growing labor movement and the emergence of various forms of nationalistic populism, some of which were of Marxist inspiration. The Protestant Pentecostal movement, which had remained heretofore relatively small, found its place among the poor masses and began to spread rapidly.[14] The Catholic church began to suffer a setback numerically, politically, and intellectually.

To regain these losses, the church launched a "new Christendom strategy" centered on the Catholic Action movement, which had started in Italy and France several decades before.[15] Educational institutions were founded, labor organizations were formed, and Christian Democratic political parties were organized throughout the continent. A new Catholic elite emerged in the various spheres of society.

Yet by the middle 1950s it was obvious that this new approach could not contain the process of de-Christianization among the masses, the growing influence of Marxism, the advance of Pentecostalism, and the independent Protestant groups. The new Christendom project could not satisfy the tremendous pastoral needs of the urban Catholic church.

In 1955 the Episcopal Conference of Latin America (CELAM) was formed to bring about a continentwide pastoral coordination. It began with the recognition that Latin America was still in a state of mission; that the majority of its people were not practicing Christians; that there was still a tremendous evangelistic work to be done and that, in order to accomplish it, there had to be a pastoral renewal. The Latin American Pastoral Institute (IPLA) was formed in the late 1950s to stimulate such a renewal. But, as some Protestants had painfully come to realize and as it soon became obvious to Roman Catholics also, the evangelization of Latin America could not be done in a vacuum; it could not be a mere spiritual endeavor; the pathetic social and economic situation of the continent could not be overlooked any longer. Meanwhile Pope John XXIII called for Vatican Council II to enable the church to cope with the problems of the day.

While this was taking place in the Catholic church, mainline Protestants were entering a new period in relation to Latin American society. The first generation of Protestants had passed away and a new political situation demanded a more effective response than the traditional social and educational work of Protestant missions.

In the 1950s the Student Christian Movement began to sponsor a series of studies on the nature and mission of the church in Latin America. These studies led to the launching (in 1961) of the Church and Society movement. At first this movement was concerned with the stimulation of the church toward greater participation in the solution of social problems. Soon, however, it began to enter into the political arena and became a critical prophetic movement against the institutional Protestant church. The Church and Society movement, through various studies on ideology, Marxism, and revolution, paved the way for a liberation theological discourse. Hence it should be no surprise that a Protestant turned out to be the first to write a book on liberation theology: The Brazilian Presbyterian theologian, Rubem Alves, in 1966 wrote a doctoral dissertation at Princeton on the theme "Toward a Theology of Liberation," published three years later under the title *Theology of Human Hope.* Yet liberation theology did not shine as a Protestant theology but primarily as an ecumenical Catholic discourse.

Vatican II served as a training ground for Latin American bishops. Thus they felt the need for a special conference to deal with the implications of the council for Latin America. Preparations began to take place amid a growing concern over the increasing gap between rich and poor. In 1966 CELAM held a meeting in Buenos Aires around the question of development. In the same year the World Conference on Church and Society was held in Geneva, with a leading role taken by Latin American Protestant theologians. A year later Pope Paul published his encyclical *Populorum Progressio,* wherein he called for the integral development of the poor and disfranchised nations of the world.

By the time the Catholic Episcopal Conference came to celebrate its second general assembly, the most pressing issue to be dealt with was not how to apply the theology of Vatican II in Latin America but, rather, how to respond to the growing impatience over the social and economic disparities between the haves and the have-nots. Thus the theme of the meeting, held in Medellín, Colombia, in August 1968, was "The Presence of the Church in the Present-Day Transformation of Latin America." It was Medellín that used the word "liberation" as the new term for what *Populorum Progressio* called "integral development." At Medellín the bishops of Latin America not only formally introduced a new method of doing theology, but gave their imprimatur to the theological trend that would most characterize Latin American theology. By making a preferential option for the poor and committing themselves to work for their integral liberation, the bishops legitimized a theology that has since flourished as a Catholic ecumenical theology.

After Medellín 1968 there followed a political radicalization of many priests, bishops, theologians, and lay men and women, as they sought to implement its commitment to the liberation of the poor. Then came a conservative backlash. After the Chilean coup d'état of September 11, 1973, liberation theology became the target of conservative right-wing bishops, priests, theologians, and politicians. A carefully orchestrated campaign was launched to renounce the commitment of Medellín to the poor and oppressed at the Third General Assembly of Latin American Bishops in Puebla, Mexico, in February 1979. In so doing, liberation theology would lose the legitimacy it received in Medellín. Thanks to the leadership of progressive bishops, the protest of thousands of Catholic basic ecclesial communities throughout the continent, the moral support of many Catholic theologians, bishops, and laity in other parts of the world, and the diligent service of an impressive number of talented Latin American theologians, Puebla did not deny the commitment of Medellín but, rather, affirmed it. As the Final Document states: "With renewed hope in the vivifying power of the Spirit, we are going to take up once again the position of . . . Medellín, which adopted a clear and prophetic option expressing preference for, and solidarity with, the poor. . . . We affirm the need for conversion on the part of the whole Church to a preferential option for the poor, an option aimed at their integral liberation."[16]

The commitment that stimulated the development of liberation theology was thus upheld at Puebla. Nevertheless the repression witnessed in many countries throughout the 1970s continues, although the pressure has eased somewhat in some countries. This situation has forced liberation theology to take various forms according to the particular national context. In highly repressive countries it functions as a theology of resistance in captivity; in situations where there is relative freedom, it functions as a theology of solidarity with the thousands of women and men who have been and are being tortured, imprisoned, or thrown out of their countries for their participation in the struggle for justice and liberation, with the millions of peasants and workers who continue the struggle, passively and actively, in the midst of brutal dictatorships, and with all those around the world who are engaged in similar struggles.

The Method

Liberation theology is not so much a new theology as a new method of doing theology. Western academic theology has been notorious for its abstractness, being a reflection upon itself without any reference to concrete problems. This was not the case in the early church, where theology followed the experience of faith and was confirmed by the work of faith. But with the development of academia, theology became a scholastic discipline—a reflection on truth for its own sake. It ceased to be *practical* and became instead *philosophical*.

At Medellín, theology became once again practical as the traditional approach was challenged by the introduction of a different method. Theological reflection was so structured that it followed the analysis of the social, economic, and political reality of Latin America. How could there be a theological reflection on "The Church in the Present-Day Transformation of Latin America" without a clear analysis of the continental situation? Thus, before *hearing* what God's revelation had to say about present-day Latin

America, the church, it was felt, had to *see* (i.e., understand) the concrete reality. Moreover, it was not enough for the church to hear the Word in the light of what it saw, but to commit itself to *do* what the Word commanded for that hour. *See, hear,* and *do* are the three words (all verbs) that characterized Medellín's theological method, and which marked the theological production that followed. For its part Puebla not only affirmed Medellín's preferential option for the poor, but also its method.[17]

Latin American liberation theology has sought to liberate theology from its academic, ivory-tower imprisonment and return it to the center of the practice of the Christian faith. It sees the theological task as inseparably bound to the obedience of faith (Rom. 1:5). It insists that Christians can think their faith only as they practice it. Since the practice of faith can take place only in society, the process of reflecting on the faith needs the help of those disciplines that are responsible for interpreting the social reality. The social sciences are thus brought into the theological task by liberation theology as mediating instruments. Through them theology gains a concrete understanding of the world in which the faith is lived, and therefore of the questions to which it must respond in order to enable Christians to test and strengthen the efficacy of their obedience.

The Christian faith, understood as the body of beliefs that are centered on the person and work of Jesus Christ and rooted in the witness of Scripture, has an ethical thrust: faith in Christ implies commitment to love God and neighbor, to trust in the transcendent power of God, and to hope for the coming of God's kingdom. *Love, trust,* and *hope* are all action verbs. As ethical imperatives of the Christian faith; they underscore the fact that to be a Christian is to be engaged in the transformation of history.

Because the Christian faith has an ethical thrust, theology must make a critical use of the social sciences. Latin American theology does not advocate the indiscriminate use of these auxiliary disciplines. It knows that there is not such a thing as a neutral science. Accordingly it calls for the critical use of those disciplines that can best interpret the concrete reality of the oppressed majorities. Why them and not the others? Because the gospel is particularly concerned with the poor and disfranchised (Lk. 1:51–53; 6:20), and because liberation theology emerges as a theological reflection of Christians who represent an oppressed people.

Being therefore a theological reflection from an oppressed continent, it is natural that it would want to look at history from the perspective of the powerless and oppressed, and that it would want to underscore the biblical insight of the gospel as good news for the poor (Lk. 4:18). For a long time theology has been done from the perspective of the powerful and mighty; it is time that it be done from the side of the weak and downtrodden. For far too long the poor have been hidden from the eyes of theology; it is time that they be rescued as a fundamental category of the gospel and as a place from which to reflect on the faith.

The Program

From the foregoing it follows that liberation theology in Latin America constitutes a socioecclesial program. It wants to lead Christians to experience their faith from within the history of exploitation and oppression of the majority of human beings around the world in order to participate in its transformation. In this respect it wants to put theology in the frontiers of world history through stirring up the social conscience of Christians by calling them to commit their lives to the poor and downtrodden of society and by enabling them to participate in the transformation of their sociohistorical reality. This means, further, that liberation theology wants to transform the church from a powerful social institution often aligned with oppressive structures into a servant community actively engaged in the establishment of a more fraternal, just, peaceful, and free society.

This new mode of being in the world is complemented by another goal: leading Christians to interpret their faith from within the struggle for liberation. Thus political questions are given priority over personal problems, since the struggle for liberation is primarily a political matter. In the process of reflecting on the faith in the light of the collective fears and hopes of the poor, personal concerns take on a new dimension as they are seen from another angle. Thus sin, conversion, reconciliation, and sanctification, among other themes of the Bible, are interpreted in relation to the larger problems of society rather than in the perspective of a private, individual, isolated self, as so often happens in traditional theological circles. This in turn enables the liberating dynamic of the gospel to be manifested in all its force, at the same time blocking its ideological instrumentalization and therefore its use as a religious whitewash.

The program of liberation theology does not stop with a new way of experiencing and interpreting the Christian faith. It wants also to lead Christians to communicate that faith, which is lived and interpreted from "below," in the light of the concrete history of the disfranchised. To do so Christians have to assume the identity of the downtrodden, including their symbols, customs, creations, fears, and struggles; and the church will have to become a community of the poor.

Latin American liberation theology is thus an attempt to articulate the faith from the perspective of the nonpersons of society. Whatever our judgment of this theological discourse, one thing is indisputable: its commitment to the oppressed and its articulation of their deepest concerns.

Questions

Such a theology raises numerous questions. Three are particularly problematic.

The first question has to do with the primacy that is given to the political dimension of faith. Granted, the Christian faith is political insofar as it confesses the lordship of Christ over history and witnesses to a total process of liberation. But is it not also a personal faith? Is not the personal (not the private) dimension of faith equally worthy of theological inquiry? Can there be true liberation in history if persons are not transformed? Is a new social order possible without a new person?

From a biblical perspective the answer is No, and most liberation theologians would concur. Some, however, put so much stress on the primacy of the political that they diminish the importance of personal transformation in the process of liberation.[18] Others, though stressing the integrity of the liberation process, hardly deal with the personal. Take, for example, the case of Gustavo Gutiérrez, for whom liberation takes place at three levels: the political, the psychological, and the religious (or spiritual). He argues that all three are part "of a single complex process which finds its deepest sense and its full realization in the saving work of Christ."[19] It is a fact, nevertheless, that he rarely goes beyond the political in his exposition of liberation.[20]

A second question that liberation theology posits (for Protestants, at least) is in regard to the old problem of nature and grace. Most Latin American liberation theologians reveal a too optimistic view of human nature and a synergistic concept of saving grace. They see women and men as autonomous agents, capable of overcoming their chains of oppression, establishing a just society, and cooperating thereby with God in the construction of the kingdom. As Juan Luis Segundo points out, this proceeds from the contemporary Catholic notion (derived from Karl Rahner and incorporated into the theology of Vatican II) "that all human beings are called to one and the same supernatural vocation and, thanks to the grace of God, possess the means needed to fulfill this vocation. . . ."[21] In other words, God's saving grace has been made extensive to all human beings as a result of the Christ event. Salvation, as Gustavo Gutiérrez has noted, is no longer a quantitative problem (i.e., how many will be saved), but rather, qualitative (i.e., a matter of how to exercise the saving grace that has been made extensive to everyone in Jesus Christ).[22] This being the case, men and women have the moral capability to cooperate with God in the construction of the kingdom by shaking off the bondage of oppression, enabling others to do likewise and building a just society.

It is questionable whether such an optimistic view of human nature can be reconciled with the biblical witness, for the Bible understands alienation not only as a rupture of human relations (injustice), but also as rebellion against God (ungodliness). As Andrew Kirk has well observed:

> The biblical teaching on alienation urges that man is structurally unfree to change the structures of his social relationships to the point where they express real freedom for all. By placing the nature of alienation within the context of man's *desire* to alter the structure of the universe, the Bible constantly demonstrates why man has *altered* his relationship

to his neighbor. Because he does not acknowledge God as Lord, he sets himself up as 'Lord' to his fellowman. Thus, he loses the capacity for a relationship of brotherly equality.[23]

By the same token, both the concept of human cooperation in the historical manifestation of God's saving grace and the universalism that undergirds it cannot be squared with the witness of Holy Scripture. While it is true that the New Testament witnesses to a universal salvation, it does so against the backdrop of God's judgment and in the context of the gospel's call to faith and repentance. Put in other terms, biblical universalism is dialectical; it encompasses grace and judgment. In Jesus Christ, sin has been overcome and grace revealed. Hence salvation can be appropriated and judgment avoided by turning from sin (repentance) and trusting in him (faith) through the enabling power of God's Spirit.

From a biblical perspective, all efforts to restore human relationships and build a just, fraternal, and peaceful society are not by themselves adequate responses to the problem of alienation. To be thoroughly free, men and women need to deal with their fundamental alienation, and this can be done only through faith in Christ and repentance. Such freedom enables them to be witnesses (not builders) of the kingdom of God, in regard both to its present manifestations in history and to its final consummation. Indeed, this freedom enables them to become incarnated in the sweat and toil of the struggle for a more just, peaceful, and fraternal society while maintaining a critical distance and a discerning attitude.

A third problem that liberation theology poses for Protestants has to do with the role of the Bible in theology. Latin American liberation theology has been described as "a critical reflection on historical/Christian praxis in the light of the Word of God accepted in faith."[24] The problem is not that the Bible is unimportant in liberation theology; the question lies with the nature of the role ascribed to it. To say that theology is reflection on praxis in the light of the Word is to make the Bible a reference point, a fundamental referent to be sure, but *only* a reference. The Bible is, in other words, a testing source of Christian praxis, a measuring stick against which theology can judge the meaning and truth of praxis. Christian historical praxis does not emerge out of the clear blue sky, however. It is grounded on a praxeological theory. If Scripture is but a testing source of historical praxis, where do Christians get their theory of right action (orthopraxis)? At first it would appear that it is derived out of life itself. Yet, by historical Christian praxis, liberation theology does not mean any kind of action but, rather, a politically transforming (revolutionary) one.

Here Marxist thought becomes especially relevant. Marxism is not just a method of social analysis, but also a revolutionary strategy—a theory of praxis. The praxeological problem with liberation theology is not that it has benefited from Marxist analysis in its attempt to understand Latin American reality but, rather, that it has given Marxian thought a privileged place in its theory of praxis while denying a similar place to the Bible. For those for whom the Bible is not just a norm of faith but of practice, such a theology of liberation would be an unsatisfactory alternative. The solution for an evangelical theology of liberation does not lie, in my opinion, in turning the definition of theology upside-down so that it would read "a critical reflection of the Word of God in the light of historical praxis and contemporary reality," as Andrew Kirk has proposed.[25] This could make Christian praxis a referent to theological reflection rather than its privileged place, as I believe it should be. The problem is not with the *order* of the theological process but, rather, with the *content* of Christian praxis. What is needed is a biblical understanding of Christian praxis informed by Marxism or any other political strategy that is capable of enlightening the process of liberation. This would keep the theological focus on the life and mission of the church (praxis) while restoring to it the normative function of the Word of God at the crossroads of history.

Challenges

If liberation theology raises critical questions for an evangelical Protestant theologian like myself, it is no less true that it challenges evangelicals themselves, the institutional church, and academic theology.

First, liberation theology challenges those who insist on the priority and normativeness of Scripture in theology and do not make a similar insistence on personal and social transformation as part of the proclamation and teaching of the Word. What is the value of a high view of the Bible if it does not lead to transformed lives, renewed communities, and liberated institutions? Or, what is the theological validity of right doctrine (orthodoxy) without correct practice (orthopraxis)? Liberation theology argues that the truth of faith is a matter of obedience before it can be a question of doctrine.

Second, liberation theology is a protest against the sterility of academic theology. Hence it challenges academic theologians to come down from their ivory towers and do their theology from the perspective of the losers rather than the winners of history. In so doing, liberation theology rebukes the tendency in academic theology toward repetition, and challenges it to become a creative enterprise by putting its resources at the service of the oppressed.

Third, liberation theology challenges the institutional church by unmasking its ethical impotence in an unjust world. It calls the church, not only in Latin America but around the world, to a radical conversion to the God who takes sides with the poor, the powerless, and the oppressed,[26] and challenges it, consequently, to make a preferential option for their integral liberation.

Liberation theology, in Latin America and elsewhere, brings theology again into the frontiers of history as a prophetic voice in the church's mission. Herein lies the genius, not just of the model we have analyzed, but of all liberation theologies throughout the third world and their radical difference from most Euro-American contemporary theologies. Whereas the latter work with the premise that the main task of theology is to establish rationally the truth of theological propositions, the former insist that the task of theology is to help the church participate in the transformation of history. Paraphrasing Karl Marx's 11th thesis against Feuerbach, "Heretofore, philosophers have interpreted the world in many ways; the point is to change it," third world liberation theologians would say, "Heretofore, theology has reflected on the predicament of human history; the point is to help the Christian community and the institutional church to participate in its transformation."

NOTES

1. For a guide to third world theological literature, see J. Verkuyl, *Contemporary Missiology* (Grand Rapids, Mich.: Wm. B. Eerdmans, 1978), pp. 261ff.

2. Cf. Marie-Louise Martin, *Kimbangu: An African Prophet and His Church,* trans. Basil Blackwell (Grand Rapids, Mich.: Wm. B. Eerdmans, 1975), pp. 13–17; David J. Bosch, "Currents and Crosscurrents in South African Black Theology," *Black Theology: A Documentary History, 1966–1979,* ed. Gayraud S. Wilmore and James H. Cone (Maryknoll, N.Y.: Orbis Books, 1979), pp. 220ff.

3. Cf. the Final Statement of the Ecumenical Dialogue of Third World Theologians, Dar es Salaam, Tanzania, Aug. 12, 1979, in Sergio Torres and Virginia Fabella, M.M., eds., *The Emergent Gospel: Theology from the Underside of History* (Maryknoll, N.Y.: Orbis Books, 1978), pp. 259ff.; Noel Leo Erskine, *Decolonizing Theology: A Caribbean Perspective* (Maryknoll, N.Y.: Orbis Books, 1981), p. 2.

4. Cf. Gustavo Gutiérrez, *Teología desde el reverso de la historia* (Lima: CEP, 1977), revised and enlarged in *La fuerza histórica de los pobres* (Lima: CEP, 1979), pp. 305–94; an English translation is forthcoming from Orbis Books.

5. See above, Torres and Fabella, *Emergent Gospel.* The subtitle is inspired by Gustavo Gutiérrez, "Two Theological Perspectives: Liberation Theology and Progressivist Theology," ibid., pp. 227–55.

6. Cf. Aloysius Pieris, "Towards an Asian Theology of Liberation: Some Religio-Cultural Guidelines," *Asia's Struggle for Full Humanity,* ed. Virginia Fabella (Maryknoll, N.Y.: Orbis Books, 1980), p. 78.

7. For the classical formulation of this view, see Hendrik Kraemer, *The Christian Message in a Non-Christian World* (New York: Harper, 1938).

8. Gerald H. Anderson, "Christian Faith and Religious Pluralism," in *Education for Christian Missions,* ed. Arthur L. Walker, Jr. (Nashville, Tenn.: Broadman Press, 1981), p. 69.

9. Third world liberation theologies reflect different emphases. Asian theologies concentrate by and large on the religio-cultural dimension, e.g., Kosuke Koyama, *Three Mile an Hour God* (Maryknoll, N.Y.: Orbis Books, 1979); Choan-Seng Song, *Third-Eye Theology* (Maryknoll, N.Y.: Orbis Books, 1979); the survey of Indian theologies in Robin H. S. Boyd, *India and the Latin Captivity of the Church* (London: Cambridge University Press, 1974); Aloysius Pieris, in Fabella, *Asia's Struggle.* Some African theologies focus on the religio-cultural dimension, e.g., John Pobee, *Toward an African Theology* (Nashville, Tenn.: Abingdon, 1979); sections of Kofi Appiah-Kubi and Sergio Torres, eds., *African Theology en Route* (Maryknoll, N.Y.: Orbis

Books, 1979); and Aylward Shorter, *African Christian Theology* (London: Geoffrey Chapman, 1975). Other African theologies focus on the sociopolitical dimension, e.g., Allan Boesak, *Farewell to Innocence* (Maryknoll, N.Y.: Orbis Books, 1976), and sections of Appiah-Kubi and Torres. Latin American liberation theologies concentrate, by and large, on the sociopolitical, e.g., Gustavo Gutiérrez, "Two Theological Perspectives: Liberation Theology and Progressivist Theology," in Torres and Fabella, *Emergent Gospel,* pp. 227ff., but the works of research centers like the Instituto de Pastoral Andina in Peru and the old Instituto Pastoral Latinoamericano in Ecuador, sociologists of religion like Aldo Bunting and Renato Poblete, and pastoral theologians like Segundo Galilea have focused on the religio-cultural dimension; cf., e.g., Thomas M. Garr, S.J., *Cristianismo y religión Quechua en la Prelatura de Ayaviri* (Cusco: Instituto de Pastoral Andina, 1972); Segundo Galilea, *Introducción a la religiosidad latinoamericana,* no. 2, *Estudios de Pastoral Popular* (Quito: IPLA, n.d.); "La fe como principio crítico de promoción de la religiosidad popular," *Fe cristiana y cambio social en América Latina,* ed. Instituto Fe y Secularidad (Salamanca: Ediciones Sígueme, 1973), pp. 151–58; Aldo Bunting, "Dimensiones del catolicismo popular y su inserción en el proceso de liberación," in ibid., pp. 130–50; Renato Poblete, "Formas específicas del proceso latinoamericano de secularización," in ibid., pp. 159–77. In the Caribbean and among North American Blacks and Hispanics, the focus has been on both, e.g., Erskine, *Decolonizing Theology;* Wilmore and Cone, *Documentary History;* and Virgilio Elizondo, *Mestizaje: The Dialectics of Cultural Birth and the Gospel* (San Antonio, Tex.: MACC, 1978).

10. Justo L. González and Catherine G. González, *Liberation Preaching: The Pulpit and the Oppressed* (Nashville, Tenn.: Abingdon, 1980), p. 11.

11. Thus Aloysius Pieris, a theologian from Sri Lanka, has remarked that "Latin American theology . . . *is the only valid theology for the Third World today,*" even though it needs to be complemented "with an Asian critique of classical theology" for it to serve as a viable model for an Asian theology of liberation (cf. Pieris, "Asian Theology," in Fabella, *Asia's Struggle,* pp. 88, 90). It should be noted that such a complement would also be relevant for Latin America in that it would help liberation theology interact more effectively with popular, aboriginal, and African religiosity.

12. It should be noted that Latin American liberation theology is neither homogeneous nor the only form of theological trend to be found there. It is nevertheless the most influential current and its various formulations have sufficient characteristics in common to merit being treated individually.

13. Cf. Gutiérrez, "Two Theological Perspectives," in Torres and Fabella, *Emergent Gospel,* pp. 242ff.

14. On Pentecostalism in Latin America, see, among others, P. Damboriana, *El protestantismo en América Latina* (Friburg: FERES, 1962); idem, *Tongues as of Fire* (Cleveland: Corpus Books, 1969); Christian Lalive D'Epinay, *Haven of the Masses* (London: Lutterworth Press, 1969); Walter Hollenwegger, *The Pentecostals* (Minneapolis, Minn.: Augsburg Publishing House, 1972); E. Willems, *Followers of the New Faith* (Nashville, Tenn.: Vanderbilt University Press, 1967); C. Peter Wagner, *Look Out! The Pentecostals are Coming* (Carol Stream, Ill.: Creation House, 1973).

15. Cf. Enrique Dussel, "The Political and Ecclesial Context of Liberation Theology in Latin America," in Torres and Fabella, *Emergent Gospel,* pp. 176ff. See also by the same author, *History and Theology of Liberation* (Maryknoll, N.Y.: Orbis Books, 1976).

16. CELAM, "Evangelization in Latin America's Present and Future: Final Docu-

ment of the Third General Conference of the Latin American Episcopate" (1134, 1135), in *Puebla and Beyond*, ed. John Eagleson and Philip Scharper (Maryknoll, N.Y.: Orbis Books, 1981), p. 264.

17. This becomes evident through a careful analysis of the structure of the final documents. Part 1 ("Pastoral Overview of the Reality That Is Latin America") corresponds to the first step: *seeing* (analysis of reality). Part 2 ("God's Saving Plan for Latin America") corresponds to the second step: *hearing* (theological reflection). Parts 3, 4, and 5 correspond to the third step: *doing;* they outline the pastoral strategy (internally: "Evangelization in the Latin American Church: Communion and Participation"; externally: "A Missionary Church Serving Evangelization in Latin America"; and spiritually: "Under the Dynamic of the Spirit: Pastoral Options"). Cf. *Puebla*, pp. viii–xii, 123–285.

For more formal discussions on the theological method of Latin American liberation theology, see Juan Luis Segundo, *The Liberation of Theology* (Maryknoll, N.Y.: Orbis Books, 1976); Raúl Vidales, *Desde la tradición de los pobres* (Mexico City: Centro de Reflexión Teológica, 1978); Enrique Ruiz Maldonado, ed., *Liberación y cautiverio: Debate en torno al método de la teología en América Latina* (Mexico City: Encuentro Latinoamericano de Teología, 1975). For two good secondary sources in English where the question of method is thoroughly discussed, see Robert McAfee Brown, *Theology in a New Key: Responding to Liberation Themes* (Philadelphia: Westminster Press, 1978); Andrew Kirk, *Liberation Theology: An Evangelical View from the Third World* (Atlanta, Ga.: John Knox Press, 1979).

18. See, e.g., Hugo Assmann, *Theology for a Nomad Church* (Maryknoll, N.Y.: Orbis Books, 1976), passim.

19. Gustavo Gutiérrez, *A Theology of Liberation* (Maryknoll, N.Y.: Orbis Books, 1971), pp. 36–37, 176–78.

20. Cf. Kirk, *Theology*, p. 59, who makes a similar observation. Robert McAfee Brown, however, argues in his popular book on Gutiérrez's theology that the reason he "devotes less qualitative attention to [the] third level than the other two . . . is . . . that most other theologies devote inordinate attention to it; its importance is widely acknowledged." Even so, Brown insists that Gutiérrez "gives much more attention to it than his critics seem to realize. He talks at great length about 'the spirituality of liberation,' . . . while maintaining that 'spirituality' cannot be talked about by itself; the three levels all imply one another. The danger comes when concern for spirituality is isolated so that it leads to neglect of concern for political and economic and physical well-being as conditions of full liberation" (Robert McAfee Brown, *Gustavo Gutiérrez*, in the Makers of Contemporary Theology series [Atlanta, Ga.: John Knox Press, 1981], pp. 52–53). However, the opposite is equally dangerous, i.e., so much concern for political, economic, and physical well-being can lead (and in some cases has led) to the neglect of spirituality as the dynamic and motif of full liberation.

21. Segundo, *Liberation,* p. 141.

22. Gutiérrez, *Theology*, pp. 151–52.

23. Kirk, *Theology*, p. 172.

24. Cf. Gutiérrez, *Theology*, pp. 13, 145.

25. Cf. Kirk, *Theology*, p. 185.

26. For a similar challenge from the first world, see James Wallis, *The Call to Conversion: Recovering the Gospel for These Times* (New York: Harper & Row, 1981).

9

A Prayer and a Question: Ecumenical Crosscurrents in Mission and Evangelism

Two Historic Events: Melbourne and Pattaya

The Ninth World Conference on Mission and Evangelism, held May 12-25, 1980, in Melbourne, Australia, under the sponsorship of the Commission on World Mission and Evangelism (CWME) of the World Council of Churches (WCC), and the Consultation on World Evangelization (COWE), held in Pattaya, Thailand, June 16-27, 1980, under the sponsorship of the Lausanne Committee on World Evangelization (LCWE), were no ordinary meetings. Indeed they constitute two of the most significant missiological events of the 1980s.

Both represent impressive traditions and stand in direct continuity with previous events. Melbourne represents the conciliar ecumenical tradition. It follows such historic conferences as Edinburgh 1910, Jerusalem 1928, Tambaran 1938, Whitby 1947, Willingen 1952, Ghana 1958, Mexico 1963, and Bangkok 1972/73.[1]

Behind Melbourne lie the bittersweet memories of two WCC conferences of the 1970s. Bangkok, which dealt with the theme "Salvation Today," provoked much controversy in and outside the WCC. Many Africans felt good about it because it stressed the importance of cultural identity in conversion and underscored their demand for a temporary moratorium on foreign missionaries. The majority of the Latin Americans present appreciated the emphasis that was given to the liberating dimension of salvation and the indigeneity of the church. The Orthodox churches, however, criticized Bangkok for overstressing the temporal at the expense of the eternal, a criticism that was aired by many evangelicals. It was precisely against the background of Bangkok that the Lausanne Congress (1974) was led to state that political liberation was not salvation.[2]

Concerned with the controversy produced by Bangkok, the Fifth General Assembly of the WCC, which met in 1975 in Nairobi, Kenya, sought to explicate what Bangkok left implicit and to balance out what to some appeared as overstatements. Hence the report of Section I ("Confessing Christ Today") underscored the church's perennial responsibility to both evangelism and social action, recognized the need to name the name of Jesus Christ for evangelism to be authentic, and noted the role of liturgy in evangelization.[3] The overall reaction to Nairobi from member churches and evangelicals generally was positive. Even so, evangelicals, following John Stott's criticism of the WCC at Nairobi, questioned the report of Section I for its lack of explicit concern with the lostness of women and men.[4] Some ecumenical leaders, on the other hand, felt uneasy with its dichotomous language (evangelism *and* social action, rather than evangelism *in* social action) and its seeming accommodation to the critics of Bangkok and the WCC. Be that as it may, Nairobi was an attempt to calm the controversy that followed Bangkok while retaining its most important missiological insights (especially the relationship between conversion and cultural identity, and salvation and social justice).

While Melbourne was surrounded by the clouds of Bangkok and Nairobi, looking ahead for a fresh way forward, Pattaya (Thailand, 1980) stood in the shadow of the evangelical "world evangelization" tradition.[5] This tradition can be dated as far back as the evangelical missionary congresses of the nineteenth century.[6] However, it takes its contemporary impetus from the World Congress on Evangelism, held in 1966 in West Berlin under the sponsorship of two North American organizations: the Billy Graham Evangelistic Association and *Christianity Today*.[7] Berlin centered on the theology of world evangelization. It attempted to re-establish the biblical basis for reaching those who were beyond the frontiers of the gospel. It brought together women and men from all over the world concerned with world evangelization but struggling to find others of like mind and a "firm foundation" from which to work.[8] In the same year, the associations of Evangelical and Independent Foreign Missions (EFMA/IFMA, the two leading consortia of missionary societies in the United States) sponsored a conference on the worldwide mission of the church, in Wheaton, Illinois.[9] If Berlin was reacting against the split between evangelists and theologians, Wheaton was reacting against theological trends in the conciliar ecumenical missionary movement, especially after the integration of the International Missionary Council with the WCC in 1961.

The process initiated at Berlin and Wheaton were continued at the International Congress on World Evangelization held in July 1974 in Lausanne, Switzerland. Lausanne 1974 gathered 4,000 Christians from all over the world. They had in common two things: (1) concern and involvement in world evangelization and (2) evangelical credentials or recommendations. The purpose was much larger than Berlin and the composition broader than Wheaton. The formal purpose was to examine what God was doing in the world and exchange ideas on how Christians might effectively "reach" with the gospel those who were beyond its frontiers ("the unreached"). But there was also a latent purpose: to explore the possibilities of organizing for world evangelism. The participants entered into a covenant "with God and with each other."[10] They also approved the creation of a Continuing Committee (the LCWE). Since its inception, the LCWE has sought to promote world evangelization through intercession, research, communication, and missiological reflection.

The LCWE called the Thailand consultation. Whereas Lausanne was the launching pad for an evangelical movement for world evangelization, Thailand was a stop on the way to enable the LCWE constituency to evaluate the work done and to strategize for the unfinished task of reaching the unreached. In this respect Thailand was for the Lausanne movement what Melbourne was for the CWME: an opportunity to evaluate the state of world mission and evangelism and to challenge the member churches of the WCC to a more relevant missionary obedience in a troubled and perplexed world.

Both meetings were significant, moreover, because of their international composition and worldwide scope. Melbourne had over 650 official and fraternal delegates, advisers and observers from all over the world and all the major Christian traditions, including Orthodox, mainline Protestants, established and radical evangelicals, Pentecostals, charismatics, and Roman Catholics. As has been the tradition in CWME conferences since Mexico 1963, Melbourne was concerned with the missionary situation of the church in the six continents.

Pattaya, to be sure, was not half as ecumenical as Melbourne, but it was equally international. It gathered 850 participants, consultants, theological observers, lay observers, and guests from all continents and many countries. (Missing were representatives from socialist countries like the Soviet Union, Poland, Cuba, and Nicaragua, although there were participants from such Eastern European countries as Yugoslavia, Romania, and East Germany.) All participants were required to be in agreement with the Lausanne Covenant, but not observers, consultants, and guests. Among the observers there was a small delegation from the Roman Catholic church, from several mainline Protestant denominations, from the CWME and the Division of Overseas Ministries of the National Council of Churches in the United States of America.

Perhaps because of the foregoing factors, the significance of these two events will be manifested in their influence over the missiological agenda of the 1980s. This is already guaranteed by the organizations that sponsored them. Melbourne will no doubt have a significant influence not only on the work of the CWME, but also of the WCC member-churches. Pattaya has already given the LCWE its agenda for the next five years. Aware of this reality, the American Society of Missiology structured its 1980 meeting around both events. Being the highest professional missiological society in

North America, this meeting has stimulated academic research on Melbourne and Pattaya. Already many articles and several books have been published giving the pros and the cons of the meetings. More important is the stimulation that these events have given those already involved in mission and world evangelism.

The Biblical and Theological Framework
of Melbourne and Pattaya

Like most events of this nature, Melbourne and Pattaya operated under particular biblical and theological frameworks, which are implicit in the themes of each conference. Melbourne's theme was a prayer: "Your Kingdom Come"; Pattaya's was a question: "How Shall They Hear?"

The Biblical Sources of the Themes

Each theme was grounded on a specific biblical passage. Melbourne was derived from the Lord's Prayer (Mt. 6:8–13). It reflects what New Testament scholars call "Jesus language," which revolves around his teaching ministry and preserves many of Jesus' own words. Jesus' teaching ministry centered on the theme of the kingdom and witnessed to the nature of God by means of an intimate filial relationship. It is a narrative rather than expository language, symbolic instead of conceptual. It belongs to the oral rather than the written tradition. Hence Melbourne sought to interpret the meaning of Jesus' prayer for the kingdom by studying various passages from Matthew's Gospel that illustrate and clarify the meaning of each part of the Lord's Prayer and its kingdom theme.

In contrast, Pattaya derived its theme from the epistle to the Romans (Rom. 10:14). It is expressed in "Pauline language," which is expository and deductive rather than narrative and inductive, conceptual instead of symbolic, and argumentative rather than descriptive. Hence the consultation did not study the theme in inductive Bible studies but in deductive biblical-theological expositions on the implications of the theme. It began with a keynote address, was followed by a series of plenary addresses on the God who speaks, the Word God has spoken, and the people through whom God speaks.

The Mood and Style of the Themes

Melbourne and Pattaya reflected different moods and formulated their respective themes in contrasting styles. For Melbourne, the mood was clearly apocalyptic. A world that had witnessed in the preceding seven years some of the most horrendous and barbaric deeds in the history of humankind (tortures, concentration camps, political assassinations, massive exiles, sexual and racial oppression, economic exploitation, and psycho-cultural alienation) could not but leave Christians in a state of shock, anxiety, and despair. This apocalyptic nightmare led the CWME to focus on the prayer that Jesus taught the church to pray. As stated in the letter sent by the conference to the churches:

> In the name of Jesus Christ we have come. Our attention focussed on the prayer Jesus taught us: "Your kingdom come." This prayer disturbs us and comforts us yet by it we are united.
>
> We meet under the clouds of nuclear threat and annihilation. Our world is deeply wounded by the oppressions inflicted by the powerful upon the powerless. These oppressions are found in our economic, political, racial, sexual and religious life. Our world, so proud of human achievements, is full of people suffering from hunger, poverty and injustice. People are wasted. "Have they no knowledge, all the evildoers who eat up my people as they eat bread?" (Psalm 14:4)
>
> The poor and the hungry cry to God. Our prayer "Your Kingdom come" must be prayed in solidarity with the cry of millions who are living in poverty and injustice. Peoples suffer the pain of silent torment; their faces reveal their suffering. The church cannot live distant from these faces because she sees the face of Jesus in them (Matthew 25).[11]

Pattaya was pricked by an equally tragic reality: an explosive world population of over 4.5 billion people, with almost 80 percent not only beyond the frontiers of the gospel but beyond the actual reach of any church or individual Christian. COWE's theme reflects a passionate concern for the salvation of billions who have not had the opportunity to hear the gospel and consider it as a personal option for their lives. This is reflected in the introduction of the concluding statement:

> We have spent 10 days together in a fellowship of study, praise and prayer. We have celebrated God's great love for us and for all humanity. We have considered before him and under his Word the command of our Lord Jesus Christ to proclaim the gospel to all people on earth. We have become freshly burdened by the vast numbers who have never heard the good news of Christ and are lost without him. We have been made ashamed of our lack of vision and zeal, and of our failure to live out the gospel in its fullness, which have weakened our obedience and compromised our witness. . . .
>
> Some two-thirds of the world's four and a half billion people have had no proper opportunity to receive Christ. We have considered the value of thinking about them not only as individuals but as people groups. Many are within easy reach of Christians. Large numbers of these are already Christian in name, yet still need to be evangelized because they have not understood the gospel or not responded to it. The

great majority of people in the world, however, have no Christian neighbors to share Christ with them.[12]

This passionate concern led the organizers to posit the Pauline question to the evangelical Christian church: How shall they hear—except preachers of the gospel be sent to them?

The Theological Focus of the Themes

Melbourne's prayer and Pattaya's question enable us to understand the theological focus of each event.

Melbourne focused its attention on God and the future. Its prayer theme disclosed a God who sees the condition of the oppressed (Ex. 2:35) and hears their cry (Ex. 3:7; Jas. 5:1–5; Acts 7:34). It showed a passionate search for the coming of God's kingdom. Hence it was a prayer of hope on behalf of the world, particularly the poor, the powerless, and the oppressed. And it was in this perspective that Melbourne dealt with the mandate for mission and evangelism.

Pattaya's interrogatory theme, on the other hand, underscored not only the fact that God speaks (Heb. 1:1), but also that Jesus Christ is God's saving Word to humankind (Rom. 10:9). Without him, women and men are lost in their trespasses and sins (Rom. 3:10ff.; Eph. 2:1). Hence COWE's theological focus was on Christ and salvation. As the Thailand Statement says: the "mandate . . . to proclaim [the] good news . . . to every person of every culture and nation, and to summon them to repent, to believe and to follow [Jesus Christ] . . . is urgent, for there is no other Savior but [him]."[13]

The Missiological Thrust of Melbourne and Pattaya

Melbourne and Pattaya were not, strictly speaking, theological events, however. That is, they were not called to discuss the church's faith but, rather, to reflect on its mission in the 1980s. Thus it is in order to ask about their respective missiological orientations.

Melbourne's missiological concentration was on the church and the macro-social reality. Three of the four study sections dealt with macro-social issues: poverty, various types of social struggles (institutional, religious, political conflicts, human rights, economic systems, and urban life) and divergent manifestations of human power (ideological, organizational, financial, punitive, military, technological, and political). Even though there were also numerous references to the church in the latter, there was an entire section dedicated to the theme of the church as a witness to the kingdom.

A close examination of the four sectional reports reveals a concern with the integral *transformation* of society and the *renewal* of the inner life and mission of the church. While Melbourne challenged the churches to hear and urgently respond to the cry of the poor, the powerless, and the oppressed by working for the transformation of the global conditions that so dehumanize and waste two-thirds of humankind, it also underscored the necessity of personal transformation through faith in Jesus Christ. Indeed section III challenged the churches to become spiritually renewed in order to be authentic witnesses of God's kingdom in a troubled and perplexed world. At the conclusion of its report, section III raised five questions corresponding to each subsection of the report:

a) Do we know Jesus Christ in such a way that we can speak convincingly of him?

b) Is our congregation reaching out and truly welcoming all those in need, and all those who seek?

c) Are we expressing the Spirit's ministry of healing for those with broken hearts, disturbed minds and sick bodies?

d) Are we sharing with all Christians the deep concern in our neighborhood and nation for better ways of living?

e) As we receive the Eucharist, God's all for us, are we giving our all to him and his needy children?[14]

It should be noted that while not all of these questions deal with mission as a cross-cultural movement, they all refer implicitly to mission as a (multiple) frontier-crossing event and are spearheaded by two questions that underscore the fundamental importance of the proclamation of the gospel to the unreached. This is congruent with paragraph 7, which not only underscores "the continual necessity" of the proclamation of the good news and the call to repentance and faith, but also acknowledges and "gladly accepts" the churches' "special obligation to those who have never heard the good news of the kingdom."[15] It can be said, therefore, that Melbourne's emphasis on the renewal of the inner life of the church had a missionary intent, since the celebration of the Eucharist, the church's healing ministry, and the lifestyle of Christians not only have a missiological dimension in themselves but also lend credibility to the communication of the gospel in local and cross-cultural contexts.

Pattaya, on the other hand, put its missiological energies on the specialized (para-church) missionary agency and the micro-social reality. COWE stressed "people groups" as the key to world evangelization. A people group was defined as "a significantly large sociological grouping of individuals who perceive themselves to have a common affinity for one another."[16] Since the majority of the people of the world are not within the reach of local churches, the leadership of the consultation reasoned that specialized cross-cultural agents and agencies are needed for their evangelization. Thus while COWE underscored the role of the local church as the principal agency for evangelization, it diminished that role by its very argument in favor of the specialized cross-cultural agency.[17]

The emphasis on "people groups" reflects COWE's concern with micro-societal issues. Since its interest was on reaching specific people, it was logical that it would seek to study the belief and value systems of these groups, their geographical, racial, linguistic, and socioeconomic situation. This meant, however, that the larger, global issues would be considered only indirectly.

This reality led a group of participants and consultants to draw up a "Statement of Concerns." Addressed to the LCWE Executive Committee, the statement affirmed:

> During the 1974 Lausanne Congress on World Evangelization it was affirmed that "Evangelism and socio-political involvement are both part of our Christian duty." The Congress also asserted that "we should share God's concern for justice and reconciliation throughout human society and for the liberation of men from every kind of oppression" (Lausanne Covenant, section 5). . . .
>
> It is a fact, nevertheless, that outside of . . . [a few] noble and commendable efforts the Lausanne Committee for World Evangelization (LCWE) does not seem to have been seriously concerned with the social, political and economic issues in many parts of the world that are a great stumbling block to the proclamation of the Gospel. This is clearly evident here at Pattaya, Thailand during this Consultation on World Evangelization. We have a working group on "Reaching Refugees," but none on those that are largely responsible for the refugee situation around the world: politicians, armed forces, freedom fighters, national oligarchies, and the controllers of international economic power.
>
> Since the world is made up not just of people groups but of institutions and structures, the Lausanne Movement, if it is to make a lasting and profound evangelistic impact in the six continents of the world, must make a special effort to help Christians, local churches, denominations and mission agencies to identify not only people groups, but also the social, economic and political institutions that determine their lives and the structures behind them that hinder evangelism. Indeed to be an effective mobilizing agent for the evangelization of the world, the LCWE (as the visible expression of the Lausanne Movement) will have to give guidelines to Christians in many parts of the world who are wrestling with the problems of racial, tribal and sexual discrimination, political imperialism, economic exploitation, and physical and psychological harassment of totalitarian regimes of whatever ideology (i.e. tortures, unjust imprisonment and forced exiles) and the liberation struggles that are the consequences of such violent aggression.[18]

The statement urged that the LCWE be given a mandate to continue with its ministry, but suggested that the latter implement four recommendations:

1. That the LCWE reaffirm its commitment to all aspects of the covenant and in particular provide new leadership to help Evangelicals implement its call to social responsibility as well as evangelism.

2. That the LCWE encourage and promote the formation of study groups at all levels, to deal with social, political and economic issues and provide specific guidance on how evangelicals can effectively apply the Lausanne's Covenant affirmation of "God's concern for justice and reconciliation throughout human society and liberation of men from every kind of oppression."
3. That, within three years, the LCWE convene a World Congress on Evangelical Social Responsibility and its implications for evangelism.
4. That the LCWE give guidelines on how evangelicals who support oppression and discrimination (thus hindering evangelism) can be reached by the Gospel and challenged to repent and uphold biblical truth, and how to give encouragement and support to Christians of all races in situations of oppression as they are seeking to be faithful to the Gospel at a great risk.[19]

Though the Executive Committee met with three of the leading sponsors, it did not give a formal reply until the entire LCWE met after COWE. The formal response, however, was preceded by the Thailand Statement. In two paragraphs that speak directly to the challenge of faithfulness to the whole of the Lausanne Covenant, and not just to parts of it, the Thailand Statement asserts:

We are also the servants of Jesus Christ who is himself both "the servant" and "the Lord." He calls us, therefore, not only to obey him as Lord in every area of our lives, but also to serve as he served. We confess that we have not sufficiently followed his example of love in identifying with the poor and hungry, the deprived and the oppressed. Yet all God's people "should share his concern for justice and reconciliation throughout human society and for the liberation of men from every kind of oppression" (Lausanne Covenant, para. 5).

Although evangelism and social action are not identical, we gladly reaffirm our commitment to both, and we endorse the Lausanne Covenant in its entirety. It remains the basis of our common activity, and nothing it contains is beyond our concern, so long as it is clearly related to world evangelization.[20]

The formal response was given in a fourfold motion. The first part simply referred to the fact that the Thailand Statement had already responded to the first recommendation. The other parts of the motion, however, were rather cool and disappointing:

(2) The Committee took note of the fact that the Executive Committee last November approved the proposal of LTEG to arrange a small consultation in cooperation with WEFTC on "The Relationship between Evangelism and Social Responsibility" in June 1982, which

would be preceded by study groups in different countries and cultures. These study groups will, in the Committee's view, fulfill the purpose of their second recommendation. The Committee does not believe that it should convene a World Congress on this topic within three years (the 3rd recommendation).

(3) The Committee does not consider that it should attempt to give the guidelines requested in their 4th recommendation.

(4) The Committee commits to LTEG a further consideration of these matters within the decisions of this Minute.[21]

Such a response makes one wonder how committed indeed is the LCWE to the whole of the Lausanne Covenant. If all that the former can do for the implementation of the covenant's commitment to social action and evangelism is "to arrange a small consultation . . . on 'The Relationship between Evangelism and Social Responsibility' " with no more than forty participants; if the committee refuses, *at least,* to "attempt to give the guidelines requested in [the] 4th recommendation"; and if the matter is further referred to a working group that is technically no longer in existence (the decision was made at COWE formally to disband the LTEG), then how seriously are Christians around the world to take the Thailand Statement, which has become the basis for the LCWE's new mandate? In my considered opinion the LCWE's response to the Statement of Concerns raises a very serious question of *integrity* on the part of the LCWE. Indeed it reflects a subtle cop-out from the scandalous situation in which evangelism finds itself in many parts of the world, and verifies the Statement of Concerns' contention that the LCWE has not been "seriously concerned with the social, political and economic issues in many parts of the world that are a great stumbling block to the proclamation of the Gospel." Hence, whatever else Pattaya said to the contrary, the fact remains that as far as the LCWE is concerned "business continues as usual."

It is a fact that Pattaya and Melbourne were both committed to the church, even if this commitment was not focused in the same direction. While Melbourne expressed its ecclesial commitment through the local church, Pattaya (in spite of its assertion to the contrary) focused on the specialized parachurch agency. This is understandable when one considers the sponsoring bodies of both meetings: an ecumenical council of churches and a parachurch committee. It is equally understandable why Melbourne would insist on the *renewal* of the church for mission and evangelization and Pattaya on the *mobilization* of the church's resources for world evangelization. For the latter and the movement it represented, church renewal was a by-product of mobilization; for Melbourne and the CWME, a precondition.

Both conferences, of course, had a point in their respective ecclesial focus, but only one point. Each affirmed the other. The local church is basic to any missionary effort, but there are situations where it cannot participate in mission except through specially gifted agents. Likewise the specialized cross-cultural agency has become a necessity in mission, but without the local church it lacks an adequate supporting base and ends up truncating the gospel call to the formation of communities of faith. Renewal without mobilization for mission ends up in a religious trip, but mobilization without church renewal becomes a lifeless, mechanistic exercise.

The Structures and Dynamics of Melbourne and Pattaya

The complementariness and diversity of these two meetings can also be appreciated by their contrasting structures and inner dynamics. Both had a long and intensive preparatory process. Both had divergent forms of organization. Both suffered (in many degrees) the tensions of pluralism and homogeneity, of openness and fear. In both there was a lot of lobbying, resistance, and solidarity. And both had strengths and weaknesses in their respective liturgical environments.

The Preparatory Process

The preparatory process for Melbourne began three years before. It involved the celebration of several worldwide consultations, regional meetings, and national study groups. There were at least six issues of the CWME's journal, the *International Review of Mission (IRM),* dedicated to some aspect of the conference. A study book was published in several languages and preparations were made for various books to be written on the theme and conclusions of the conference in the major languages of the earth. Intercessory groups were organized throughout the world and prayer aids were prepared. There were numerous consultations with local leaders and many visits made by the CWME staff to various regions to secure an adequate across-the-board representation. Some of the most extensive preparations were made in Australia itself, where not only local study groups were organized, but a fascinating itinerary was prepared for the international visitors. Participants were thus sent after the first week of the conference to practically all corners of Australia to minister to local churches and study groups.

Preparation for Pattaya began around the same time as for Melbourne (though both were originally scheduled to be held several months apart). In a way, however, all LCWE-sponsored activities since Lausanne were part of this process. This includes the three consultations sponsored by the Theology and Education Group and their respective reports, the various publications of the Strategy Group, the annual Prayer Calendar prepared by the Intercessory Group and the information bulletin, *World Evangelization,* and later the *COWE Newsletter* published by the Communications Group. But the backbone of the Pattaya process began to take shape as the seventeen study groups were organized around the world. Some of them, like the one on Reaching Large City Dwellers in the United States, which sponsored an impressive preconsultation in Chicago, Illinois, were very successful in reaching their preparatory goal. Others were not. Equally complicated was the selection of participants, since the Participants' Committee had to rely on a complicated screening process to assure that the right kinds of people were invited.

The Parts and the Whole: The Organization

Both meetings not only had different types of sponsors but totally different organizational schemes. The day-to-day operation of Melbourne was in the hands of a Steering Committee appointed by the CWME, which included some of its own members and other delegates. COWE, on the other hand, was in the hands of a Program Committee, appointed by the LCWE. Both meetings were presided over by the chairpersons of the respective sponsoring bodies.

But whereas at Melbourne there was considerable plenary debate on the final reports and decisions, at Pattaya there was no debate in the plenary; participants were only allowed to vote Yes or No, even though they were urged to make suggestions in writing. Furthermore, Melbourne was structured as a public conference, while Pattaya was declared from the beginning a "private consultation." This meant that whereas at Melbourne there was a large number of accredited journalists, at Pattaya there was no accredited press. Melbourne had thus "freedom of the press"; Pattaya had its own news staff. (Interestingly enough, the members of this team represented rank-and-file evangelical publications.)

In spite of Melbourne's more pluralistic and open environment and Pattaya's more homogeneous and closed atmosphere, there were tensions in both.

Lobbying, Resistance, and Solidarity

At Melbourne there were ecclesiological, theological, missiological, and ideological tensions. Some Orthodox, for example, felt rather uncomfortable with both the strong evangelical and Latin American presence, a feeling that was shared by at least one German Lutheran to whom I talked. They felt that there was too much evangelical theology in the documents and too much emphasis on the sociologically poor. The Orthodox lobbied for a strong trinitarian theology and emphasized the importance of liturgy in mission and evangelism.[22]

Some representatives from the United States, Western Europe, and Australasia, and a few Asians, felt that the conference had been dominated by a Latin American perspective on the kingdom. Some of them resented the strong criticisms of the North Atlantic nations. "It seems as if all the pagans were now in the West," commented one respected North American mission executive.[23]

Many delegates were upset with the conference's refusal to make an explicit condemnation of the Soviet invasion of Afghanistan. One African delegate said to Eugene Stockwell that in turning down an amendment condemning the Soviets, which a Pakistani delegate tried to attach to a resolution by David Bosch calling for solidarity with those who were in situations of oppression but for whom it was not possible to name publicly the responsible powers, Melbourne abdicated its "prophetic role, and . . . placed a weapon in the hands of any government that wants to silence criticism of its policies in WCC assemblies—all they will have to do is threaten retaliation against the country's delegates."[24] The amendment was unacceptable not only to the Soviet delegation (perhaps for the same reason the main resolution refused to name specific people and countries), but also to many other delegates, among them several Latin Americans. I myself argued that if the amendment was accepted it would open the door for other issues that were equally significant for the third world (including the twenty-year-long economic boycott of the United States against Cuba, the Palestinian issue, and the Iranian conflict). The Bosch resolution had a pastoral concern. It stated that "while some oppressive countries and oppressed people could be identified publicly, others could not for the simple reason that such a specific public identification . . . may endanger the position—even the lives—of many of our brothers and sisters . . . [including] martyrdom . . . something we dare not do from a safe distance." Its purpose was then to assure those "unnamed brothers and sisters in many unnamed countries" that the conference did not "forget them" and that "it identified strongly in their suffering for the Kingdom of God."[25] The condemnatory amendment, however, appeared to many of us as a betrayal of the resolution's intent. Consequently, in rejecting the proposed amendment, the conference did not abdicate its prophetic role but, rather, exercised its pastoral ministry to those who suffered in silence.

For their part, evangelicals lobbied passionately for a strong statement on the billions of unevangelized people and the importance of cross-cultural missions today. Some of them felt, with the Orthodox, that there was not enough transcendence in the discussion on the kingdom and criticized the conference for its weak Christology (its failure to take seriously the doctrine of substitutionary atonement). Some Latin Americans, on the other hand, criticized the report of section III for its ambiguity and lack of clarity in reference to sociopolitical issues. They were unhappy with the strong evangelical language of this report.

The attempt to produce a manifesto on mission and evangelism in the 1980s (in conformity with a request made several years before by the Central Committee of the WCC) resulted in a bitter controversy. A preliminary draft prepared at the request of a specially appointed commission was severely criticized and was withdrawn for lack of support, even though it served to gather different opinions and to develop an annotated agenda for the eventual preparation of such a document in the near future.

But Melbourne did not have a franchise on tensions. Pattaya had its share of internal controversy in spite of the efforts of the leadership to avoid it. I've already discussed the most overt one: the Statement of Concerns on the Future of the Lausanne Committee for World Evangelization. But there were other controversial episodes.

Curiously one of them had to do with Melbourne. A nonscheduled voluntary meeting was held one evening for those interested in hearing reports on the Melbourne Conference. Surprisingly enough, the attendance was over 250. Allan Cole, from the Church Missionary Society of Australia, and Waldron Scott, from the World Evangelical Fellowship (WEF), were asked to give their own impressions. Cole was acidly critical, to the delight of some. Scott was also critical but reflected a positive attitude and empathetic spirit, something that pleased the small pro-Melbourne group and enraged many rank-and-file "established evangelicals." Arthur Glasser, who had gone to Melbourne as the reporter for *Christianity Today,* was asked to share his article on Melbourne, and Bruce Nichols, from the WEF's Theological Commission, shared with a limited number part of his own written report. Glasser's views on Melbourne were like Scott's, positively critical, while Nichols's were closer to Cole's. Neither Glasser nor Nichols, however, was asked to speak formally. Emilio Castro, director of the CWME, who was there as an observer from the WCC, was then asked to respond to the presentations of Scott and Cole. His response was eloquent and evangelistically passionate.

When the meeting was opened for discussion, an avalanche of opinions, questions, and critical remarks followed. Toward the end of the session, John Stott, in an unusual and untypical way, went to the podium and challenged Emilio Castro directly on the grounds that Melbourne had not listened to the challenge that he had given the WCC at Nairobi when he chided the former for not being passionately concerned for the lost.[26] Because the audience was split between those who were sympathetic toward Castro and Melbourne and those who were acidly critical of what went on, the Program Committee became worried and sought a formal response from the Lausanne Theology and Education Group (LTEG). John Stott, convener of the LTEG, had prepared a

> possible "Response" which, after an introduction, had two sections, first "Good News for the Poor" and secondly "World Evangelization." This was not accepted, mainly on the grounds *(a)* that it was selective and superficial, responding to only some issues in the 4 section reports and not at all to the plenary papers, and *(b)* that, because not all LTEG members had yet had time to study the section reports, [the LTEG was] not yet ready to respond with integrity and care.[27]

But since there was concern that many were confused and could interpret the silence as an endorsement of Melbourne from the Lausanne leadership, it was agreed that John Stott write a brief note in the *Daily Communiqué.* And so it was. On June 26 the daily news sheet contained the following comment by Stott:

The Lausanne Theology and Education Group has met during COWE and has given some brief consideration to the CWME conference (held at Melbourne in May 1980) in the light of the reports of its four sections. Since most of us were not ourselves at Melbourne, and since we have not yet had time to study the documents thoroughly, we feel able at this stage to only make a preliminary and tentative comment.

First, we know that at Melbourne the cries of the poor and the oppressed were heard. We ourselves in the Lausanne Covenant (1974) have said that "we are disturbed by the poverty of millions and shocked by the injustices which caused it." At the same time, we confess that we and our whole evangelical constituency have not been active enough in the quest for a more just, free, compassionate and humane society.

Secondly, we welcome the excellent material in the report of Section III about the indispensable place of proclamation within the church's witness. At the same time we miss any clear and urgent call to world evangelization.

Thirdly, we have recommended to LCWE that they authorize (preferably with WEF) a serious study of, and considered response to, the major issues which were raised and debated at Melbourne, with special reference to world evangelization.[28]

A second episode was a statement from the women present to the Lausanne Executive Committee. Many of them (and many men) were upset with the lack of female presence in the program and the apparent insensitivity shown by the COWE leadership toward their own spiritual gifts. Though moderate in tone, their statement turned out to be incisive if for no other reason than the fact that it highlighted the statistical reality of the consultation in relation to them. They noticed that while

72% of all evangelicals engaged in cross-cultural evangelization are women, yet:

58 of the 650 invited participants are women	or 9%
3 of the 50 members of the Lausanne Committee are women	or 6%
1 of the 34 members of the 4 Working Groups of LCWE is a woman	or 3%
None of the 9 Subcommissions or working group chairpersons are women	0%
2 of 18 Consultants to the Mini-Consultations are women	11%
None of the Plenary speakers are women	0%
None of the Bible study leaders are women	0%
None of the 7 Regional Group Chairpersons are women	0%
4 of the 74 alphabetically-grouped prayer group leaders were women	5%
5 of the observers invited by LCWE were women	

They also noted that

> 5 out of the 5 Executive Assistants are women   100%
> There are 46 staff women, 18 lay observer women, 28 guest women
> 159 of the 261 non-participants are women   or 61%

The women (and supporting men) offered several suggestions to help the LCWE "involve women in all levels of the church where they can be vital to the cause of world evangelization making a very special and unique contribution to evangelism."[29]

There did not appear to be any formal response from the LCWE Executive Committee. At least I did not see any in the official *Daily Communiqué*. However, in his closing message Leighton Ford spoke directly to the issue when he acknowledged this lacuna and asked how it was possible that our sisters should not be allowed and encouraged to make their own contribution, as members of the body of Christ, to the cause of world evangelization. As if to reinforce the whole issue, he asked his wife to lead in prayer at the outset of his message. This was a courageous and Christian gesture on the part of the moderate Ford.

A third incident was perhaps the saddest and most unfortunate. Some twenty-eight Latin Americans (of the seventy who were present), led by two executives of the Luis Palau Evangelistic Team, met secretly to consider the possibility of forming a Latin American Association of Evangelicals because the newly organized Latin American Council of Churches (CLAI) did not represent them and was too closely related to the WCC. (The meeting was called in secret because in the Latin American delegation there were two CLAI leaders and many sympathizers.) The gesture was not harmful in any way. But one of the executives of the Palau Team took advantage of the fact that he was on the staff of COWE's Information Service and wrote a story that was put on the Associated Press telex. Three days later the story appeared in one of Thailand's English daily newspapers. A day after, COWE's Information Service made the story part of the press release that was sent to its larger constituency all over the world. The whole issue caused an uproar in the Latin American delegation.

The two issues that were most embarrassing and offensive were the comment on Emilio Castro's presence at COWE and the accusation against the Latin American Council of Churches for claiming to represent the majority of Latin American Protestants and for being an advocate of liberation theology. Many of those who were not at the secret meeting, and some who were, demanded an open meeting of all the Latin Americans at COWE to deal with the problem. Some fifty came, including Emilio Castro and the writer of the article. The meeting, chaired by Bruno Frigoli, a member of the LCWE Executive Committee, enabled the issue to be clarified. The author of the article stated that it was his own doing and did not have the approval of the twenty-eight who had met. He further admitted not to have had all the facts straight as to Castro's presence at COWE and apologized publicly to him. The CLAI representatives made it clear that at no time had the latter claimed to speak for *all* Latin Protestants and that it did not have an official position on liberation theology. It was then agreed that a new press release should be prepared by the author of the article and me.

The two of us met immediately to write the press release, as the close of the consultation was drawing near. We submitted it to the director of information, Stan Izon, for his approval. He told us that he had to get the approval of the director of COWE, David Howard. The release was briefly modified and mimeographed on the COWE official Information Service letterhead. I was then assured by the director of information that it would be put on the Associated Press telex, and would be distributed the next day to all the participants and sent to the LCWE constituency, as had the previous one. To my knowledge, no one received it and, contrary to the first story, which was sent to the entire LCWE constituency, this new release was not distributed.

The latter incident marks, in my opinion, one of the lowest points of COWE and reflects its greatest liability. COWE, in the words of an observer, was "the closest meeting" he had ever attended. The flow of information was almost as tightly controlled as that of conferences sponsored by orthodox communist organizations. And the way in which the COWE Information Service so eagerly dispatched the news of the twenty-eight Latin Americans who had attacked liberation theology, questioned the presence of Emilio Castro, and proposed to set up an anti-CLAI association[30]; the way in which it deliberately withheld the one news release that expressed a real consensus of the majority of the Latin American delegation only demonstrates the bias of at least a few COWE executives. Indeed it left a lot to be desired in contrast to the openness of Melbourne and the courtesies afforded evangelical leaders there.

Liturgical Pomp and Evangelical Monotony

Worship is always an important ingredient in any international Christian event. Melbourne and Pattaya had their share of liturgical moments. Unfortunately, however, both suffered the one-sided syndrome and reflected contrasting weak spots, at least for some of the participants.

There were two ecumenical worship services at Melbourne to which the general public was invited: one at the Roman Catholic cathedral and the other at the city coliseum. The first was a formal, colorful, and liturgically pompous occasion. Bishops, archbishops, and metropolitans marched through the aisles with their elaborate robes accompanied by the heads of African Independents, Latin American Pentecostals, and Western mainline free-church denominations. Representatives from the various cultures and regions of the world offered a symbolic gift of products from their part of the world. A group of liturgical dancers gave an impressive performance while a distinguished, learned Greek Orthodox bishop (Anastasio Yannaulatos) gave a theological meditation. The rest of the conference participants occupied the side pews, witnessing to the event, as it were, on the fringes. In the middle pews sat the general audience from the various churches of Melbourne.

The second service was a direct contrast. It was a festival of faith (much like the medieval "festivals of fools"), with bands, clowns, a mixed ecumenical choir, a vibrant singing congregation of nearly 15,000 persons, two moving testimonies from Nicaragua and South Korea, and a challenging sermon from the general secretary of the WCC, Phillip Potter, who had been hospitalized the entire week and spoke from a chair due to his illness.

Besides these two ecumenical services, there were daily liturgies and a concluding eucharistic service. But contrary to the two public ecumenical events, which complemented each other, the daily liturgies and especially the concluding service reflected a baffling liturgical one-sidedness, dominated by the older traditions. There was hardly any liturgical contribution from the traditional free churches (Baptist, Mennonite, Congregational, Methodist, Presbyterian, etc.) and far less from the more recent ones (Pentecostal and African Independent churches). This, in my considered opinion, was the lowest point of Melbourne.

Pattaya went to the other extreme with its traditional evangelical liturgy. The music was centered on the old gospel song repertoire. Worship services were by and large led by the traditional evangelistic song leader. The reading of the Word was always in function of the sermon or lecture. The level of participation was minimal.

There were, nevertheless, two exceptions to the static, almost boring, liturgical monotony of COWE. One of them was the time allotted every morning at the end of each devotional hour for group prayer. This was a highlight of the worship experience. The other exception was the occasion when third world participants took part in worship. In this context, a Thai "Dance Drama" presentation proved to be, for me, liturgically meaningful, even though it was not presented, strictly speaking, as a liturgical activity but, rather, as a culturally relevant way of communicating the gospel, in one of the evening plenary sessions.

Outside of these noble exceptions, COWE was a countersign of the liturgical vitality and diversity in world evangelicalism. Missing from the majority of the worship sessions were not only the excitement of Black African rhythms and the mystery of Asian music, but also the ecumenical creativity of the charismatic movement, the richness of Anglican liturgy, the depth of Methodist hymnody, the contribution of our female colleagues, the spontaneity of Pentecostals, the breath of the Reformed tradition, and the commonality and simplicity of the Anabaptist groups. This is the tragic result of closed structures, a dictum which, when applied to liturgy, was as true of Pattaya as of Melbourne.

Mutual Challenges and Unresolved Questions

Melbourne and Pattaya were complementary in more ways than one. They certainly had their share of challenges for each other and left numerous unresolved questions.

The Cry of the Oppressed

Evangelicals who attended Melbourne were hardly in agreement with one another as to the importance and significance of the conference. The majority did agree on one important issue: the cry of the poor, the powerless, and the oppressed. Bruce Nichols readily acknowledged that raising this issue loud and clear was the most significant contribution of the conference. "Melbourne," he said, "has given me a fresh realization of the enormity of human suffering in the world."[31] Arthur Glasser agrees with Nichols. He said: "I am . . . convinced that most evangelicals at Melbourne felt Bruce Nichols . . . was right when he said at a private gathering: 'We evangelicals must realize that the crisis issue of the 80's will be the growing gap between the rich and the poor.' "[32] Interestingly enough this was also one aspect that caught John Stott's attention, even though he did not attend Melbourne. In his short explanatory statement at COWE, he acknowledged the fact "that at Melbourne the cries of the poor and the oppressed were heard." He then went on to confess: ". . . we and our whole evangelical constituency have not been active enough in the quest for a more just, free, compassionate and humane society."[33] These selected testimonies suffice to demonstrate that Melbourne's challenge at least rang loud and clear at Pattaya.

This being the case, it is all the more striking to see the LCWE backing off from the recommendation of the Statement of Concerns mentioned earlier. If it is true that Pattaya *heard* the challenge of Melbourne, why then did the LCWE refuse to call a World Congress on Evangelical Social Responsibility and its Implications for Evangelism? Why did it refuse to offer "guidelines on how evangelicals who support oppression and discrimination (thus hindering evangelism) can be reached by the Gospel and challenged to repent . . ."? Is it enough for the LCWE to say that it believes that both evangelism and social action are important? Can such a crucial question be adequately dealt with in a small consultation? Are well-balanced statements an adequate response to the cry of the billions of poor, powerless, and oppressed people in the world? Eugene Stockwell is right in stating that "Pattaya can be justifiably criticized for its evident unwillingness to take seriously the issues of social justice which to many are not just auxiliary matters but are at the very heart of any evangelization which is to be credible and authentic."[34] As for the Lausanne movement, it has yet to demonstrate in concrete ways how seriously it takes the cry of the poor and oppressed. Perhaps the LCWE may never solve this question and evangelicals may have to look elsewhere for leadership in the promotion of a worldwide evangelistic movement that has biblical, theological, and ethical integrity. As Waldron Scott has pointed out: "It seems unlikely. . . that the Lausanne Committee will be a major force in the 1980s for promoting a style of evangelism based on a holistic theology and a clear-sighted vision of the definitive contextual realities of this decade. Within evangelical circles we will have to look to groups other than LCWE for leadership along these lines."[35]

The Reality of a World without Christ

If Melbourne challenged Pattaya to hear the cry of the oppressed, Pattaya took Melbourne to task for not seeing the billions of women and men who live outside the frontiers of the Christian faith. On the same page where he criticized Pattaya for its unwillingness to take seriously the challenge of social justice, Stockwell notes that Melbourne had been attacked often at COWE "(with some justification . . .) for a failure to issue a clear call to evangelization."[36] The criticism had already been raised in Melbourne by those evangelicals who were present. It would almost seem that outside of several noble exceptions, noted above, Melbourne did not reflect the same passionate concern for the billions of unreached women and men that it showed for the poor, the powerless, and the oppressed. Why would a world conference on mission and evangelism show so much compassion for the poor and so little concern for those who do not know Jesus Christ?[37] Was it a slip of the hour or a deeper problem?

To be sure, there were many at Melbourne who would insist that the imbalance was not intentional but, rather, fruit of the conference's deep shock over the apocalyptic situation facing the poor and oppressed of the earth. It is a fact, nevertheless, that the CWME does not have the most impressive record when it comes to the evangelization of the billions who have *never* heard the gospel, even though it has been all along theoretically committed to their cause. Moreover, in its previous conferences the CWME has not addressed itself loud and clear to this problem. In fact Melbourne demonstrated that at least one sector of the CWME constituency does not seem to be overly concerned with the question of the unreached. One can only hope that in the immediate future the CWME might be able to take up this challenge and put into action its theoretical commitment.

The Problem of Hermeneutics

A third challenge of Melbourne and Pattaya is hermeneutics. The problem of biblical and theological interpretation remained one of the greatest unresolved questions between many evangelicals and a significant sector of the conciliar ecumenical movement.

Some evangelicals have criticized Melbourne for watering down the principle of *sola scriptura*. For them Melbourne's theology suffered from a biblically deficient hermeneutic. One of the most vocal was Bruce Nichols, a missionary from New Zealand who lives in India and serves as executive secretary of the WEF's Theological Commission. "The crisis in the WCC, and also among some who call themselves evangelical, is the same as it was at Nairobi 1975," said Nichols. "It is a Biblical hermeneutical crisis in which the context determines the interpretation of the text." Arguing that behind Melbourne's hermeneutic of "the Good News to the poor" was the hermeneutical system of Ernst Käsemann, who happened to have been one of the keynote speakers,[38] Nichols goes on to assert that such hermeneutical method relativized the "unique objectivity and authority" of Scripture in that it puts the Scriptures alongside contextual considerations. He insists that what Melbourne needed was "the rule of Scripture interpreted by a Biblically determined hermeneutic."[39]

It is questionable whether Käsemann's hermeneutical circle can be equated with the hermeneutic behind Melbourne's concept of "the poor." A simple comparison between Käsemann's starting point (the situation of the biblical text) and theological conclusions (resistance to the idols) and that of the most articulate historically committed contextual hermeneutics, especially those that come from Latin America, casts a cloud of doubt on Nichols's assertion. For whereas Käsemann starts with the historical situation of *the text,* contextual hermeneutics starts with the historical situation of the *exegete,* and whereas Käsemann ends up with a theology of *resistance,* the former (and the Melbourne documents) end up with a theology of *transformation.* To be sure, there are coincidences in both approaches, but the methods are different and so are the conclusions.

Nichols's claim of "a biblically determined hermeneutic" raises further doubts. In so arguing he is claiming for himself an "ideologically free" or culturally presuppositionless hermeneutic. What Nichols seems to be implying is that Käsemann and the hermeneutic of Melbourne are ideologically biased. But would not the same dictum apply to his own claim? Is there such a thing as "a biblically determined hermeneutic"? Many serious evangelical scholars would not dare answer this question affirmatively. They would insist that whereas the Bible is God's authoritative Word, our hermeneutics cannot claim to be determined by it. We can rigorously attempt to arrive as close to the original meaning of the text as possible, but that is no guarantee that we will have an ideologically free interpretation. In fact not even the biblical writers themselves were free from their ideological and cultural biases.

The issue in biblical interpretation is always *from where* do we read the text and *what do we do* with its message? Nichols, and certain evangelicals like him, become upset when other evangelicals look at the text from a different sociohistorical situation and arrive at a different understanding of its message. Hence when he questions Melbourne's interpretation of the poor he is not simply questioning Käsemann's new hermeneutic; he is questioning an exegesis that comes from the other side, *the underside of history,* and he is doing so not simply as an evangelical but especially as an *established* evangelical with a classical Western philosophical mind-set and a middle-class ideology.

That the hermeneutical problem was not a franchise of Melbourne will become evident once all the Pattaya reports are published. In the revised draft report of COWE's working group (mini-consultation) on the urban poor, we read a very similar interpretation of the poor as that of Melbourne. The report states:

> Through our ministry and mission in urban areas we had known the reality of poverty and its debilitating, dehumanizing consequences worldwide. We had known, too, the problem of riches, the great gap between rich and poor, and the often ruthless exercise of power which reduces people to poverty and keeps them in it. What we had not known, and has shaken us to see, is the amount of space devoted in Scripture to the poor and to God's dealings with them and for them.[40]

The report goes on to note the number of references in both Testaments to the poor and concludes that "the majority of the references . . . indicate that the poor are the . . . oppressed, the powerless, the destitute, the downtrodden." It further points out that poverty is never taken for granted.

> It causes concern, anger and protest. It is challenged and opposed. And its source is seen as injustice and oppression by the powerful. To try to dodge any word about the poor is like standing under an avalanche confident in [one's] ability to duck.[41]

Such a statement, grounded on a fairly thorough analysis of the biblical language of poverty, is no different from Melbourne's statement on the poor in Scripture. Interestingly enough, there is even a methodological similarity, for the COWE Urban Poor report begins with the situation of the poor around the world. Only after it has adequately described the situation does the report go on to consider the poor in the Bible. And while its conclusions are more restricted than Melbourne's counterpart (after all, COWE concentrated specifically on evangelization, while Melbourne was a conference on mission as well as evangelism), it is interesting to note its suggestion that Christians "must first create and bring [the poor] to find a place where the language of faith, hope and love can be experienced in action before the Gospel can be articulated in terms that will make sense in their situation."[42] By *action,* the report means, among other things, service, hospitality, consciousness-raising, and solidarity with "the struggle for justice, against racism, homelessness, poverty, wrongful imprisonment, exploitation. . . ."[43]

Just as certain sectors in COWE used a similar hermeneutic and arrived at similar (though not identical) conclusions, so nonevangelicals criticized Melbourne for its imbalance and bias toward the poor. Perhaps one of the better examples of this sort of criticism is that of David Stowe, well-known mission executive of the United Church of Christ (USA), who has commented that Melbourne was "more a conference on social action and church renewal than a missionary conference." It was characterized by "an exclusively liberationist style." He argues that the four major sectional themes revealed "the liberationist pattern" and that "liberation theology. . . provided the frame of reference for [its] thinking. Other perspectives intruded from time to time, but overall the freeing of human lives from oppression, injustice, and deprivation was the hinge on which the Conference turned."[44] Hence, while Stowe and Nichols do not have the same theological commitment, nor do they formulate their criticism in the same way, when all is said and done they end up with a similar indictment on Melbourne, an indictment that reflects, nevertheless, similar philosophical mind-sets, class identities, and ideological presuppositions.

We see thus the perennial presence of nontheological factors in the theological task. Melbourne and Pattaya, their respective scriptural bases, theological framework, and concepts of mission and evangelism notwithstanding, reflect the influential role of ideology, cultural tradition, organizational affiliation, political system, even personality, in the reflection of faith and the church's mission.

A prayer and a question, eschatology and soteriology, Gospels and Epistles, Jesus and Paul, social justice and personal witness, the poor and the lost—Melbourne and Pattaya are complementary events and represent common concerns for the Christian world mission. But, if history teaches anything, it may be many years before these two events will be recognized as such by both the conciliar ecumenical and the Lausanne evangelism movements. Even so we would do well to take to heart Eugene Stockwell's words of wisdom: "The prayer and the question, neither of which belongs to any one of us or to any group, remain valid and pressing—an agenda for the world Christian community worthy of continued exploration and committed sacrificial service."[45]

NOTES

1. For a historical analysis on these conferences, see "Edinburgh to Melbourne," *International Review of Mission* 67, no. 267 (July 1978): 249–370; also in Gerald H. Anderson, ed., *Witnessing to the Kingdom: Melbourne and Beyond* (Maryknoll, N.Y.: Orbis Books, 1982), pp. 9–28.

2. Cf. "The Lausanne Covenant," article 5, in J. D. Douglas, ed., *Let the Earth Hear His Voice* (Minneapolis, Minn.: Worldwide Publications, 1975), p. 4.

3. Cf. "Confessing Christ Today," report of Section I, Fifth General Assembly of the World Council of Churches, *Breaking Barriers: Nairobi 1975*, ed. David M. Paton (Grand Rapids, Mich.: Wm. B. Eerdmans; London: SPCK, 1975), pp. 43–57.

4. See John R. W. Stott, "Response to Bishop Mortimer Arias," *International*

Review of Mission 65, no. 257 (January 1976): 30–34. In this same volume, see Mortimer Arias's speech "That the World May Believe," pp. 13–26.

5. The expression "world evangelization" has become (from the 1960s on) a code for the concept of mission among a significant number of Christians who identify themselves as evangelicals. It suggests a dissociation from those who speak of "mission and evangelism" or "world mission," as is the case in conciliar ecumenical circles. Its fundamental intent is to avoid any distraction from evangelism as the most important missionary responsibility of the church. Some evangelicals have questioned the theological and practical validity of such reasoning, arguing that while mission may be larger than evangelism and the latter has a fundamental place in the church's mission, it is theologically and practically impossible to divorce evangelism from such tasks as theological education, social service, and advocacy for justice.

The debate came to a head in Thailand. Some had come determined to hold not only to the primacy of evangelism but to dissociate it from its historic and practical relation to other aspects of the church's mission. Commenting on their "victory" at COWE, C. Peter Wagner has said: "From beginning to end, COWE took a clear and distinct stand on [the] issue [of] the primacy of evangelism. . . . While recognizing that the cultural mandate is indeed part of holistic mission, COWE refused to go the route of the WCC and make it either primary or equal to evangelism." Referring to an issue that will be commented on in this chapter, Wagner makes the point that COWE's stance on the primacy of evangelism "did not come without opposition. A very vocal minority . . . attempted to dislodge evangelism as primary in the mission of the church. . . . This teaching seems to me to be a historical repeat of the change of the meaning of 'mission' now refocused on the word 'evangelism.' There is a significant group of evangelicals who are advocating not only 'holistic mission' but also 'holistic evangelism'. . . . COWE not only said 'No' to the WCC position of the primacy of social service but also to those evangelical brethren who are attempting to load the word evangelism with meanings it never has had. If they had prevailed a new Word would have to be invented, but COWE held the line at that point" (C. Peter Wagner, "Lausanne's Consultation on World Evangelization: A Personal Assessment," quoted in Waldron Scott, "The Significance of Pattaya," Annual Meeting of the American Society of Missiology, August 1980, p. 13 [mimeographed]).

Wagner's argument follows the line of Arthur Johnston in his *The Battle for World Evangelism* (Wheaton, Ill.: Tyndale, 1978). This book articulates the uneasiness of some North American evangelicals with the Lausanne Covenant and in particular its principal architect, John Stott, for accepting a broader definition of mission "to include both evangelism and service" (p. 301). In Johnston's opinion, at Lausanne Stott "dethroned evangelism as the historical aim of mission" (p. 303). What Johnston did with Stott in the aftermath of Lausanne, Wagner did during and after Pattaya to those who in his opinion wanted to take the battle beyond the territory of mission into that of evangelism itself: he distorted their position and attacked them on the basis of a fabricated argument (cf. C. Peter Wagner, *Church Growth and the Whole Gospel: A Biblical Mandate* [New York: Harper & Row, 1981], pp. 97ff.).

Wagner does not take into account the argument that the issue at Pattaya was not the primacy of evangelism but, rather, the *relationship* between evangelism and other aspects of mission, especially social justice, a matter that had already been dealt with in the functional definition agreed by the combined LCWE Theology and Education Working Group and Strategy Working Group. As Waldron Scott has pointed out, the two working groups agreed that "the *nature* of world evangelization is the communication of the Good News, the *purpose* of world evangelization is to give individuals and groups a valid opportunity to accept Jesus Christ, and the *goal* of world evangelization is to persuade men and women to accept Jesus Christ as Lord and Savior and to serve him in the fellowship of his church" (Scott, "Pattaya," p. 14).

The argument of those at Pattaya who were on the opposite side of Wagner is this. It is practically impossible to communicate the gospel, enable women and men to hear its message, and persuade them to accept Jesus Christ if the church is not *living* in conformity with the gospel, if there are *obstacles* that inhibit people from hearing the message, and if Jesus Christ is *not being honored as Lord* in the church. This in fact is the point that Charles W. Forman eloquently brings out in his critique of Thailand: "I think, as Peter Wagner says . . . that evangelism should not be loaded with meanings it never had. It is better to keep it as a word meaning the verbal sharing of the gospel message, and to use other words for other aspects of the Christian mission. But still, it cannot be considered in separation from those other aspects. It is intrinsically linked with them. It is doubtless true, as Pattaya declared, that evangelism comes first. But evangelism which is not troubled by people's hunger and nakedness does not come first. In fact it comes at the very last. Evangelism by people who are deaf to criticisms of their own wealth, does not come first. Evangelism which refuses to face the sources of exploitation and oppression in this world, for fear of offending its comfortable supporters, does not come first. So the evangelism which comes first is not just any kind of evangelism, but an evangelism which is closely linked to the personal and social attitudes of the evangelist" (Charles W. Forman, "A Response to 'The Significance of Pattaya' by Waldron Scott," Annual Meeting of the American Society of Missiology," p. 2; mimeographed).

For further consideration of the background and nature of the controversy discussed in this note, see John R. W. Stott, *Christian Mission in the Modern World* (London: Falcoln, 1975); Edward Dayton, David A. Fraser, *Planning Strategies for World Evangelization* (Grand Rapids, Mich.: Wm. B. Eerdmans, 1980); David J. Bosch, *Witness to the World* (London: Marshall, Morgan and Scott, 1980); and my own *The Integrity of Mission* (New York: Harper & Row, 1979).

6. For a summary of this tradition, albeit controversial for its one-sidedness, see Arthur Johnston, *World Evangelism,* pp. 23ff.

7. Cf. Carl F. H. Henry and Stanley Mooneyham, eds., *One Race, One Gospel, One Task,* 2 vols. (Minneapolis, Minn.: Worldwide Publications, 1967).

8. Cf. "The Focus of Thailand," *COWE Newsletter* 1 (November 1979): 1.

9. Cf. Harold Lindsell, ed., *The Church's Worldwide Mission: Proceedings of the Congress on the Church's Worldwide Mission,* April, 4–16, 1966, at Wheaton College, Wheaton, Ill. (Waco, Tex.: Word Books, 1966).

10. "Lausanne Covenant," introduction, in Douglas, *Let the Earth,* p. 3.

11. Conference on World Mission and Evangelism, "Your Kingdom Come"—A Message to the Churches, Melbourne (May 12-24, 1980), p. 1 (mimeographed). See also *International Review of Mission* 69, no. 275 (July 1980): 253; and Gerald H. Anderson, ed., *Witnessing to the Kingdom,* p. 7.

12. COWE, "The Thailand Statement," Pattaya, Thailand (June 16-27, 1980), pp. 1-2 (mimeographed).

13. Ibid., p. 2.

14. Conference on World Mission and Evangelism, "The Church Witnesses to the Kingdom," Final Report, Section III, Document No. G 11 revised, Melbourne (May 12-24, 1980), pp. 12-13 (mimeographed). See also *International Review of Mission*

69, nos. 276–77 (October 1980–January 1981): 419; and Gerald H. Anderson, ed., *Witnessing to the Kingdom*, p. 148.

15. Ibid., p. 3; *International Review of Mission* 69, nos. 276–77: 409; and Gerald H. Anderson, ed., *Witnessing to the Kingdom*, pp. 134–35.

16. Edward R. Dayton, *That Everyone May Hear: Reaching the Unreached,* special COWE edition (Monrovia, Calif.: MARC, 1979), p. 22.

17. The Thailand Statement recognizes "the local church as the principal agency for evangelism" and insists that its "total membership must . . . be mobilized and trained." But it also states that the "great majority of people in the world . . . can . . . be reached only by cross-cultural messengers of the gospel" (cf. pp. 2, 3).

18. David Gitari, Vinay Samuel, Orlando Costas, Andrew Kirk, Ronald Sider, Clarence Hilliard, Peter Kuzmic, et al., "A Statement of Concerns on the Future of the Lausanne Committee for World Evangelization," Pattaya, Thailand (June 16–27, 1980), pp. 1–2 (mimeographed).

19. Ibid., p. 2.

20. Thailand Statement, p. 2.

21. John R. W. Stott, Memo to Members of the Lausanne Theology and Education Group (Aug. 22, 1980), p. 4 (mimeographed).

22. For an Orthodox evaluation of Melbourne, see Michel Oleska, "An Orthodox Witness," in Gerald H. Anderson, ed., *Witnessing to the Kingdom*, pp. 77-94.

23. But note Eugene Stockwell's bold attempt to deal with the challenge to the "conversion of the pagan west" in "After Melbourne, What?", Ibid., pp. 95-101.

24. Eugene L. Stockwell, "So . . . What Really Did Happen at Melbourne? Some Initial Uncertain Estimates" (May 29, 1980), p. 4 (mimeographed).

25. David J. Bosch, "Resolution," World Conference on Mission and Evangelism, Melbourne (May 12-25, 1980) (mimeographed).

26. Cf. Stott, "Response to Arias," *International Review of Mission* 64, no. 255 (July 1975), p. 31.

27. Stott, "Memo."

28. John R. W. Stott, "Comment on Melbourne," *Thailand 80 Daily Communiqué* (June 26, 1980), p. 2.

29. Faith Annette Sand, Becky Manley Pippert, Carol A. Glasser, Claudia Mitchell, Waldron Scott, Ray Bakke, et al., "Some Reflections on a Holistic Approach to Evangelism," Pattaya, Thailand (June 16-27, 1980), p. 1.

30. This new organization has since been created at the Latin American Evangelical Consultation held from April 19-23, 1982 in Panama City. Cf. "Acta de Panamá," Confraternidad Evangélica Lationaméricana, Panamá, April 23, 1982 (mimeographed).

31. Bruce J. Nichols, "Theological Reflections on Melbourne," p. 2 (mimeographed).

32. Arthur F. Glasser, "An Evangelical Appraisal of Melbourne 1980," COWE, orientation paper for an informal meeting following the evening plenary session (June 19, 1980), p. 4 (mimeographed).

33. Stott, "Comment," p. 2.

34. Eugene L. Stockwell, "What Did I Hear . . . How Shall They Hear?" p. 13 (mimeographed).

35. Scott, "Pattaya," p. 13. Cf. Waldron Scott's bold attempt to present a corrective to this loophole in his "The Fullness of Mission," in Gerald H. Anderson, ed., *Witnessing to the Kingdom*, pp. 42-56.

36. Stockwell, "What Did I Hear. . .?" p. 13.

37. But cf. Gerald H. Anderson in his "Introduction" to his edited work on Melbourne, who argues that the Conference did express concern for the unevangelized. He admits, however, that "the missionary and evangelistic nature of the . . . Conference . . . is not to be found primarily in its statements *about* the mandate for world evangelization. Rather, it is in the challenge and commitment that permeated the conference, calling for the total liberation/redemption of all human beings, and requiring a style of missionary witness that is profoundly contextual and incarnational" (ibid., p. 3).

38. Cf. Ernst Käsemann, "The Eschatological Royal Reign of God," Melbourne Doc. no. G.04 (May 12–24, 1980), p. 8 (mimeographed). See *Your Kingdom Come: Mission Perspectives* (Geneva: World Council of Churches, 1981).

39. Nichols, "Reflections," p. 5.

40. COWE, "Revised Draft Report on Reaching City Dwellers—Inner City (Urban Poor)," p. 6 (mimeographed).

41. Ibid.

42. Ibid., p. 23.

43. Ibid., p. 24.

44. David M. Stowe, "Report on the Melbourne Conference on World Mission and Evangelism," Annual Meeting of the American Society of Missiology (June 30, 1980), pp. 3, 6.

45. Stockwell, "What Did I Hear. . .?" p. 14.

10

The Whole World for the Whole Gospel: Recovering a Holistic Legacy for the 1980s

"The whole gospel for the whole world" is a slogan that has been around Protestant circles since the early decades of the twentieth century. By 1925 the Eastern Baptist Theological Seminary of Philadelphia, Pennsylvania, had adopted it as its motto. In a way this phrase represented the original spirit of the social gospel advocated by theologians like Walter Rauschenbusch. In 1928 the words became part of the ecumenical movement at the Second World Missionary Conference in Jerusalem.

While it could be argued that the spirit behind this guiding principle can be traced to the early Christian church, the honor of first making its content and intent conscientiously a fundamental characteristic of life, faith, and witness, at least in Protestant history, must go to the Wesleyan movement in the eighteenth century. Early Methodists, under the guidance and inspiration of their founder, John Wesley, sought to mold their mission around a holistic concept of the gospel and an integral vision of the world. They integrated faith and work, personal piety and social concern, evangelization, fellowship, liturgy, and diakonia. Little wonder that Wesley defined his pastoral ministry in terms of the whole world. "I see the whole world as my parish," he said.[1]

Ironically such a noble legacy was lost in the aftermath of World War II. Indeed in many parts of the world during the first two decades of the second half of the twentieth century, Protestant Christianity, at least, bogged down in an either/or mentality. Hence it can be said that the 1950s became the evangelization and spirituality decade, while the 1960s turned out to be the social action and secularization years. Fortunately a shift began to take place in the early years of the 1970s in practically all the continents. This shift can be described as a movement toward a more holistic approach to mission and evangelism. At the heart of this trend seemed to be a deep and sincere longing for the recovery of the wholeness of the gospel. This reality is evidenced by the most universal missiological documents of the decade: the Lausanne Covenant (1974), the Confessing Christ report of the Fifth General Assembly of the World Council of Churches (1975), and the Apostolic Exhortation on Evangelism in the Modern World, *Evangelii Nuntiandi* (1975).

Interestingly enough, the quest for the recovery of the wholeness of the gospel has been accompanied by a similar quest for the recovery of the totality of the world. Unfortunately, however, this latter search has not received as much attention in missiological literature as the former. In the three documents mentioned above, for example, the focus is on the content of the gospel rather than on the nature of the world. This reflects a common tendency in Western holistic theologies: the whole world ends up occupying a junior role in comparison to the whole gospel. This is why many third world theologies have insisted that the wholeness of the gospel can be perceived only when the world is kept in perspective. In fact, many of them insist that it is not possible to hear the whole gospel in our time without seeing the world in its complexity.

"The whole gospel for the whole world" implies a claim on the totality of the world. Hence a vision of "the whole world" is essential for a faithful and relevant proclamation of the whole gospel.

The World as Object and Context of the Gospel

The Scriptures are clear as far as the place of the world in God's economy is concerned. The gospel is no more and no less than God's message to the world. It announces God's love for the world. It underscores the divine claim on the world because it is God's creation and reason for the incarnation. "God so loved the world that he gave his only begotten Son . . ." (Jn. 3:16).

Johann Baptist Metz reminds us that the world God has so loved "is not merely a world of things; it is actually *man's world*; a world in which understanding-acting man has always . . . played a part, because in God's action in the world the subject is always man, and, therefore, it always deals with the world of man's existence."[2] It is to this world of human beings that Jesus Christ was sent. In his life, death, and resurrection, God has declared forever to be on the side of humanity, not willing that any should perish, but that all should have everlasting life. Not only that, but the whole creation, which according to the apostle Paul was subjected to futility on account of human sin, has been filled with hope as a result of the death and resurrection of Jesus. In Christ God has promised ultimately to liberate creation from its "bondage to decay" (Rom. 8:20–21). Hence, the *whole* world, the world of humans *and* the world of things, is the object of the gospel.

The world is also important in God's economy because it is the context in which the good news of salvation was first given and received and is today proclaimed and heard. Outside the world there is no gospel and certainly no Christian mission. For Christians have no other mission than that which has been given them in Jesus Christ, a mission which takes place in the concrete struggles of history. Likewise they have no other gospel than that which announces the historical reality of the Carpenter from Nazareth, who was born of a humble virgin, who died on a cross as the representative of sinful humanity, who was raised from the dead and continues to make himself present in the struggles of history by the Holy Spirit, and who will bring to consummation God's kingdom.

This world, which is the context of the gospel and the setting for its mission, is a complicated sociocultural mosaic and a dynamic, multidimensional phenomenon. It is not a static object, but an active subject. While it is shaped by the historical actions of women and men, it shapes in turn their perceptions and productivity. Thus the makeup and dynamic of the world affects profoundly our understanding of the gospel. This implies that, if we want to share faithfully, in word and deed, the whole gospel with the whole world, we shall need not just to understand its original context and the historical development of its interpretation, but, especially, to be aware of the multiple situations from which it is being currently interpreted and proclaimed.

Yet our problem is not simply one of understanding, but also of incarnating the gospel in today's world. We can communicate the good news of salvation effectively only to the extent that it is made flesh in concrete situations. In such situations the power of the gospel can be seen at work. Only thus can its message be received as good news in the ears of the world. Hence one basic requirement of Christian mission is the immersion of the community of faith in the various situations that make up the world. Put in other terms, mission presupposes an experiential knowledge of human society rather than an intellectual understanding of an abstract world.

The Fullness of the World and the Wholeness of the Gospel

What has been said does not mean, of course, that generalizations about our world are neither possible nor important in mission. Indeed it is a sociological fact that all sociohistorical situations, every piece of the human mosaic, are glued together by common elements. Identifying them, knowing their basic characteristics, and understanding their function in human society is essential for an effective communication of the gospel in each situation. In fact such an awareness enables us not only to have a fuller vision of the world but also to live and share the gospel holistically.

A World of Culture

It should be pointed out, first of all, that the world which is claimed for the whole gospel is one of cultures. The more than four-and-a-half billion people who inhabit planet earth and are spread throughout six continents and thousands of islands are not, as I have argued elsewhere in this volume, isolated individuals. They are linked together by family, linguistic, ideological, educational, religious, political, and economic ties. The cultivation of those relationships defines their respective modes-of-being or cultures.

Culture is thus the result of human interaction. It is a universal reality that encompasses both the creative activity of human beings in history and the product of their endeavor.[3] From this perspective culture can be defined as the total set of values, norms, attitudes, and creations that distinguishes a people from another, that conforms their conceptions of time and determines their relationship with their living space.[4]

It is a fact that the more people interact with one another, the more complex their culture becomes. In order to communicate effectively with them, one needs to identify the signs, symbols, and myths that shape their respective lifestyles. Getting to know in depth the myths, symbols, and signs of a given people is especially crucial in the communication of the gospel, since it seeks not only an intelligent, meaningful transmission, but also an effective response to its call to faith and repentance, its invitation to become part of the Christian fellowship, and its commitment to the transformation of history.

Enrique Dussel, following the thought of Paul Ricoeur, has underscored the importance of penetrating what he calls a people's "ethical-mythical nucleus" in order to evangelize them in depth. By this he means that the gospel, in order to achieve its transformational objective, must penetrate "the value system" of those that are being evangelized. The ethos of a people, says Dussel, is the total complex of attitudes that predetermines its collective behavior. These attitudes, he adds, are referrable "to an ultimate meaning, a radical premise, a kingdom of ends and values that justify all action. These values find themselves covered up in symbols, myths and structures of double meaning."[5] It is this system of attitudes and values that the gospel must penetrate to have a historically significant impact on a given people. Dussel illustrates his point with a reference to the second-century "Apologist" church fathers. Not only did they address the gospel to the personal needs of their contemporaries, but they critically confronted the very foundation of their Greco-Roman culture with the gospel. In so doing they were instrumental in the evangelical transformation experienced by Greek culture, whenever its traditional symbols, values, and attitudes were enriched, changed, and substituted with new ones. Hence not only were persons brought to personal conversion, but their social reality was transformed by the impact of the gospel.

A people's collective identity is of paramount importance in reaching the largest number of those who lie beyond the frontiers of the Christian faith. Evangelization is not only done *qualitatively* better through groups, but is also *quantitatively* more effective when women and men are approached in their respective communal settings.

Edward Dayton and David Fraser, working on a concept launched by the Strategy Working Group of the Lausanne Committee for World Evangelization in 1977, suggest that the most effective way to evangelize the largest number of human beings is to do it "one people at a time." They define a people as "a significantly large sociological grouping of individuals who perceive themselves to have a common affinity for one another. This common affinity can be based on language, religion, ethnicity, residence, occupation, class or caste, situation, or a combination of any of these."[6] Dayton and Fraser argue that a "people" can be said to have been evangelized when at least 20 percent of its members have become Christians, participate responsibly in the fellowship of the church, and faithfully propagate the gospel among their neighbors.

This cross-cultural approach to evangelization has a lot in its favor. For one thing, it recognizes the importance of groups and the need to come to terms with a people's self-understanding in order to evangelize them effectively. For another, it distributes the responsibility of the church's world evangelizing mission fairly and realistically: the missionary agency is to evangelize the first 20 percent of a given people and thereafter the local church takes over.

In my opinion, however, this approach has at least two basic problems. On the one hand, it defines a "people group" much too narrowly. People in general and groups in particular cannot be defined solely on the basis of their perceptions. Sometimes perceptions are distorted by sociohistorical conditions and forces. A people group may thus "perceive" itself falsely. Its "common affinity" may be superficial. Such a subjective definition lacks, therefore, precision. What is needed is a broader concept of a group that sees the latter not simply as a unit of individuals with a superficial self-understanding, but rather, as part and parcel of a people with a cultural ethos. This will allow for psycho-social variations, but will maintain the fundamental ingredient of a collective identity: the "ethico-mythical nucleus." Without such a concept, one is unable properly to identify *real* groups and is hindered thereby from penetrating the gospel deep into the "collective soul" of a people. In such cases the response of the group to the gospel turns out to be spurious, which amounts to failure at the crucial task of evangelizing a people at their cultural root and implies, in turn, failure to do justice to the demands and goals of the whole gospel.

On the other hand, Dayton and Fraser's view of a group seems atomistic. To be sure, they readily acknowledge that groups are not islands, being shaped and molded by numerous forces inside and outside themselves. They also insist that such variables (forces) need to be taken into account in the analysis of the needs of each group. Yet they fail to discuss the interrelationship between "people groups" as such. It is a fact, especially in urban areas, that women and men usually belong to various groups at the same time. In such cases a natural cross-fertilization between groups takes place. They can influence and resist each other. Without an awareness of group linkage, it is not possible to assess realistically evangelistic progress or stagnation. Hence it is not enough to understand the "needs," "system of meanings," "behavior," and "larger context" of a group for an effective evangelization,[7] as Dayton and Fraser propose. There also has to be awareness of the interconnecting links with other groups, for, as women and men exist in relationship, so do groups.

A World of Institutions

The world wherein Christians live and witness today is not only one of peoples and cultures but also of institutions. Sociologists tell us that socio-cultural relations develop a permanent character through the subdivision of group life in large areas of social interaction, such as the state, law, family, and religion. These are the areas of life that give continuity to culture and enable it to develop its creative function. Consequently they are designated "institutions" because they establish and fix group life.

Social institutions produce complex systems of norms and relationships, such as private and social property, the monetary system, marriage, and religions. These systems order the life of peoples. Without them social institutions disappear.

From these systems we derive our organizations (schools, government agencies, business enterprises, and voluntary associations). Organizations serve as vehicles for the transmission of culture in general and mediate social institutions in particular. Schools and churches, for example, transmit cultural values while mediating the institutions of education and religion. Government agencies are vehicles of political norms and relationships and mediators of the state. Business enterprises mediate the economy of a society and transmit the principles upon which it is established.

In the Bible institutional life occupies a significant place. We find through-out its pages countless references to such institutions as the family, the state, the economy, education, and religion. The fact that biblical faith originates in the life and work of a nation amid a community of nations, and that the corporate life of this nation is held accountable to the sovereign lordship of God, is indicative of the importance of institutional life in the process of God's revelation.

It is no less significant, moreover, that in both the Old and the New Testaments the mission of God is oriented by the manifestation of his kingdom. This gives a public and, therefore, institutional character to God's mission in history. God's mission deals not simply with the private affairs of humankind but with its social and institutional concerns. His message is not only addressed to people in the light of their institutional connections, but expresses itself in institutional forms. This is why mission involves not only a public announcement, but also a public celebration, a celebration that reaches its climax in the observance of baptism and the Lord's Supper—the two Christian ordinances that witness to the institutional character of the church, for they give the Christian fellowship outward identity and historical continuity. When the church proclaims and teaches the whole gospel it does so not just as a redeemed fellowship, but also as a social institution. As such the church bears witness to the institutional dimension of the gospel and calls the institutions of society to submission to the lordship of Christ.

Jitsuo Morikawa, the Japanese-American who directed for many years the evangelistic program of the American Baptist churches, began in the 1960s to raise the issue of dealing evangelistically with the institutions of society. In 1977 I had the opportunity to interview Morikawa on this issue. I asked him how the church could deal evangelistically with the world of institutions. "By confronting them with the moral issues involved in their behavior," he answered. He went on to say that the church has to raise, time and again, the question of what institutions exist for in the light of the gospel and the new order of life which it proclaims. In his opinion, the church "has to bring them to accountability by challenging them at the moral and practical, political levels." In other words, institutions that order life have themselves to be brought to order by the message of God's kingdom. Since "the church is itself an institution," added Morikawa, it "must also be confronted with the moral [challenge] of the gospel." Accordingly, "we have to address the church as an institution with a similar question: 'What is the church for?' " This will lead to an evaluation of its policies, systems of relationships, and organizational patterns, in the light of the gospel, and force it to change in conformity with the values of God's kingdom.[8]

These insights from an Asian-American prophet should not be taken lightly. Indeed they reinforce our contention that to communicate the good news relevantly, deeply, and critically throughout the whole world we need to take account of the institutions of society and contextualize its message amid them. Failure to do so will make the gospel's call to faith and repentance, its invitation to the Christian fellowship, and its challenge to participation in the transformation of history a spurious exercise. Those who respond (immersed as all human beings are in the world of institutions) will most likely do so with only part of their self and will not be able to affect decisively their socio-historical reality. The practical consequence of such an anomaly is that while there might be an increasing number of people embracing the Christian faith, there may be few who will be leaven, light, and salt in their respective social realities—in a word, many may call themselves Christians who are in fact anything but true followers of Jesus Christ. When this happens, the gospel is truncated, its demands cheapened, and its saving power diluted.

It would be very difficult to deny that this is exactly what is happening in too many regions of the contemporary world, where there seems to be a strange silence in the church's evangelistic endeavors with regard to social institutions. Missionary and evangelistic programs have by and large reflected a sociological ignorance or naiveté as far as the institutional aspect of human life is concerned. This has often inhibited Christians and their churches from proclaiming the gospel to social institutions. It has also contributed to the shallow, privatistic, and historically alienating communication of the Christian faith that is largely responsible for what Uruguayan Jesuit theologian Juan Luis Segundo has described as a "massified Christianity" and Ecuadorean evangelical theologian René Padilla has labeled "culture Christianity."[9]

Unfortunately theological seminaries have not been helpful in the reversion of this tragic reality. I remember my utter frustration as a seminarian in the tumultous 1960s, immersed in an inner-city ministry in the Hispanic community of a midwestern city and not being able to receive any relevant orientation from the particular seminary I was attending that would help me cope with the enormous institutional issues that I was having to face. While we were forced to take several courses in Greek and Hebrew, philosophy of religion and apologetics, not a single sociologically related course was offered. To be sure, we had ministry courses, but none of them dealt with the institutional dimension of the gospel. I decided to transfer to a more liberal seminary to see, among other things, if I could get this situation corrected. There I found ample studies in history, theology, pastoral care, and communication theory, but I was not given help as a Hispanic pastor to deal with the educational, economic, political, and cultural oppression that our community was suffering. Thus, to carry on my pastoral and evangelistic ministry in a contextually relevant manner, I had to work my way through "the school of hard knocks."

If Christian theological schools today want to be dedicated not only in word but also in deed to the communication of the whole gospel in the whole world, they shall have to develop at all levels a deeper understanding of this element of the human mosaic. This demands more than a theoretical awareness of the role of institutions in North American and other societies. It demands a firsthand encounter with them at the point of their most negative manifestations, namely, in cross-cultural, oppressive situations. Students and faculty will need to experience the world of institutions from the side of those who suffer its impact the most, whether it be the religious experience of the poor masses of the third world, the educational deformation that takes place in the urban ghettos, the mechanisms of economic exploitation that are usually present among poverty-stricken masses, or the gloomy and depressed atmosphere that one finds in politically repressive contexts. The sinful character, the human limitations, and the transcendent possibilities of social institutions will become so much clearer and deeper if they are seen from the side of the disfranchised and outcast. This in turn will help teachers and students to focus their teaching and learning more realistically and penetratingly, enabling them further to develop more effective missional responses to the challenge of institutions. This is another way of stating what Ronald J. Sider has said in another context, namely, "if it is true that God is on the side of the poor and oppressed and therefore that God's people must also be on the side of the little ones, then visible, tangible identification with the oppressed and weak is a *sine qua non* of seminary education."[10]

A World of Structures

Institutions are interconnected by networks of global relations. These networks determine the life and function of institutions. Therefore they are denominated "structures" and constitute a third dimension of our contemporary world.

Understood thus, structures distinguish themselves by their invisibility.

They are neither persons nor things, buildings nor even organizations, says Brazilian ecumenical theologian Rubem Alves. He adds that "structures are global relations [that] cannot be seen. They are to society what the mind is to the body: the controlling logic of behavior." He explains that

> No matter how painfully an executive is aware of the need to humanize the economy by making it responsive to human values, there is nothing he can do to change the logic of profit. For this is the dominant global relationship that governs the rules of his game. No matter how painfully aware a militarist may be of the absurdity of war, he cannot eliminate the logical presuppositions behind his uniform.[11]

According to Alves, the aim of these structures is the monopoly of power. They have a threefold component: economic, military, and scientific domination, which, in turn, respond to a single, unifying logic, namely, that of purchase and possession. Alves likens such logic to dinosaurs, those mammoth prehistoric animals which turned out to be as absurd as they were powerful. And this, he contends, is the reality behind the forces that are determining our contemporary life, which exploit and oppress poor nations, degrade human life, and pollute the environment.

The reality of structures, as described by Alves, is not foreign to biblical revelation. Indeed it is similar to the Pauline concept of "thrones, dominions, principalities and powers" that operate in "heavenly places" (cf. Eph. 1:21; 3:11; 6:12; Col. 1:16; 2:10; Rom. 8:38; 1 Cor. 2:8; 15:24–26). For a long time, biblical scholars associated these beings with demons. And, while their link to the evil one cannot be disputed, today we find an increasing number of scholars who, taking their cue from the context in which Paul uses these terms, have begun to see them as invisible forces that determine institutional behavior and cultural relations.[12] Paul describes these forces as moral rules, rituals, traditions, philosophical convictions, laws, and lifestyles. They are links between everyday life and the universal experiences of humanity. Frequently they respond to great economic and political interests whose ultimate goal is domination and subjugation. In this case they can be liberated from their oppressive function and transformed into vehicles of justice and liberation.

Such a possibility stems from Paul's assertion that the "principalities and powers" were created to help Christ in his government of the world (Col. 1:16). Unfortunately they refused their God-given role in creation, usurping Christ's authority. They rebelled against God's rule and tried to act like him. They became rebellious and oppressive structures.

This corruption of power, this rebellion against the creator, was one reason why God's Son went to the cross. Whatever else we may say about the cross, one reality stands out: it marked a decisive battle between Christ and these invisible corrupt powers. Paul tells us that in his death, Christ "disarmed the principalities and powers and made a public example of them, triumphing over them . . ." (Col. 2:15). For this reason the church has been exhorted not to be intimidated by them but to make known to them "the manifold wisdom of God" (Eph. 3:10). Whether they be multinational corporations that control, destabilize, and deform the economies of entire nations; the current syndrome of militarization and nuclear armaments that we see around us; the dehumanizing structure of orthodox communism; the destructive powers of racism and sexism; or the myth of scientific and technological omnipotence that prevails in so many modern centers of learning, unmasking the powers and proclaiming to them God's judgment and liberation in Christ is a fundamental aspect of the church's evangelizing mission.

Any church, mission agency, or theological institution that claims the whole world as its mission field and wants to proclaim faithfully the whole gospel must make the kerygmatic encounter with the structures that dominate and oppress human life a fundamental component of its agenda. We must avoid deluding ourselves, however. This is not an easy task. Because churches, mission agencies, and schools are assailed by the same invisible forces that dominate and control the institutions of society, especially in a consumer society, the powers that be have a way of creeping in and permeating all institutions, *including those that are committed to Christ*. The temptation to accommodate to the "spirit of the age" rather than to the spirit of Christ, to compromise Christian convictions rather than to stand firm on the Lord's calling, to be more loyal to public-relations techniques than to the values of God's kingdom is ever before us. Subtle and overt pressures are brought to bear upon institutions that are committed to God's liberating mission, that are actively unmasking the principalities and powers and proclaiming Christ's triumph and authority over them.

The letter of Ephesians seems aware of this reality when it states that "we are not contending against flesh and blood, but against the principalities, against the powers, against the world rulers of this present darkness, against the spiritual hosts of wickedness in the heavenly places" (Eph. 6:12). Therefore, in order to resist the evil moment, we have to heed carefully its exhortation to "take the whole armor of God": to gird our loins with God's truth, to put on "the breastplate of righteousness," to have our feet "shod" with the "equipment of the gospel . . . taking the shield of faith . . . the helmet of salvation, and the sword of the Spirit, which is the word of God," and praying "at all times in the Spirit" with intensity and supplication (Eph. 6:13–18). Whatever else this exhortation may mean, one implication stands out: the battle against the principalities and powers requires not technological knowhow and speculative knowledge but commitment to God's truth and justice, obedience to God's Word, and sensitivity to God's Spirit.

To take head-on oppressive structures like consumerism, technology, militarism, multinational capitalism, international communism, racism, and sexism, we need a spirituality of missional engagement: a devotional attitude, a personal ethic, a continuous liturgical experience that flows out of and expresses itself in apostolic obedience.[13] Prayer, Bible study, personal ethics, and worship will not mean withdrawal from the world but an immersion in its sufferings and struggles. Likewise participation in the struggles of history will not mean an abandonment of piety and contemplation, but an experience of God from the depths of human suffering.

Mission without spirituality cannot survive any more than combustion without oxygen. The nature of the world in which we live and the gospel that we have been committed to communicate therein demand, however, that it be a spirituality of engagement and not of withdrawal. Such a spirituality can only be cultivated in obedience and discipleship, and not in the isolated comfort of one's inner self. By the same token, it can only be verified in the liberating struggles against the principalities and powers that hold so many millions in bondage.

World and Gospel: The Challenge of Mission

The world that the Scriptures claim for the gospel is as crowded, complicated, and captive as it has ever been. It is a conglomeration of billions of women, men, and children, clustered in a variety of cultures and social groups. They all need to hear God's total message of liberation and life through his Son Jesus Christ. Such a world is also a complex web of institutions that need to be called to accountability by the new order of life that has broken through in the incarnation, death, and resurrection of Jesus Christ. It is a network of global relationships that determines the life of people and their institutions, that deforms God's creation and opposes the work of his kingdom. Such a demonic and oppressive network needs to be resisted by God's People and overcome by the liberating power of the gospel as it is incarnated in concrete life situations.

If we can enable Christian women and men around the world to see the billions who have yet to hear the good news of salvation, to commit their lives to their integral evangelization, and to acquire the necessary analytical tools and communications skills to facilitate such a task; if we can enable them to have prophetic courage and confront social institutions with the demands of the gospel; and if we can foster in them a "spirituality for combat" (M. M. Thomas), we shall have been indeed faithful to the whole gospel and sensitive to the fullness of the world to which God has sent us. We shall have recovered a holistic legacy and shall be far better equipped to meet the challenge of the 1980s.

NOTES

1. John Wesley, "L. I. 285f: to James Harvey" [March 20, 1739] in Philip S. Watson, *The Message of the Wesleys—A Reader of Instruction and Devotion* (New York: Macmillan, 1964), p. 31.

2. Johann Baptist Metz, *Teología del mundo*, trans. from German by Constantino Ruiz-Garrido (Salamanca: Ediciones Sígueme, 1970), p. 26. Eng. trans.: *Theology of the World* (New York: Seabury, 1969).

3. Cf. Plutarco Bonilla, "Teología y cultura latinoamericana," unpublished address delivered at the Council of Hispanic Ministries of the United Church of Christ (May 3, 1979). It should be remembered that while culture has to do with the totality of human achievements, it is also related to the particular way of life of a people. As such it is but one aspect of social interaction.

4. Cf. Beatriz Melano Couch, "¿Cultura de la pobreza o cultura de dependencia?" *Los pobres: encuentro y compromiso*, ed. ISEDET (Buenos Aires: La Aurora, 1978), pp. 186ff.

5. Enrique Dussel, *Historia de la Iglesia en América Latina* (Barcelona: Editorial Nova Terra, 1974), p. 58.

6. Edward Dayton and David Fraser, *Planning Strategies for World Evangelization* (Grand Rapids, Mich.: Wm. B. Eerdmans, 1980), pp. 37, 138; Edward R. Dayton, *That Everyone May Hear* (Monrovia, Calif.: MARC, 1979), p. 22.

7. Cf. Dayton and Fraser, *Strategies*, pp. 146–92.

8. Jitsuo Morikawa, personal interview, Louisville, Ky. (Sept. 15, 1977).

9. Cf. Juan Luis Segundo, *The Liberation of Theology* (Maryknoll, N.Y.: Orbis Books, 1976), pp. 213ff.; René Padilla, "Evangelism and the World," in *Let the Earth Hear His Voice*, ed. J. W. Douglas (Minneapolis, Minn.: Worldwide Publications, 1975), pp. 125f. For a further discussion of this topic, see my *Integrity of Mission: The Inner Life and Outreach of the Church* (New York: Harper & Row, 1979), pp. 13–24.

10. Ronald J. Sider, "The Christian Seminary: Bulwark of the Status Quo or Beachhead of the Coming Kingdom?" Inaugural lecture, Eastern Baptist Theological Seminary (Oct. 31, 1978), p. 22.

11. Rubem Alves, *Tomorrow's Child: Imagination, Creativity and the Rebirth of Culture* (New York: Harper & Row, 1972), p. 21.

12. For bibliographical details, see H. Berkhof, *Christ and the Powers*, trans. from Dutch by John Howard Yoder (Scottdale, Pa.: Mennonite Publishing House, 1962), passim; Richard J. Mouw, *Politics and the Biblical Drama* (Grand Rapids, Mich.: Wm. B. Eerdmans, 1976), p. 86. For additional helpful exegetical and theological comments, see Albert H. van den Heuvel, *Those Rebellious Powers* (London: SCM Press, 1966), passim; James Wallis, *Agenda for Biblical People* (New York: Harper & Row, 1976), pp. 56ff.; and Ronald J. Sider, *Christ and Violence* (Scottdale, Pa.: Herald Press, 1978), pp. 43ff.

13. For a recent systematic treatment of missional spirituality, see the excellent work of Michael Collins Reilly, S.J., *Spirituality for Mission* (Maryknoll, N.Y.: Orbis Books, 1978).

11

Evangelization in the United States: An Agenda for the 1980s

One of the characteristics of the Christian church in the United States during the 1970s was the resurgence of the concept and practice of evangelization, especially in mainline circles. When mainline churches began to take evangelization out of the closet (after a decade of being set aside as old garments to be given eventually to the "goodwill industries" that kept alive minority, conservative-evangelical, and fundamentalist churches and parachurch organizations) some of us began to wonder if the new popularity of evangelization might not be one more fad in a fad-prone land.[1] Others warned of the danger of falling into the pendulum syndrome: the idea that since social action had been the concern of the 1960s it was in order during the 1970s for the pendulum to swing toward evangelization.[2]

Fairly soon, however, it became clear that the awakened interest in evangelization was not a franchise of American mainline Christians. Indeed the years 1974 and 1975 witnessed three major world events on evangelism: the International Congress on World Evangelization (Lausanne, Switzerland, 1974), the Synod of Catholic Bishops (Rome, 1974), and Section I of the Fifth Assembly of the World Council of Churches (Nairobi, Kenya, 1975). These events bore witness to the fact that evangelization was on the agenda in all the major sectors of the Christian church around the world. When we look at the years 1970–73 and 1976–79, we note an avalanche of regional and national meetings all over the world that underscored the centrality of evangelization and challenged Christians and churches to make it a top priority in their missional agendas.[3]

What is interesting about all of these efforts is the fact that they represent a quest for a fuller, deeper, and more integral evangelistic action. If it is true that the 1970s repossessed the centrality of evangelization lost in the social activism of the 1960s, it is no less true that it remembered negative and positive challenges of the 1960s. Hence, during the 1970s not only was the church reminded of the bankruptcy of any Christian social action that is not accompanied by a passionate concern for those who have not had a chance to hear intelligently and respond personally to the gospel; but, conversely, during the same decade, Christians were warned that an evangelistic action that is not incarnated in the social agonies and struggles of women and men is in biblical, theological, and historical terms both a betrayal of the gospel and an alienating drug.

So the 1970s marked a quest for totality in evangelization. But no sooner had Christians begun to accept the fact that sharing the good news of salvation in word and deed was both a Christian indicative and imperative than they were faced with the challenge of a new decade. As stated in the letter sent by the Melbourne Conference to the member churches of the WCC:

> We meet under the clouds of nuclear threat and annihilation. Our world is deeply wounded by the oppressions inflicted by the powerful upon the powerless. These oppressions are found in our economic, political, racial, secular and religious life. Our world, so proud of human achievements, is full of people suffering from hunger, poverty and injustice. People are wasted. . . . The poor and the hungry cry to God. . . . People suffer the pain of silent torment; their faces reveal their suffering.[4]

A month later, the Pattaya Consultation stated in its concluding document:

> We have become freshly burdened by the vast numbers who have never heard the good news of Christ and are lost without him. We have been made ashamed of our lack of vision and zeal, and of our failure to live out the gospel in its fullness, which have weakened our obedience and compromised our witness. . . . Some two-thirds of the world's four and a half billion people have had no proper opportunity to receive Christ.[5]

An apocalyptic nightmare, informed by the scandalous and lengthy list of horrendous and barbaric deeds, and the tragic reality of an explosive world population of over four-and-a-half-billion people, with almost 80 percent lying outside the frontiers of the gospel and beyond the actual reach of any church or individual Christian—these are initial and general glimpses of the challenges before the world church in the 1980s.

American Society in the 1980s

Without pretending to be socioanalytically scientific, allow me to outline some basic contours of American society in the 1980s.

A Decade of Gloom

First of all, the 1980s appear to be a decade of gloom. Practically all the forecasts predict very tough days ahead—economically, socioculturally, politically, and militarily.

The economic gloom was humorously illustrated on the ABC Nightline program the night that President Ronald Reagan delivered his economic message to a joint session of Congress (Feb. 18, 1981). The editorial cartoonist summarized the president's address with a picture of a typical family watching the president on television deliver the following message: "My fellow Americans, I regret to tell you that we are in a terrible economic mess. Good night!"

Energy and food are two aspects of the current economic malaise. The rapidly increasing cost of oil has put a tremendous burden on the average consumer, created enormous loss of real income for industrial nations like the United States, and sent the non-oil-producing nations of the third world to the brink of crisis.[6] In 1980 the United States "sold more food abroad—$40 billion worth—than at anytime in its history, despite a partial embargo on sales to . . . the Soviet Union." For a nation that has been used to eating relatively inexpensively on account of continuous food surpluses, "the massive shipments of grain abroad which have been a boon to the American balance of payments and a boost to farmer income," have meant higher food prices for the American consumer.[7] A gap "between supply and demand for food and energy and rapid depletion of forests and arable lands" all over the world has sharpened the already alarming problem of wide income disparities and the increase in global population.[8]

Unemployment in the United States continues to rise. According to the Bureau of Labor Statistics, the unemployment rate had risen to 9 percent by March 1982. Among Blacks it was 18 percent, and among all minorities, 16.6 percent. This was complicated by cuts in the federal budget, which curtailed or eliminated some 300 needed domestic and social programs. With an already alarming scarcity of adequate housing for the urban poor (in New York City there are nearly 36,000 people who have nowhere to go at night), with deteriorating conditions in the large urban school systems, a growing crisis in mass transportation, the continuous increase of drug addiction and other similar social ills, the future of American society looks gloomier every day.

The sociocultural crisis of American society is not exhausted, however, by the economic situation. Indeed, during recent decades American society has been experiencing a progressive erosion in the structure and role of the family.[9] The crisis of the American family is particularly manifested in the alarming rate of divorces. During the 1960s there was an increase of 34 percent in the divorce rate; in the 1970s it increased to 79 percent.[10] Such a pathological trend has especially damaged the world of children. "Divorce is one of the most serious and complex mental health crises facing children of the 80's," according to Albert Solnit of the Yale Child Study Center.[11]

Divorce has led to remarriage, which in turn has created a new phenomenon in mainstream American culture: the new extended family. According to one recent study, "There are roughly 3.5 million households, one out of every seven in this country, in which at least one parent has remarried and at least one child is from a previous union."[12] Such a situation is threatening to destroy the most basic unit of society. Given the individualistically oriented lifestyle that characterizes mainstream society, it is doubtful that a loose family relationship like the new extended family can satisfy and undergird the need for intimate relationship and support that is foundational to the well-being of any society. Hence, if the trend persists, by the end of the 1980s mainstream American society will find itself in a communal limbo.

The fact that in a time of such severe frugality in social and domestic programs, military spending is being greatly increased further complicates the picture. The resurgent militarism and confrontational attitude of the Reagan administration, its pronuclear stance, its alliances with inhuman and unscrupulous regimes like those in Chile, Argentina, and South Korea, and its growing military involvement in El Salvador and Guatemala make the threat of war an even greater reality.

What has possessed a nation that less than a decade earlier managed to get out of its largest and most painful war to fall again into the trap of military schemes and political alliances with unpopular oligarchies in response to deeply rooted social, economic, and political problems in the third world? Where has the commonsense gone in a society that has had to bear the enormous cost of decades of oppressive policies and institutions and is now willing to embark, almost fanatically, on an economic and political course that is sure to aggravate further the already chaotic situation of its cities, the impoverished reality of its ever-growing racial minorities, the sad state of its senior citizens and youth, and the heavy burden of a significant sector of its labor force?

A Period of Illusions

It is not easy to answer these questions, especially since we often find ourselves on both sides of the track, being at the same time the possessed and the possessor, the victim and the aggressor, the prisoner of fear and hope. The famous phrase, "They that refuse to learn from the past are condemned to repeat it," is certainly true of the situation in the United States today. Fear, especially in times of uncertainty, often leads people to run away from their immediate past and escape into castles of illusions. The first two years of the decade of the 1980s has revealed an American society steadily falling under the spell of several dangerous illusions.

There is, for example, the illusion of a revived "American Dream." Of course, there is nothing illusory about the search for a better way of life. Struggling for social and political freedom, wanting a secure job, saving to buy one's own home, enjoying an annual vacation, having one's children receive the best possible education, living secure from external military threats, counting on good police protection, and having access to sound medical care—these are all legitimate aspirations.

But when only a limited number of people have any possibility of ever seeing such aspirations materialize, when the fulfillment of expectations is contingent upon limiting the well-being of others, and when a dream causes one to distort reality, then the dream ceases to be a positive, guiding vision and becomes a deadly illusion, an alienating ideology. The American dream was always the private possession of certain sectors of society. For the people on the fringes it was an illusion, since they had very little hope of ever seeing the dream come true.

If in the past the American dream was the personal possession of middle-class Americans, today it has become their private illusion. For, on the one hand, they are relatively worse off than they were five years ago; on the other, many economists have argued that even with a reduction in taxes and a significant cut in the federal budget, it is unlikely that inflation will be effectively controlled within several years.[13] But, what is worse is the fact that all over the world there is an ever decreasing availability of natural resources while a handful of people accumulate a vast amount of wealth and the overwhelming majority live in material deprivation. This, in fact, is the pattern in the United States: the current policies have guaranteed a boom for the wealthy and a setback for the poor, while middle Americans remain about the same, which in the long run means that their economic situation will get worse. When President Ronald Reagan quoted Franklin D. Roosevelt's words, "We have nothing to fear but fear itself," Reagan was certainly referring to the wealthy, not to the middle sectors, and much less to the poor.

Another illusion is that of a new Pax Americana. The notion that only a militarily strong United States can guarantee planetary peace has been generally held by a significant sector of the population, at least during the twentieth century and especially in the post-World War II period. In the nineteenth century the Pax Americana was limited to the Americas, as evidenced by the Monroe Doctrine (1823) and a history of numerous interventions in the life of neighbors, like the Indian nations of the North American West, the Latin Caribbean, Mexico, Central America, and the Panamanian isthmus. Indeed it was the role of the United States as the police of the Americas that prepared it to be the police of the so-called free world in the post-World War II period. In recent years it has been generally felt, however, that with the shattering experience of Vietnam, the illusion of a Pax Americana would fade from the American consciousness. But Vietnam was followed by Angola, Ethiopia, Iran, Nicaragua, Grenada, Afghanistan, and El Salvador. The thought that giving up the old role has only meant making available more space for the number one enemy of the free world to move in (international communism) has led to the renewal of the old belief that only a militarily strong United States can guarantee the peace of the free world.

The evidence of a new Pax Americana is all around us. Indeed it started with the Carter administration and has moved into full swing with the Reagan presidency. For the first time in thirty years, the United States has a military general as secretary of state, but with one difference, acutely pointed out in an article ("The United States: A Nation Hungry for Heroism") that appeared in the Mexican weekly, *Proceso*: whereas General George C.

Marshall represented a victorious World War II army, General Alexander Haig is a member of a defeated army in Vietnam.[14] A five-year military buildup plan promises to double the current defense budget, pushing it from $171 billion in fiscal 1981 to $367.5 billion in 1986. By the end of the five-year plan, the United States will have spent $1.5 trillion. *Time* magazine has noted that "in the celebrated Reagan analogy the $1.5 trillion . . . would be a stack of $1,000 bills 103.5 miles high."[15] A testing ground close to home and part of the old Pax Americana is El Salvador. In this tiny Central American republic the United States decided to "draw the line" against the enemy of peace and freedom: international communism.

It doesn't take much imagination for us to see the illusion of such thinking. For one thing, the world knows too well that military aggression, no matter how much it has been provoked, is never a guarantee of peace. For another, there is no real future in adventures like Vietnam, whether for the United States or the Soviet Union (as Afghanistan has shown). There is no such thing as a good war or a bad peace.

It is a fact, nevertheless, that for all the criticism that has been aired by the media, allied nations, some members of Congress, and grassroots organizations,[16] there are too many Americans who appear spellbound by the illusion of a new Pax Americana.

Another illusion that seems to have captivated important sections of American society in the 1980s is the notion of a Christian society. For many years it was a common assumption of American Christians that the United States was a nation built on Christian principles and values. The process of secularization came to a head in the 1960s with a general decline in church attendance, a seemingly decreasing interest in the transcendent, and a rejection of traditional patterns of personal morality. In the 1970s the pendulum began to move in the opposite direction with a religious awakening that touched not only liberal social activists but especially a significant number of young people, particularly in the college community. Yet, as Richard F. Lovelace has pointed out, the religious awakening of the 1970s lagged in the area of social and cultural transformation. But was it not the conviction that conservative Christians have remained "passive under the growing might of social evil" that prompted the launching of the so-called Moral Majority movement? Lovelace, at least, seems to think so when, among other things, he notes how Jerry Falwell has begun to recover "the impulse toward 'reformation of manners' that motivated 19th century evangelicals."[17] Interestingly enough, the presupposition behind the Anglo-American evangelicalism of past centuries was the conviction that Britain and the United States were Christian nations and that the challenge before the church in each period of religious awakening (e.g., the Wesleyan revival in England and the first and second awakenings in North America) has always been to call the nation back to its Christian roots. Hence the traditional connection between evangelism and revivalism.

Because many Americans are convinced that the United States is a society founded upon Christian principles and values with the church as its mentor, they have sought to solve the nation's problems by reinstating traditional Christian values in the center of political power. They have thus become actively engaged in politics and have begun to lobby for legislation that will outlaw what they consider to be "unchristian practices" (like abortion) and reenact others that, according to them, had been wrongly put aside (like prayer in public schools).

But, is the assumption of a Christian American society historically valid? It is well known that many of the "founding fathers" were deists. Can a nation that had racism, sexism, classism, and deism built into its system, or has had from its beginning what William Appleman Williams has referred to as an "empire-building" way of life ever pass for a Christian society?[18] Can a people that have enriched themselves with the land and resources of their weak neighbors, that permit, consciously or unconsciously, the destruction of the environment and endorse the building of a nuclear arsenal that threatens to wipe out human life from the face of the earth be a God-fearing nation? Can a society that allows its weak children to live in inadequate housing, to be undernourished, to be harassed by the police and denied fair legal aid, to be out of work and out of funds, to be denied access to a sound education, to be victims of drug pushers and other agents of vice, to be manipulated by a consumerist media—can such a society ever pretend to be theistic let alone Christian?

The answer is no! For the Bible is clear: to know God is to practice justice (Jer. 21:16). This is what the Lord requires, says Micah: ". . . to do justice, and to love kindness, and to walk humbly with . . . God" (Mic. 6:8). The vision of the Old Testament is for the abrogation of warmongering nations, the transformation of "swords into plowshares," and the eradication of war from the face of the earth (Isa. 2:4; Mic. 4:3). In the New Testament the apostle James warns us that the true worship of God is "to visit orphans and widows in their affliction, and to keep oneself unstained from the world" (Jas. 1:27). Jesus called "blessed" the "peacemakers," the "pure in heart," the "merciful," those who "hunger and thirst for righteousness," the "meek," those who "mourn" and the "poor in Spirit." He further stated that they shall be called "children of God," and promised that they "shall see God," "be satisfied," "obtain mercy," "be comforted," and "inherit the earth" as well as the "kingdom" (Mt. 6:3-9). All of this can be summed up in the Johannine concepts of love of neighbor and exercise of justice (1 Jn. 3:10).

The idea of a Christian society is not only an illusion as far as the United States is concerned, but anywhere else in the world. All Christendom projects—from the Edict of Milan (A.D. 313) to the present—have been and will always be illusory, because the church has not been called to manage the world but, rather, to bear witness to the kingdom of God in the world. Nor does the gospel envision the establishment of a Christian society. Rather, it announces a new world order that can neither be exhausted by historical structures nor be relegated to the beyond. The fundamental problem with Christendom projects is that they confuse the kingdom of God with the institutional church, the gospel with culture, and the power of the cross with the power of the sword.

The Gospel in the 1980s

While the 1980s do not promise to be a decade of roses, they do give us an opportunity to *hear* the gospel with greater clarity and *see* it at work in sharper focus. If the 1970s gave us the theological space to repossess the wholeness of the gospel, the 1980s can help us recover its cutting edge. Therefore I want briefly to explore the meaning of the gospel as revealed in the biblical witness and its implications for our historical context.

As has been noted throughout this volume, the New Testament writers describe the gospel as God's saving message to the world. The underlying presupposition of that message is God's sovereign and gracious rule over all creation. This was in fact the theme of Jesus' ministry. He came proclaiming the kingdom of God in the power of the Holy Spirit (Mk. 1:14–15; Lk. 4:14–15; Mt. 4:23). He was not only the herald but the bearer of the kingdom.

In Jesus' life and ministry, women and men were reminded of God's claim upon their lives as their creator. They were summoned to honor, glorify, and obey the only lawful rule of heaven and earth. The gospel is both a *reminder* of God's creation and sustaining sovereignty over the world and the accountability of every living thing to its Lord as well as a *call* to the fulfillment of the purpose of creation.

Implicit in the kingdom theme is the recognition of a fundamental gap between God's sovereignty and holiness and humankind's frail and rebelling existence. The whole of creation has been corrupted by the irresponsible and rebellious action of women and men. The effect of this action has been so deep that it has left humankind spiritually impotent (Rom. 3:10ff.). Accordingly no creature is capable of positively responding to the call of the creator. To do this, there needs to be a radical transformation in the fundamental attitudes and relationships of women and men toward God, their neighbor, and their environment, a transformation in their heart and, consequently, in their way of life.

This is why the theme of the kingdom appears in the New Testament not just as a symbol of God's sovereignty, but also as an eschatological hope—the promise of a radically new world order. This promise involves the reconciliation "of all things," or the overcoming of all antagonisms between humankind and nature, peoples and cultures, classes, sexes, generations, and races (Col. 1:19–20; Eph. 1:19–23; 2:17–18; Lk. 4:18–21); it incorporates the Old Testament vision of the messianic age: an era of love, freedom, justice, and peace (Isa. 2:2; 11:1–2, 3b–10; 42:4; 51:4; 66:1ff.; Jer. 31:33; Am. 5:24); and encompasses the cosmic transformation envisioned in both the Old Testament and the New Testament: the hope of new heavens and a new earth (Isa. 65:17ff.; Rom. 8:23ff.; Rev. 21:5).

According to the New Testament the biblical promise of a new world order is embodied in the person and work of Jesus Christ. He was not only a sign of the presence of God's rule in history, but also an anticipation of the messianic age. Hence he was anointed by the Spirit to preach, teach, and heal with power and, in so doing, announced the presence of the kingdom and summoned women and men to repentance and faith in anticipation of the age to come. But it was in his death and resurrection that the kingdom of God broke through, unveiling the new world order and making possible the fulfillment of its promise. Hence the apostle Paul can speak of the messianic age as an accomplished fact: ". . . the Father. . . has delivered us from the dominion of darkness and transferred us to the kingdom of his beloved Son, in whom we have redemption, the forgiveness of sins. . . . For in him all the fullness of God was pleased to dwell, and through him to reconcile to himself all things, whether on earth or in heaven, making peace by the blood of his cross" (Col. 1:13-14, 19-20).

Because in the death and resurrection of Jesus the kingdom of God has come, the world need not live in fear and hopelessness. According to Paul those who trust in Jesus Christ are *saved* in hope, and this hope becomes extensive to the whole created order which "waits with eager longing for the revealing of the children of God" in order to be "set free from its bondage to decay and obtain the glorious liberty of the children of God" in the final and definitive day of redemption (Rom. 8:19-23).

Thus the gospel of the kingdom that Jesus proclaimed in his ministry and embodied in his life has become, through his death and resurrection, the good news of his saving name. The event of Jesus Christ has become the focal point of the kingdom of God, the densest moment of salvation history. In the words of the apostle Peter, there is now "salvation in no one else, for there is no other name under heaven . . . by which we must be saved" (Acts 4:12). This is the name that the church has been led to confess by the gracious witness of the Spirit; this is the reality it has been blessed to embody through the regenerating experience of the Spirit; and this is the message it has been sent to proclaim in the power of the Spirit.

But how shall we interpret this message in our historical situation? How shall we understand the new world order that it announces? It seems to me that in the 1980s we need to highlight the gospel as a message of life and joy.

In the American society of the 1980s we need to emphasize the fact that the gospel is above all else the glad tidings of the new creation that God is bringing into being through Jesus Christ. Contrary to the impression given by some old- and modern-day evangelists, the gospel is not a message of hell and brimstone but, rather, of grace and forgiveness, justification and new birth. It is true that there is no gospel without judgment. But it is equally true that Jesus Christ suffered God's judgment on sin at the cross and overcame the power of death by the resurrection.

If there was ever a time in which we needed to stress the life and joy of the new creation, it is now. Our society needs to know that there is the possibility of life *on this side of the grave*—"abundant life, vigorous life, love life and eternal life."[19] This possibility lies in Jesus Christ, the one who incarnated eternal life, who rejected apathy and refused to become used to the ways of death, the one who lived passionately for others and gave his life that others might live. Our society needs to be made aware of the dangerous consequences of its obsession with success, achievement, and power. Such obsession brings apathy, or indifference, and leads slowly to death. Affluence and work, military might and political power do not guarantee "life before death" but rather "death before life." Yet the gospel does guarantee both life before *and* after death, because it is rooted in the life and love of Jesus Christ. As José Míguez Bonino has noted: "The meaning of our life before death and the confidence in a life after death have only one sole guarantee: the love of Jesus Christ."[20] And as Jürgen Moltmann has also said: "Jesus' life is inspired not just by the wish for a life after death, but by the will for life *before* death, yes, even *against* death. When the sick are healed, lepers are accepted, and sins are not punished but forgiven, there *life* is present. Freed life, redeemed life, divine life is there, in this world, in our times, in the midst of us. Where Jesus is, there is life."[21] And where there is true life, there is real joy— shared joy, not selfish pleasure; joy in the midst of pain, not indifference to and freedom from suffering; joy in small things, not masquerades of hilarious celebrations over mighty, successful, and false achievements.

In the gloomy climate of American society in the 1980s, where false dreams and deadly illusions cover up a perplexed, confused, humiliated, lonely, and deeply saddened population, full of anxieties and broken in spirit, the church needs to emphasize the joy and gladness of the gospel. In so doing it will provide a challenging alternative to a schizophrenic style of life, organized on one side around wealth, power, pleasure, and fun, and on the other around a growing psychological and sociological impoverishment, a dreadful fear of becoming politically, economically, and militarily weak, full of self-defeated guilt feelings and in a melancholic and insensitive mood.

Evangelization in the 1980s

Because the gospel is a message of life and joy, it is to be experienced and shared. When John the Baptist sent his disciples to inquire of Jesus whether he was the one to come or if he should look for someone else, Jesus showed him what was happening in his ministry: the physically deformed were experiencing healing and transformation, the poor were receiving the good news that salvation had drawn near, and those who were not scandalized with a Messiah who took the form of a servant and identified himself with the outcast were blessed. Jesus then told them to "Go and tell John" what they had heard and seen (Mt. 11:4). In other words, he exhorted them to bear witness to the new world order of life, freedom, justice, and peace that was being revealed. I suggest that this is how Christians in the United States ought to understand evangelization in the 1980s.

The New Testament concept of witness-bearing stands both for the giving of a faithful account of a historical fact and for the interpretation of the theological significance of that account from the perspective of a personal conviction. While the former sense appears predominantly in relation to the reporting of the gospel events by the apostles (eyewitnesses of the death and resurrection of Christ), the latter appears in relation to evangelism, as the book of Acts, the Johannine literature, and the Pauline epistles so clearly demonstrate. In this sense, to witness is to confess one's conviction about the theological truthfulness of the history of Jesus Christ.

An evangelistic witness (*mártus*) is, therefore, a person who testifies (*marturéin*) from within a personal knowledge (experience) of Jesus Christ as the crucified and risen Son of God and therefore as the embodiment of God's reign. This testimony (*marturía*) is sealed by the readiness of the witness to stand by his or her affirmation, even at the cost of death.[22]

Bearing a personal witness, however, does not mean giving an isolated, private testimony to individuals from an abstract and ahistorical situation. On the contrary, bearing witness involves a joyful *public* declaration by one who has experienced abundant life in Jesus Christ and participates in his passionate commitment to the poor, the powerless, and the oppressed. Only from within such a transforming experience and radical commitment can there be an authentic evangelistic witness. It was this hard reality that led so many socioreligious and learned leaders of his day to become scandalized at Jesus. Yet what was so hard for the powerful and the wise to understand and accept, the poor, the ignorant, and the handicapped were able to grasp (Mt. 11:25). As Paul reminded the Corinthian church:

> Not many of you were wise according to worldly standards, not many were powerful, not many were of noble birth; but God chose what is foolish in the world to shame the strong, God chose what is low and despised in the world, even things that are not, to bring to nothing things that are, so that no human being might boast in the presence of God. He is the source of your life in Christ Jesus, whom God made our wisdom, our righteousness and sanctification and redemption . . . [1 Cor. 1:26–30].

It is a fact that, at a time when important sectors of mainline Christianity have become stagnant and dry, and when leading sectors of the evangelical, fundamentalist, and charismatic movements have embarked on a neo-Christendom project incorporating the illusion of a Pax Americana and an exclusivist, revived "American dream," large sectors of the church of the poor and disfranchised are bearing vigorous witness to the gospel—without fanfare, financial resources, and academically qualified personnel. Black, Hispanic, Asian, and Native American churches and Christians, in partnership with a minority from the mainstream society that has identified itself with the poor, the powerless, and the oppressed of the land, are witnessing to the new world order announced in the gospel—*outside* the realm of economic wealth, military might, and political power, and *inside* the world of millions who are being wasted by numerous forms of social, economic, and political evils. Within such a witnessing engagement, the Holy Spirit is beginning to give more liberating and inclusive visions, even as it was promised by the prophet Joel:

> And it shall come to pass afterward,
> that I will pour out my spirit on all flesh;
> your sons and your daughters shall prophesy,
> your old men shall dream dreams,
> and your young men shall see visions.
> Even upon the menservants and maidservants
> in those days, I will pour out my spirit [Joel 2:28–29].

Yes indeed, even in the dark 1980s, the old and the young, the menservants and the maidservants, the people on the fringes of American society, are beginning to have visions: visions of a more wholesome and fraternal society; visions of a *pax humana*, more enduring, lasting, and inclusive than the Pax Americana; visions of an outpouring of the Spirit on all flesh, the Spirit of the living God—not the God of theologians, who is often held captive in the hands of the theological academy; not the God of philosophers, who is often reduced to an abstract concept; not the God of the rich and mighty, who is treated as private property that can be manipulated for their own self-interest; not the God of a success-crazy and achievement-oriented society, which is indifferent and apathetic to a suffering world; *but* the God and Father of our Lord Jesus Christ, who has pitched his tent among the poor and disfranchised of the world and has become part of our frail history, suffering for us and with us.

Evangelization in the United States means bearing witness in the power of the Spirit to the new world that God has promised in Jesus Christ. Such a witness can only be given from within situations where the signs of that new world are present, where love and freedom, justice and peace are being experienced—even if in small and limited ways. And the one place where this is happening is in *the other* American church—the church of the disfranchised racial minorities, which has been living in and witnessing from the underside of American history.

For a long time Christians and churches in mainstream society have seen their brothers and sisters in the minority church as a mission station, or at best an interesting ecclesial nucleus that does things differently. In the 1980s, however, they are having to learn from them what it means to bear a joyous and lively witness to a messianic order of life. Indeed, by and large it is the church of American minorities that is not only growing numerically by leaps and bounds and has been enjoying a continuous process of evangelistic mobilization but, more important, is the one nucleus of American Christianity that has *experienced* the gospel as life and joy in an environment of death and misery. This is the one portion of the American church community that is being blessed with fresh and liberating visions in an age of deadly illusions, false dreams, and alienating ideologies. This is the one segment of the universal church in the United States that knows how "to sing the Lord's songs in a foreign land" (Ps. 137:4). This is, therefore, that prophetic unit that is best able to teach mainstream Christians, denominations, and local churches how to evangelize in the 1980s. It is my sincere conviction that, if and when mainstream sisters and brothers start attending to the living teach-in of their minority counterparts, if and when their churches begin to follow in the footsteps of minority churches and apply their model of evangelization to the concrete situation of mainstream society, there will be a transformation in the personal and collective lives of women, men, and children such as the United States has never known.

NOTES

1. See my article "Evangelism and the Gospel of Salvation," *International Review of Mission* 63, no. 249 (January 1974): 37.

2. Cf. Alfred Krass, *Beyond the Either/Or Church* (Nashville, Tenn.: Tidings, 1973), pp. 7ff.

3. E.g., the Methodist World Mission Consultation (Jerusalem, 1974); the Orthodox Consultation on "Confessing Christ Today" (Bucharest, Hungary, 1974); the Pan African Christian Leadership Assembly (Nairobi, Kenya, 1976); the Second Latin American Congress on Evangelism (Lima, Peru, 1979); the Third General Assembly of the Latin American (Catholic) Bishops Conference (Puebla, Mexico, 1979).

4. "Message from Melbourne 1980," *International Review of Mission* 69, no. 275 (July 1980): 253.

5. COWE, "The Thailand Statement," Pattaya, Thailand (June 16–27, 1980), pp. 1–2 (mimeographed). Cf. Lausanne Committee for World Evangelization, "The Thailand Statement," *International Bulletin of Missionary Research* 5, no. 1 (January): 29–31.

6. Leonard Silk, "A Growing Interdependence," *New York Times*, section 12 (Feb. 8, 1981), pp. 1, 10.

7. Ann Crittenden, "Food Trade: Increasing Dependence," ibid., p. 9.

8. Clyde H. Farnsworth, "Toughening Attitudes on World Trade," ibid., p. 11.

9. Cf. Myron R. Chartier, "Marriage and Family: A Priority for Ministry," unpublished paper (Philadelphia: Eastern Baptist Theological Seminary, n.d.).

10. W. Shrum, "Religion and Marital Stability: Change in the 1970s?" *Review of Religious Research* 21 (1980): 135–47.

11. Cf. L. B. Franke, "The Children of Divorce," *Newsweek* (Feb. 11, 1980), pp. 58–59, 61–62, 63.

12. Michael Norman, "The New Extended Family," *New York Times Magazine* (Nov. 23, 1980), p. 44.

13. Steven Rattner, "Economists Find Reagan Proposal for Cutting Taxes Favors Wealthy," *New York Times* (March 15, 1981), pp. 1, 29.

14. Arid Dorfman, "Estados Unidos: un pueblo hambriento de heroismo," *Proceso*, no. 224 (Feb. 16, 1981), p. 36.

15. Ed Magnuson, "A Bonanza for Defense: The Administration Proposes a Record Military Build-up," *Time* (March 16, 1981), p. 26.

16. "Green Berets Going to Assist El Salvador," *Philadelphia Inquirer* (March 14, 1981), pp. 1, 12a. See also James McCartney, "How Haig's Scare Campaign on El Salvador Backfired," ibid., p. 12a; Tom Fiedler, "Reagan Now Wants to Play Down Salvador," ibid. (March 13, 1981), pp. 1, 12a; Felipe Llerandi, "A Savior for El Salvador," ibid., p. 12a; and Gabriel García Marquez, "El Kissinger de Reagan," *Proceso* (Feb. 16, 1981), p. 37.

17. Richard F. Lovelace, "Completing an Awakening," *Christian Century* 48, no. 9 (March 18, 1981): 297.

18. Cf. William Appleman Williams, *Empire as a Way of Life* (New York: Oxford University Press, 1980).

19. Jürgen Moltmann, *The Open Church: Invitation to a Messianic Lifestyle* (London: SCM Press, 1978), p. 19.

20. José Míguez Bonino, *Espacio para ser hombres* (Buenos Aires: Tierra Nueva, 1975), p. 60. English trans.: *Room to be People* (Philadelphia: Fortress Press, 1979).

21. Moltmann, *Church*, p. 24.

22. For a detailed treatment of the use of these terms in the New Testament, see H. Strathmann "Mártus, marturéin, marturía," *Theological Dictionary of the New Testament*, vol. 4, ed. Gerhard Friedrick, trans. and ed. from German by G. W. Bromiley (Grand Rapids, Mich.: Wm. B. Eerdmans 1967), pp. 489–512.

Epilogue: Outside the Gate

So Jesus also suffered outside the gate in order to sanctify the people through his own blood [Heb. 13:12].

These words were originally addressed to Jewish Christians for whom the meaning of Jesus Christ and his sacrifice on the cross had remained nebulous. The writer of the epistle to the Hebrews wanted to strengthen their faith by clarifying what it meant to believe in Jesus in their particular socioreligious situation. Hence throughout the epistle he describes Jesus as the Son of God (1:2ff.), a new (and greater) Moses (3:2ff.), the great high priest (4:15ff.), the mediator of a new covenant (9:15), the author and perfecter of the faith (12:2), the one who is perpetually the same: the faithful savior (13:8), and the great shepherd of the sheep (13:20). He is described in our text as the man of God who died outside the gate of the Holy City.

In the providence of God these words have been extended to us who live geographically, culturally, religiously, and chronologically very far from its original recipients. Let us consider several implications that spring from this text and its context.

A New Place of Salvation

First of all, the death of Jesus outside the gate implies a new place of salvation. In the Old Testament the temple, which had replaced the ancient tabernacle, was understood not just as a place of worship, but especially as the central location of salvation. Sacrifices were regularly offered by the priests on behalf of the people to atone for their sins. Once a year the high priest would enter the Holy of Holies, symbol of the very presence of God, and sprinkle the blood of a ram over the "mercy seat" on his behalf and the blood of a goat on behalf of the nation. After that he would take a live goat, put his hands upon it, and send it with their iniquities to the wilderness, the place of sin and the evil one (cf. Lev. 16:1ff.). In this context salvation was confined to the temple, inside the walls of the Holy City. It was understood as a "benefit": the continuous liberation (or forgiveness) of the people from the wrath of God. Through animal sacrifices the people were made whole and kept in communion with God.

With Jesus there came a fundamental shift in the location of salvation: the center was moved to the periphery. Jesus died in the wilderness among the outcast and disfranchised. The unclean and defiled territory became holy ground as he took upon himself the function of the temple.

With the change of location came also a shift in focus. The concept of salvation was now seen in a broader and more radical perspective. No longer was it understood in terms of a mere benefit. The focus was now on commitment to a life of service. Jesus died "to sanctify the people," that is, to set them apart for ministry. This ministry is described by the writer of Hebrews as the confession of the name of Jesus by way of sharing one's material possessions with the poor and powerless and working for their general well-being (cf. 13:15–16). Salvation means, in other words, freedom to confess Jesus Christ in the service of outsiders.

It is a fact, nevertheless, that throughout church history Christians have had a hard time accepting the explicit teaching of this text. They have been, by and large, like their ethnocentric counterparts among the diverse elements in ancient Israel. Israel was saved from slavery in order to be God's priestly people amid the nations, but became instead, through the efforts of some leaders, an exclusive community that saw its election as a national privilege rather than a call to serve the world. Far too many Christians have interpreted God's salvation through Jesus Christ as a private possession, a personal privilege, rather than freedom for service. As a result the church has become an exclusive fellowship, a club of "insiders" (as the synagogue became with Ezra, despite the efforts of Deutero Isaiah).

This is clearly demonstrated in the phenomenon of Christendom. Contrary to popular thought, Christendom is *not* the sum total of Christians in the world. It is, rather, a "historical project" that has taken various shapes and forms from the time when it was introduced in the Edict of Milan (A.D. 313), when Constantine made Christianity the state religion. Whatever its form, however, Christendom is the vision of a society organized around Christian principles and values with the church as its manager or mentor. In a Christendom society, people are divided between "insiders" and "outsiders." Insiders are those who live within the compounds of the church. The church is always the legitimate religious institution who administers salvation to those who come within its fold through a sophisticated clergy-class (or a combined clergy-laity elite) and the observance of clearly defined rituals and practices. Because the church is the manager or mentor of such a society, it follows that all of life must be legitimized by the church: the state has its blessings and protects in turn the church's privileged status; businesses are legitimized by its teachings and support in turn the church's operating costs; the military are upheld by the church's prayers and the spiritual care of its chaplains, and provide in return protection from outside intruders; education is stimulated by church schools and transmits in turn the values and principles that are foundational for its Christian society.

There are those who may argue that such a picture may have been true of the Middle Ages in Europe or the early colonial period in the Americas, but is no longer the case, at least, in an increasingly pluralistic and secular Western Europe and North America. But is this a valid argument? Pluralism and secularization notwithstanding, in most of the countries of Western Europe and Canada there is a strong relationship between public institutions and the church. As for the United States, there has always been an alliance between religion and the other institutions of society. Witness, for example, the public role of religious symbols (the Bible and prayer in public ceremonies) and the role of clergy in society.

The problem with Christendom does not lie with society as such but with the church. As a "historical project," Christendom dominates the church's mental structures. It causes the church to see society as an extension of itself and its inner life as a reflection of its culture. Therefore those who lie outside its ecclesiastical compounds, those who are not heirs of the "appropriate" religious traditions, those who do not have the same cultural background, those who do not "speak" the same "language," even if they call themselves "Christians," do not share in the "spiritual," social, economic, and political "blessings" of salvation. They are not "insiders," but "outsiders." For all practical purposes, they share the same fate as everyone else in the "wilderness": they are lost. The fact of the matter is that in North American Christendom the lost are not simply those who do not profess a personal faith in Jesus Christ, but especially those who are "outside" the domain of established religious institutions.

In a real sense, the old maxim of the church fathers, "outside of the church, there is no salvation," is applicable today to everyone who is not directly or indirectly, practically or formally part of the North American ecclesiastical compound. To be sure, the latter is as complex as it is sophisticated; it has invisible walls and a hidden gate. It is pluriform and goes by different names. It can be a socioreligious network, denomination, or spiritual community. It can be labeled mainstream Christianity or established evangelicalism, United Presbyterian or Roman Catholic, American or Southern Baptist, United Methodist or United Church of Christ, Episcopalian or Assembly of God, Brethren or Schwenkfelder. Its form and identity notwithstanding, it is evidenced in the past history and present situation of North American society.

It is in this context that we need to hear the words of the epistle to the Hebrews. Jesus died "outside the gate," outside the religious compound, outside the comfort and security of the redeemed community. In so doing, Jesus reiterated and confirmed the voice of those truly radical prophets of Israel:

> In that day there will be five cities in the land of Egypt which . . . swear allegiance to the Lord. . . . And the Lord will make himself known to the Egyptians; and the Egyptians will know the Lord in that day. . . . In that day there will be a highway from Egypt to Assyria . . . and the

Egyptians will worship with the Assyrians. In that day Israel will be the third with Egypt and Assyria, a blessing in the midst of the earth . . . [Isa. 19:18, 21, 23–24].

Voices like this were unpopular and rare in nationalistic Israel, but they laid the foundations for Jesus' life and work. Jesus unequivocably shifted the whole concept of salvation—from benefit and privilege to commitment and service. To be saved by faith in Christ is thus to come to Jesus where he died for the world and gave his life for its salvation; it is to commit oneself to those for whom he suffered.

Salvation lies outside the gates of the cultural, ideological, political, and socioeconomic walls that surround our religious compound and shape the structures of Christendom. It is not a ticket to a privileged spot in God's universe but, rather, freedom for service. This is why Jesus said: "If any man would come after me, let him deny himself and take up his cross and follow me. For whoever would save his life will lose it, and whoever loses his life for my sake will find it" (Mt. 16:24–25).

A Fuller Understanding of Mission

The death of Jesus outside the gate implies, second, a fuller understanding of mission.

In the Old Testament, it was generally thought, though not without some opposition, that the mission of Israel was to be a showcase for the nations to see. Israel was the center of the world (Ezek. 5:5) and Jerusalem (or Zion) its holy mountain (Ps. 6:2): the place where the nations had to come in order to be saved (Mic. 4:1ff.). The mission of Israel was to be the priests of Yahweh's holy mountain (Ex. 19:6). The nations were to come to Mount Zion to learn from Israel the ways of Yahweh. As stated by the prophet Micah: ". . . many nations shall come, and say: 'Come, let us go up to the mountain of the Lord, to the house of the God of Jacob; that he may teach us his ways and we may walk in his paths' "(Mic. 4:2).

The fact that the Northern Kingdom and later Judah were taken in captivity and dispersed throughout the nations did not change this self-understanding of many of the descendants of Jacob. From Babylon, far away from Mount Zion, far removed from the Holy City, a faithful remnant kept their eschatological vision alive; it continued to dream about the promised land and refine its missiological self-understanding. In time, some of its representatives were able to go back and rebuild the temple. Those who remained continued to meditate on the Law in the synagogues that had been built partially as substitutes for the temple. Having built houses, planted gardens, and taken wives (Jer. 29:5–6), they settled permanently in the land of exile, but year after year sought to make a pilgrimage to Jerusalem. To be sure, their very life and piety enabled them to bear witness to their neighbors about Yahweh, and some of them became followers of the God of Abraham,

Isaac, and Jacob. Such conversions, however, were interpreted in terms of proselytization: it meant that gentiles became Jews, and were expected to make pilgrimages to Jerusalem. They became signs of the definitive messianic kingdom when the nations would come to Mount Zion to learn from Israel the ways of Yahweh. So mission, even in the dispersion, continued to be understood primarily as bringing the periphery to the center.

The death of Jesus not only changed the location of salvation, but also clarified the nature of mission. By shifting salvation to the periphery, the mission of the people of God has undergone a complete about-face. Mission is no longer "coming" but "going" (as anticipated by Isaiah in 19:23-25). Bearing witness to God's saving grace means going to the crucified Son of God, outside the gate of our sacred compounds, to share in his suffering death for the world. This is what the author of Hebrews has in mind when he states: "Therefore let us go forth to him outside the camp, and bear the abuse he endured" (13:13). The fact that Jesus wrought salvation outside the Holy City does not mean that we have now a new fixed salvific center but, rather, a permanent, *moving* center in the periphery of life. Salvation is to be focused on that person who has assumed the perpetual identity of the outsider. We can know Jesus only as the crucified Son of God suffering and dying for the world amid the outcasts and rejects.

Since Jesus died outside the gate, mission has become the crossing of the walls and gates of our secured and comfortable compounds, the continuous movement toward him to bear "the abuse he endured" for the world. It is only in this continuous movement toward his cross, in our identification with him and his cause, in our participation in his suffering death outside and for outsiders that we can be authentic witnesses of God's saving grace. Only thus can we lift him up and enable women and men to be drawn to him (Jn. 12:32).

If Christian mission means encountering the crucified Christ in the world of the outsiders and sharing in his suffering for the rejects and outcasts, then it follows that all its traditional aspects must be interpreted from the perspective of the periphery. The *planting* and *growth* of the church must not be thought of in terms of building sacred compounds but, rather, of sojourning (cf. Isa. 19:23) communities, like Abraham who lived in tents sojourning "in the land of promise, as in a foreign land" (Heb. 11:9). The church is to be a *paroikia*, a temporary abode, a tent in the wilderness, not a fortress or an insulated castle. *Diakonia*, or the ministry of mercy, is to be understood in terms of sharing one's possessions and living just lives, as Hebrews 13:1-5 states: "Let brotherly love continue. Do not neglect to show hospitality to strangers. . . . Remember those who are in prison . . . and those who are ill-treated. . . . Let marriage be held in honor and let the marriage bed be undefiled. . . . Keep your life free from love of money. . . ." As for *worship*, it is to be a living celebration of the name of Christ amid the crossroads of life, not a religious whitewash to soothe a bad conscience. We can only offer sacrifices of praise to God and confess the name of Christ if we are on the move toward him "outside the gate," if we are sojourners, if we live just lives and share what we have with those who are in need. Worship, evangelism, and service have Christian value if they are done "outside," in solidarity with the crucified Jesus and his permanent commitment to the outcast.

A New Goal of Salvation and Mission

The death of Jesus outside the gate implies thus a new place of salvation and a fuller understanding of mission. Neither salvation nor mission is, however, an end in itself. The context of the text suggests a third implication of Jesus' death: a new goal of both salvation and mission.

The fallacy of many in Israel, reflected in the theological debates found in the Old Testament, is that Israel grew too wrapped up in itself and lost sight of its universal mission. (The Yahwists's appeal that "by you all the families of the earth shall bless themselves" [Gen. 12:36] did not prevail.) God's goodness was selfishly interiorized. Instead of setting a worthy example of justice, freedom, and well-being, and thus being a faithful witness to the nations, Israel's ruling class blindly copied the latter's evil ways, becoming like them. Israel cherished the status quo—except when it was in slavery and captivity! But the more God delivered it from bondage, the more it sought to privatize God, and the less it remembered God's promise of universal salvation: the creation of "new heavens and a new earth," as it is so eloquently described in the prophecies of Isaiah (Isa. 65:17). Israel saw itself as an end rather than a means.

There are many Christians, ecclesiastical bodies, and missionary organizations today that tend to think of "the outside" as the end. They tend to conceive their freedom for service and their movement toward Jesus, their solidarity with his suffering for the outcast, as the ultimate goal of their Christian vocation. In so doing, they become sheer activists—pilgrims without a destination, prophets without a vision, witnesses without hope.

The encouragement of such activism is certainly not the intent of the writer of Hebrews. Indeed the exhortation to move outside and participate in the suffering of the crucified Son of God is grounded on the vision of "the city which is to come" (Heb. 13:14) "whose builder and maker is God" (11:10). The periphery, the wilderness, the world of sin and evil, of suffering and injustice, is not seen as a permanent dwelling. Service therein is a checkpoint on the way to the new Jerusalem, symbol of the new creation: the definitive transformation of the world by the power of God.

Salvation and mission without the new Jerusalem run into a dead end; they are turned into circular socioreligious exercises, exhausted by their immediacy and impotent in the face of the future. This is not what the writer of Hebrews is talking about, however. The writer is, rather, saying that the death of Jesus has made it possible for women and men to be ultimately free from the power of sin and death, so that they can look forward to an entirely new world, and therefore work in the "desert" without fear and intimidation, knowing that ultimately the desert will become God's garden and the sin-prone city will be made anew by the power of the living God.

Jesus died outside the gate, and in so doing changed the place of salvation and clarified the meaning of mission. No longer can I see God's saving grace as an individual benefit, a privileged possession, or a religious whitewash that enables me to feel good and continue to live the old way because my bad conscience has been soothed and my guilt feelings washed away. On the contrary, because salvation is to be found in the crucified Son of God who died outside the gate of the religious compound, to be saved by faith in him is to experience a radical transformation that makes me a "debtor" to the world (Rom. 1:14) and calls me forth to share in his suffering by serving, especially, its lowest representatives: the poor, the powerless, and the oppressed. Nor am I allowed to use the cause of evangelism to build ecclesiastical compounds that insulate Christians from the basic issues of life and impede them to follow through in their calling to take up the cross, deny themselves, and follow Jesus through the crossroads of life.

But the cross is not the end of Jesus; it is not God's last word. Jesus not only died, but rose from the dead and shall yet bring forth the new creation in all its fullness and glory. It is the resurrection and the new creation that constitute God's last and definitive words. They validate the cross as a necessary and decisive checkpoint in God's plan to create a new earth and a new heaven. If we are saved from the power of selfishness and decay and are exhorted to move in mission outside the comfort and security of our ecclesiastical compounds, it is in order that we might serve the world and witness to the new creation by helping to transform the wilderness of an unjust, oppressive, and torn world into a garden of justice, freedom, and well-being.

Therefore let us not be co-opted by the structures of Christendom but, rather, let us become apostolic agents in the mobilization of a servant church toward its crucified Lord, outside the gate of a comfortable and secure ecclesiastical compound. Let us not sell our missional birthright for the mess of pottage of a cheap social activism but, rather, let us be prophets of hope in a world of disillusionment and false dreams, pressing forward to the city of God—the world of true justice and real peace, of unfeigned love and authentic freedom. Amen.

Selected Bibliography
(in English)

I. Periodicals

Africa Now, Sudan Interior Mission, Cedar Grove, N.J., U.S.A.
Africa Theological Journal, Lutheran Theological College, Makumira, Tanzania.
African Ecclesiastical Review, Pastoral Institute of Eastern Africa, Gaba, Kampala, Uganda.
Ching Feng: Quarterly Notes on Christianity and Chinese Religion and Culture, Christian Center on Chinese Religion and Culture, Hong Kong.
The Church and the Jewish People, World Council of Churches, Geneva, Switzerland.
The Ecumenical Review, World Council of Churches, Geneva, Switzerland.
Evangelical Missions Quarterly, Evangelical Missions Information Service, Springfield, Pa., U.S.A.
Evangelical Review of Theology, World Evangelical Fellowship Theological Commission, New Delhi, India.
Global Church Growth Bulletin, Overseas Crusades Ministries, Inc., Santa Clara, Calif., U.S.A.
IAMS Newsletter, International Association for Mission Studies, Leiden, Netherlands.
International Bulletin of Missionary Research, Overseas Ministries Study Center, Ventnor, N.J., U.S.A.
International Review of Mission, Commission on World Mission and Evangelism, World Council of Churches, Geneva, Switzerland.
Journal of Religion in Africa, E. J. Brill, Leiden, Netherlands.
Latin America Evangelist, Latin America Mission, Coral Gables, Fla., U.S.A.
Latin America Fraternity Theological Bulletin, Mexico, D.F., Mexico.
Maryknoll Magazine, Catholic Foreign Mission Society of America, Maryknoll, N.Y., U.S.A.
Ministerial Formation, Program on Theological Education, World Council of Churches, New York, N.Y., U.S.A.
Missiology: An International Review, American Society of Missiology, Pasadena, Calif., U.S.A.
Missionalia, The South African Missiological Society, Pretoria, South Africa.
Newsletter, Center for the Study of Islam and Christian–Muslim Religions, Selly Oak Colleges, Birmingham, England.
Occasional Essays, Latin American Evangelical Center for Pastoral Studies, San José, Costa Rica.

Religion and Society, Christian Institute for the Study of Religion and Society, Bangalore, India.

The Southeast Asia Journal of Theology, Association of Theological Schools in Southeast Asia, Singapore.

Sparks, Institute of Slavic Studies, Wheaton, Ill., U.S.A.

Theological Journal, Japan Lutheran Theological College and Seminary, Tokyo, Japan.

Today's Mission, Today's Mission, Inc., Pasadena, Calif., U.S.A.

Update Latin America, Washington Office on Latin America, Washington, D.C., U.S.A.

World Mission, Society for the Propagation of the Faith, New York, N.Y., U.S.A.

II. General Works on Mission and Introduction to Missiology

Allen, R.

1964   *Missionary Principles.* Grand Rapids, Mich.: Wm. B. Eerdmans.

1965   *The Ministry of the Spirit.* Grand Rapids, Mich.: Wm. B. Eerdmans.

1966   *Missionary Methods: St. Paul's or Ours?* Grand Rapids, Mich.: Wm. B. Eerdmans.

Anderson, Gerald H., and Stransky, Thomas F., eds.

1974   *Mission Trends No. 1: Crucial Issues in Mission Today.* New York: Paulist Press; Grand Rapids, Mich.: Wm. B. Eerdmans.

1975   *Mission Trends No. 2: Evangelization.* New York: Paulist Press; Grand Rapids, Mich.: Wm. B. Eerdmans.

1977   *Mission Trends No. 3: Third World Theologies.* New York: Paulist Press; Grand Rapids, Mich.: Wm. B. Eerdmans.

1979   *Mission Trends No. 4: Liberation Theologies.* New York: Paulist Press; Grand Rapids, Mich.: Wm. B. Eerdmans.

1981   *Mission Trends No. 5: Faith Meets Faith.* New York: Paulist Press; Grand Rapids, Mich.: Wm. B. Eerdmans.

Barrett, David.

1982   *World Christian Encyclopedia.* New York: Oxford University Press.

Bavink, J. H.

1960   *An Introduction to the Science of Missions.* Philadelphia: Presbyterian and Reformed Publishing Company.

Beyerhaus, Peter, and Hallencreutz, Carl F., eds.

1969   *The Church Crossing Frontiers: Essays on the Nature of Mission in Honor of Bengt Sundkler.* Lund, Sweden: C. W. K. Gleerup.

Costas, Orlando E.

1974   *The Church and Its Mission: A Shattering Critique from the Third World.* Wheaton, Ill.: Tyndale House.

1979   *The Integrity of Mission: The Inner Life and Outreach of the Church.* New York: Harper & Row.

Engel, James F., and Norton, Wilbert.

1977   *What's Gone Wrong with the Harvest?* Grand Rapids, Mich.: Zondervan.

Fenton, Horace L.

1973   *Myths about Mission.* Downers Grove, Ill.: InterVarsity Press.

Goldsmith, Martin.
1976   *Don't Just Stand There: A First Book on Christian Mission.* Downers Grove, Ill.: InterVarsity Press.
Griffiths, Michael.
1980   *Shaking the Sleeping Beauty: Arousing the Church to Its Mission.* Leicester, England: InterVarsity Press.
Hoekendijk, J. C.
1966   *The Church Inside Out.* Philadelphia: Westminster Press.
Hoffman, Ronan.
1960   *Pioneer Theories of Missiology.* Washington, D.C.: Catholic University of America.
Hopkins, Paul A.
1977   *What Next in Mission?* Philadelphia: Westminster Press.
Kane, J. Herbert.
1974   *Understanding Christian Missions.* Grand Rapids, Mich.: Baker Book House.
Neill, Stephen C.; Anderson, Gerald H.; Goodwin, John.
1970   *Concise Dictionary of Christian World Mission.* Nashville, Tenn.: Abingdon.
Samuel, L. Vinay, and Sugden, Chris.
1981   "Christian Mission in the Eighties: A Third World Perspective," Partnership Booklet no. 2. Bangalore, India: Partnership in Mission—Asia.
Scott, Waldron.
1980   *Bring Forth Justice: A Contemporary Perspective on Mission.* Grand Rapids, Mich.: Wm. B. Eerdmans.
Song, C. S.
1975   *Christian Mission in Reconstruction: An Asian Analysis.* Madras: Christian Literature Society; and Maryknoll, N.Y.: Orbis Books.
Sundkler, Bengt.
1963   *The World of Mission.* London: Lutterworth Press.
Taylor, John Vernon.
1966   *For All the World.* London: Hodder and Stoughton.
Trueblood, Elton.
1972   *The Validity of the Christian Mission.* New York: Harper & Row.
Verkuyl, J.
1978   *Contemporary Missiology.* Grand Rapids, Mich.: Wm. B. Eerdmans.
Warren, Max.
1977   *I Believe in the Great Commission.* Grand Rapids, Mich.: Wm. B. Eerdmans.

III. Theologies of Mission

Anderson, Gerald H., ed.
1961   *The Theology of the Christian Mission.* New York: McGraw-Hill.
1967   *The Christian Mission in Theological Perspective.* Nashville, Tenn.: Abingdon.
Anderson, Wilhelm.
1955   *Towards a Theology of Mission.* London: SCM Press.

Barth, Karl.
1962   *Church Dogmatics,* vol. 4, pt. 3, 2nd half: 830–901. Edinburgh: T & T Clark.
Bassham, Rodger C.
1980   *Mission Theology.* Pasadena, Calif.: William Carey Library.
Beyerhaus, Peter.
1971   *Missions: Which Way? Humanization or Redemption.* Grand Rapids, Mich.: Zondervan.
Blauw, Johannes.
1974   *The Missionary Nature of the Church.* 3rd ed. Grand Rapids, Mich.: Wm. B. Eerdmans.
Boer, Harry R.
1961   *Pentecost and Missions.* Grand Rapids, Mich.: Wm. B. Eerdmans.
Bosch, David J.
1980   *Witness to the World: The Christian Mission in Theological Perspective.* London: Marshall, Morgan & Scott; Atlanta, Ga.: John Knox Press.
Braaten, Carl E.
1977   *The Flaming Center: A Theology of the Christian Mission.* Philadelphia: Fortress Press.
Comblin, José.
1977   *The Meaning of Mission.* Maryknoll, N.Y.: Orbis Books.
Hahn, F.
1965   *Mission in the New Testament.* Naperville, Ill.: Alec R. Allenson.
Hillman, Eugene.
1965   *The Church as Mission.* New York: Herder & Herder.
Jeremias, J.
1958   *Jesus' Promise to the Nations.* London: SCM Press.
Lindsell, Harold.
1979   *An Evangelical Theology of Missions.* Grand Rapids, Mich.: Zondervan.
Moltmann, Jürgen.
1977   *The Church in the Power of the Spirit.* New York: Harper & Row.
1978   *The Open Church: Invitation to a Messianic Lifestyle.* London: SCM Press.
Newbigin, Lesslie.
1961   *A Faith for This One World?* New York: Harper & Row.
1964   *Trinitarian Faith and Today's Mission.* Richmond, Va.: John Knox Press.
1978   *The Open Secret.* Grand Rapids, Mich.: Wm. B. Eerdmans.
Niebuhr, H. Richard.
1956   *The Purpose of the Church and Its Ministry.* New York: Harper & Row.
Niles, D. T.
1961   *Upon the Earth.* New York: McGraw-Hill.
Peters, George W.
1972   *A Biblical Theology of Missions.* Chicago: Moody Press.
Rowley, H. H.
1955   *The Missionary Message of the Old Testament.* London: Carey Press.

Stott, John.
1975   *Christian Mission in the Modern World.* London: Falcon Books.
Vicedom, George F.
1965   *The Mission of God: An Introduction to a Theology of Mission.* St. Louis, Mo.: Concordia.

IV. Historical Perspectives of Mission

Beaver, R. Pierce.
1962   *Ecumenical Beginnings in Protestant World Mission: A History of Comity.* New York: Nelson.
1964   *From Missions to Mission.* New York: Friendship Press.
1967a   *The Christian World Mission: A Reconsideration.* Calcutta: Baptist Mission Press.
1967b   *To Advance the Gospel: Selections from the Writings of Rufus Anderson.* Grand Rapids, Mich.: Wm. B. Eerdmans.
1968   *The Missionary between the Times: A Christian Encounter With a World in Upheaval.* Garden City, N.Y.: Doubleday.
1970   *All Love Excelling.* Grand Rapids, Mich.: Wm. B. Eerdmans.
1980   *American Protestant Women in World Mission: A History of the First Feminist Movement in North America.* Grand Rapids, Mich.: Wm. B. Eerdmans.
————ed.
1977   *American Missions in Bicentennial Perspective.* Pasadena, Calif.: William Carey Library.
Berg, J. van den.
1956   *Constrained by Jesus' Love: An Inquiry into the Motives of the Missionary Awakening in Great Britain in the Period between 1698 and 1815.* Kampen: J. H. Kok.
Boberg, John T., S.V.D., and Scherer, James A., eds.
1972   *Mission in the 70's: What Direction?* Chicago: Chicago Cluster of Theological Schools.
Carey, William.
1934   *An Enquiry into the Obligation of Christians to Use Means for the Conversion of the Heathen.* Leicester, 1792; reprinted. London: Baptist Missionary Society.
Chaney, Charles L.
1976   *The Birth of Missions in America.* Pasadena, Calif.: William Carey Library.
Danker, William.
1971   *Profit for the Lord.* Grand Rapids, Mich.: Wm. B. Eerdmans.
———— and Kang Wi Jo, eds.
1971   *The Future of the Christian World Mission: Studies in Honor of R. Pierce Beaver.* Grand Rapids, Mich.: Wm. B. Eerdmans.
DuBose, Francis M.
1979   *Classics of Christian Mission.* Nashville, Tenn.: Broadman Press.
González, Justo L.
1969   *The Development of Christianity in the Latin Caribbean.* Grand Rapids, Mich.: Wm. B. Eerdmans.

Hamilton, J. Taylor, and Hamilton, Kenneth G.
1967   *History of the Moravian Church: The Renewed* Unitas Fratrum *1722-1957.* Bethlehem, Pa., Winston-Salem, N.C.: Interprovincial Board of Christian Education, Moravian Church in America.

Harnack, Adolf von.
1908   *The Mission and Expansion of Christianity in the First Three Centuries,* 2 vols. New York: G. P. Putnam's Sons.

Harr, Wilber C., ed.
1962   *Frontiers of the Christian World Mission since 1938: Essays in Honor of Kenneth Scott Latourette.* New York: Harper & Row.

Hogg, William Richey.
1952   *Ecumenical Foundations: A History of the International Missionary Council and Its Nineteenth Century Background.* New York: Harper & Row.

Kane, J. Herbert.
1975   *A Global View of Christian Missions: From Pentecost to the Present.* 2nd ed. Grand Rapids, Mich.: Baker Book House.
1978   *A Concise History of the Christian World Mission.* Grand Rapids, Mich.: Baker Book House.

Latourette, Kenneth Scott.
1970   *A History of the Expansion of Christianity,* 7 vols. Grand Rapids, Mich.: Zondervan.

Merk, Frederick, and Kerm, Lois Bannister.
1966   *Manifest Destiny and Mission in American History: A Reinterpretation.* New York: Random House.

Myklebust, Olav Guttorm.
1955-57   *The Study of Missions in Theological Education,* 2 vols. Oslo: Hovedkommisjon Forlaget Land og Kirke.

Neill, Stephen.
1965   *A History of Christian Missions.* Grand Rapids, Mich.: Wm. B. Eerdmans.

Oldham, J. H.
n.d.   *International Missionary Organization. For the Crans Meeting 22-28.* June 1920. London: Privately printed.

Van Leeuwen, Arend Th.
1964   *Christianity in World History.* New York: Charles Scribner's Sons.

Warneck, Gustav.
1906   *Outline of a History of Protestant Missions from the Reformation to the Present Time.* New York: Revell.

Warren, Max, ed.
1971   *To Apply the Gospel: Selections from the Writings of Henry Venn.* Grand Rapids, Mich.: Wm. B. Eerdmans.

V. Mission and the Religions

Anderson, Gerald H., and Stransky, Thomas F., C.S.P., eds.
1981   *Christ's Lordship and Religious Pluralism.* Maryknoll, N.Y.: Orbis Books.

Anderson, J. N. D.
1970   *Christianity and Comparative Religion.* Downers Grove, Ill.: Inter-Varsity Press.
Cox, Harvey.
1977   *Turning East: The Promise and Peril of the New Orientalism.* New York: Simon and Schuster.
Cragg, Kenneth A.
1959   *Sandals at the Mosque: Christian Presence amid Islam.* New York: Oxford University Press.
1968   *Christianity in World Perspective.* London: Lutterworth Press.
1969   *The House of Islam.* Belmont, Calif.: Dickenson Publishing Co.
1977   *The Christian and Other Religions: The Measure of Christ.* London/Oxford: Mowbrays.
Davis, Charles.
1970   *Christ and the World Religions.* London: Hodder and Stoughton.
Dawe, Donald G., and Carman, John B., eds.
1978   *Christian Faith in a Religiously Plural World.* Maryknoll, N.Y.: Orbis Books.
Freytag, W.
1957   *The Gospel and the Religions.* London: SCM Press.
Hallencreutz, Carl.
1966   *Kraemer towards Tambaram.* Lund, Sweden: C.W.K. Gleerup.
1970   *New Approaches to Men of Other Faiths, 1936–1968: A Theological Discussion,* Research Pamphlet no. 18. Geneva: World Council of Churches.
1977   *Dialogue and Community: Ecumenical Issues in Inter-Religious Relationships.* Uppsala, Sweden: Swedish Institute of Missionary Research; and Geneva: World Council of Churches.
Hick, John.
1973   *God and the Universe of Faiths: Essays in the Philosophy of Religion.* London: Macmillan.
———, ed.
1974   *Truth and Dialogue: The Relationship between World Religions.* London: Sheldon Press.
Hocking, W. E., chairman.
1932   *Rethinking Missions: A Layman's Inquiry after One Hundred Years.* New York: Harper & Row.
Hume, Robert E.
1959   *The World's Living Religions.* New York: Charles Scribner's Sons.
Kraemer, H.
1938   *The Christian Message in a Non-Christian World.* New York: Harper & Row.
1956   *Religion and the Christian Faith.* London: Lutterworth Press.
1960a   *The Communication of the Christian Faith.* London: Lutterworth Press.
1960b   *World Cultures and World Religions: The Coming Dialogue.* London: Lutterworth Press.
1962   *Why Christianity among All Religions?* London: Lutterworth Press.

Ling, Trevor.
1974   *A History of Religion East and West: An Introduction and Interpretation.* New York: Macmillan.
McCurry, Don M., ed.
1979   *The Gospel and Islam.* Monrovia, Calif.: MARC.
Miller, William M.
1976   *A Christian's Response to Islam.* Nutley, N.J.: Presbyterian and Reformed Publishing Company.
Neill, Stephen.
1970   *Christian Faith and Other Faiths: The Christian Dialogue with Other Religions.* 2nd ed. London: Oxford University Press.
Panikkar, Raymond.
1964   *The Unknown Christ of Hinduism.* London: Darton, Longman & Todd; revised and enlarged edition, 1981, London: Darton, Longman & Todd; and Maryknoll, N.Y.: Orbis Books.
1973   *The Trinity and the Religious Experience of Man.* London: Darton, Longman & Todd; and Maryknoll, N.Y.: Orbis Books.
Pickthall, Mohammed Marmaduke, trans.
n.d.   *The Meaning of the Glorious Koran.* New York: Mentor Books.
Rahula, Walpola.
1959   *What the Buddha Taught.* Bedford, N.Y.: Gordon Fraser Gallery.
Samartha, S. J.
1974   *The Hindu Response to the Unbound Christ.* Madras, India: Christian Literature Society.
1982   *Courage for Dialogue.* Maryknoll, N.Y.: Orbis Books.
———, ed.
1971   *Living Faiths and the Ecumenical Movement.* Geneva: World Council of Churches.
1974   *Living Faiths and Ultimate Goals.* Maryknoll, N.Y.: Orbis Books.
1975   *Towards World Community: The Colombo Papers.* Geneva: World Council of Churches.
1977   *Faith in the Midst of Faiths: Reflections on Dialogue in Community.* Geneva: World Council of Churches.
———, and Taylor, J. B., eds.
1973   *Christian–Muslim Dialogue.* Papers presented at the Broumana Consultation, July 12–18, 1972. Geneva: World Council of Churches.
Schlette, Heinz Robert.
1966   *Towards a Theology of Religions.* Trans. W. J. O'Hara. New York: Herder & Herder.
Sharpe, Eric J.
1975   *Comparative Religions: A History.* New York: Charles Scribner's Sons.
1977   *Faith Meets Faith: Some Christian Attitudes to Hinduism in the Nineteenth and Twentieth Centuries.* London: SCM Press.
Smith, Wilfred Cantwell.
1957   *Islam in Modern History.* Princeton, N.J.: Princeton University Press.
1965   *The Faiths of Other Men.* New York: Mentor Books.

1967   *Questions of Religious Truth.* New York: Charles Scribner's Sons.

1980   *Towards a World Theology.* Philadelphia: Westminster Press.

Taylor, John B.

1963   *The Primal Vision: Christian Presence amid African Religions.* London: SCM Press.

1971   *Thinking about Islam.* London: Lutterworth Press.

Tillich, Paul.

1963   *Christianity and the Encounter of the World Religions.* New York: Columbia University Press.

Van Straelen, Henry.

1966   *The Catholic Encounter with the World Religions.* London: Burns & Oates.

Vicedom, George F.

1963   *No Other Name: The Choice between Syncretism and Christian Universalism.* Philadelphia: Westminster Press.

Wilkins, Ronald J.

1979a   *Religions of the World.* Dubuque, Iowa: Wm. C. Brown Co.

1979b   *Religion in North America.* Dubuque, Iowa: Wm. C. Brown Co.

Wilson, Howard A.

1978   *Invasion from the East.* Minneapolis, Minn.: Augsburg Publishing House.

World Council of Churches.

1977   *Dialogue in Community.* Statement and Reports of a Theological Consultation, Chiang Mai, Thailand, April 18-27, 1977. Geneva: World Council of Churches.

VI. Mission–Church Relations

Alexander, Calvert.

1967   *The Missionary Dimension: Vatican II and the World Apostolate.* Milwaukee, Wis.: Bruce Publishing Company.

Berquist, Peter, and Lefever, Henry.

1974   *The Crisis of Dependency in Third World Ministries: A Critique of Inherited Missionary Forms in India.* Madras, India: Christian Literature Society.

Beyerhaus, Peter, and Lefever, Henry.

1964   *The Responsible Church and the Foreign Mission.* Grand Rapids, Mich.: Wm. B. Eerdmans.

Bühlmann, Walbert.

1976   *The Coming of the Third Church.* Slough, England: St. Paul Publications; Maryknoll, N.Y.: Orbis Books.

Coggins, Wade T., and Frizen, E. L., eds.

1977   *Evangelical Missions Tomorrow.* Pasadena, Calif.: William Carey Library.

Foreign Mission Conference of North America.

n.d.   *Foreign Missions Conference of North America: Annual Reports 1893-1950.* New York: Foreign Missions Conference of North America.

Hollis, Michael.
1968   *Mission, Unity and Truth. A Study of Confessional Families and Churches in Asia.* London: Lutterworth Press.
Wagner, C. Peter, ed.
1972   *Church/Mission Tensions Today.* Chicago: Moody Press.
Webster, Douglas.
1964   *Local Church and World Mission.* New York: Seabury Press.
Wilson, Samuel, ed.
1980   *Mission Handbook: North American Protestant Ministries Overseas.* 12th ed. Monrovia, Calif.: MARC.

VII. Mission, Social Justice, and Development

Abrecht, Paul, ed.
1978   *Faith, Science and the Future.* Geneva: World Council of Churches.
Adler, E.
1974   *A Small Beginning: An Assessment of the First Five Years of the Programme to Combat Racism.* Geneva: World Council of Churches.
Barnet, Richard J., and Müller, Ronald E.
1974   *Global Reach: The Power of the Multinational Corporations.* New York: Simon and Schuster.
Camara, Dom Helder.
1972   *Revolution through Peace.* New York: Harper Colophon Books.
Comblin, José.
1979   *The Church and the National Security State.* Maryknoll, N.Y.: Orbis Books.
Commission on the Churches' Participation in Development.
1975   *To Break the Chains of Oppression.* Results of an Ecumenical Study Process on Domination and Dependence. Geneva: World Council of Churches.
Corporate Information Center/National Council of Churches.
1973   *Church Investments, Corporations and Southern Africa.* New York: Friendship Press.
Corson-Finnerty, Adam Daniel.
1982   *World Citizen: Action for Global Justice.* Maryknoll, N.Y.: Orbis Books.
Dickinson, Richard D. N.
1975   *To Set at Liberty the Oppressed.* Geneva: World Council of Churches.
Elliott, Charles.
1975   *Patterns of Poverty in the Third World.* New York: Praeger.
Escobar, Samuel, and Driver, John.
1978   *Christian Mission and Social Justice.* Scottdale, Pa.: Herald Press.
Fenton, Thomas P., ed.
1975a   *Education for Justice. Participant's Workbook.* Maryknoll, N.Y.: Orbis Books.
1975b   *Education for Justice. A Resource Manual.* Maryknoll, N.Y.: Orbis Books.
Gatti, Enzo.
1974   *Rich Church—Poor Church?* Maryknoll, N.Y.: Orbis Books.

Goodall, Norman.
1964   *Christian Mission and Social Ferment.* London: Epworth Press.
Goulet, Denis.
1974   *A New Moral Order: Studies in Development Ethics and Liberation Theology.* Maryknoll, N.Y.: Orbis Books.
Holmes, Lionel, ed.
1978   *Church and Nationhood.* A collection of papers originally presented at a consultation in Basel, September 1976. New Delhi, India: World Evangelical Fellowship.
Hope, Marjorie, and Young, James.
1971   *The Struggle for Humanity: Agents of Nonviolent Change in a Violent World.* Maryknoll, N.Y.: Orbis Books.
Schumacher, E. F.
1973   *Small Is Beautiful.* New York: Harper & Row.
Sider, Ronald J.
1977a   *Rich Christians in an Age of Hunger: A Biblical Study.* New York: Paulist Press; Downers Grove, Ill.: InterVarsity Press.
1977b   *Evangelism, Salvation and Social Justice.* Bramcote, England: Grove Books.
Thomas, M. M.
1977   *Towards an Evangelical Social Gospel.* Madras, India: Christian Literature Society.
————, and Devanandan, P. D., eds.
1960   *Christian Participation in Nation-Building.* Bangalore, India: CISRS.
Verkuyl, Johannes.
1970   *The Message of Liberation in Our Age.* Grand Rapids, Mich.: Wm. B. Eerdmans.
1973   *Break Down the Walls.* Grand Rapids, Mich.: Wm. B. Eerdmans.
Verkuyl, Johannes, and Schulte Nordholt, H. G.
1974   *Responsible Revolution.* Trans. and ed. Lewis Smedes. Grand Rapids, Mich.: Wm. B. Eerdmans.
Weingartner, Erich, ed.
1976   *Church within Socialism: Church and State in East European Socialist Republics.* Rome, Italy: IDOC International.
Winter, J. A.
1971   *The Poor: A Culture of Poverty or a Poverty of Culture?* Grand Rapids, Mich.: Wm. B. Eerdmans.
World Council of Churches.
1978   *Church and State: Opening a New Ecumenical Discussion.* Geneva: World Council of Churches.

VIII. Mission, Evangelism, and Church Growth

Chaney, Charles L., and Lewis, Ron S.
1977a   *Design for Church Growth.* Nashville, Tenn.: Broadman Press.
1977b   *Manual for Design for Church Growth.* Nashville, Tenn.: Broadman Press.

Conn, Harvie M., ed.
1969   *Theological Perspectives on Church Growth.* Nutley, N.J.: Presbyterian and Reformed Publishing Co.
Dayton, Edward R.
1979   *That Everyone May Hear: Reaching the Unreached.* Monrovia, Calif.: MARC.
———, and Fraser, David A.
1980   *Planning Strategies for World Evangelization.* Grand Rapids, Mich.: Wm. B. Eerdmans.
DuBose, Francis M.
1978   *How Churches Grow in an Urban World.* Nashville, Tenn.: Broadman Press.
Glasser, Arthur F.; Hiebert, Paul G.; Wagner, C. Peter; and Winter, Ralph D.
1976   *Crucial Dimensions in World Evangelization.* Pasadena, Calif.: William Carey Library.
Green, Michael.
1970   *Evangelism in the Early Church.* Grand Rapids, Mich.: Wm. B. Eerdmans.
1979   *Evangelism—Now and Then.* Downers Grove, Ill.: InterVarsity Press.
Hesselgrave, David J.
1978   *Communicating Christ Cross-Culturally.* Grand Rapids, Mich.: Zondervan.
1980   *Planting Churches Cross-Culturally: A Guide for Home and Foreign Mission.* Grand Rapids, Mich.: Wm. B. Eerdmans.
———, ed. and contributor.
1978   *Dynamic Religious Movements: Case Studies of Rapidly Growing Religious Movements around the World.* Grand Rapids, Mich.: Zondervan.
Hogue, Dean R., and Roozen, David A., eds.
1979   *Understanding Church Growth and Decline: 1950–1978.* Princeton, N.J.: Pilgrim Press.
Johnston, Arthur.
1978   *The Battle for World Evangelism.* Wheaton, Ill.: Tyndale House.
Kelly, Dean M.
1977   *Why Conservative Churches Are Growing.* 2nd ed. New York: Harper & Row.
Krass, Alfred C.
1978   *Five Lanterns at Sundown.* Grand Rapids, Mich.: Wm. B. Eerdmans.
1982   *Evangelizing Neo-Pagan North America.* Scottdale, Pa.: Herald Press.
Lausanne Committee for World Evangelization.
1978a   "The Pasadena Consultation—Homogeneous Unit Principle," paper no. 1. Wheaton, Ill.: Lausanne Committee for World Evangelization.
1978b   "The Willowbank Report—Gospel and Culture," paper no. 2. Wheaton, Ill.: Lausanne Committee for World Evangelization.
1978c   "The Lausanne Covenant—An Exposition and Commentary by John Stott," paper no. 3. Wheaton, Ill.: Lausanne Committee for World Evangelization.

1978d   "The Glen Eyrie Report—Muslim Evangelization," paper no. 4. Wheaton, Ill.: Lausanne Committee for World Evangelization.

1980a   "Christian Witness to Refugees," paper no. 5. Wheaton, Ill.: Lausanne Committee for World Evangelization.

1980b   "Christian Witness to the Chinese People," paper no. 6. Wheaton, Ill.: Lausanne Committee for World Evangelization.

1980c   "Christian Witness to the Jewish People," paper no. 7. Wheaton, Ill.: Lausanne Committee for World Evangelization.

1980d   "Christian Witness to Secularized People," paper no. 8. Wheaton, Ill.: Lausanne Committee for World Evangelization.

1980e   "Christian Witness to Large Cities," paper no. 9. Wheaton, Ill.: Lausanne Committee for World Evangelization.

1980f   "Christian Witness to Nominal Christians among Roman Catholics," paper no. 10. Wheaton, Ill.: Lausanne Committee for World Evangelization.

1980g   "Christian Witness to New Religious Movements," paper no. 11. Wheaton, Ill.: Lausanne Committee for World Evangelization.

1980h   "Christian Witness to Marxists," paper no. 12. Wheaton, Ill.: Lausanne Committee for World Evangelization.

1981a   "The Thailand Statement 1980," *International Bulletin of Missionary Research* 5, no. 1 (January): 29–31.

1981b   *How Shall They Hear?* Proceedings and Report from the Consultation on World Evangelization, Pattaya, Thailand, 1980. Minneapolis, Minn.: Worldwide Publications.

McGavran, Donald A.

1955   *Bridges of God: A Study in the Strategy of Missions.* New York: Friendship Press.

1959   *How Churches Grow.* London: World Dominion Press.

1965   *Church Growth and Christian Mission.* New York: Harper & Row.

1974   *The Clash between Christianity and Cultures.* Grand Rapids, Mich.: Baker Book House.

1979   *Ethnic Realities and the Church: Lessons from India.* Pasadena, Calif.: William Carey Library.

1980   *Understanding Church Growth.* 2nd ed. Grand Rapids, Mich.: Wm. B. Eerdmans.

——, and Arn, Winfield C.

1973   *How to Grow a Church.* Glendale, Calif.: Regal Books.

1977   *Ten Steps to Church Growth.* New York: Harper & Row.

McQuilkin, J. Robertson.

1973   *How Biblical Is the Church Growth Movement?* Chicago: Moody Press.

Morikawa, Jitsuo.

1979   *Biblical Dimensions of Church Growth.* Valley Forge, Pa.: Judson Press.

Owens, Owen D.

1981   *Growing Churches for a New Age.* Valley Forge, Pa.: Judson Press.

Padilla, C. René, ed.

1976   *The New Face of Evangelicalism.* London: Hodder & Stoughton; Downers Grove, Ill.: InterVarsity Press.

1982   "The Unity of the Church and the Homogeneous Unit Principle,"
     International Bulletin of Missionary Research 6, no. 1 (January):
     23–30.

Peters, G. W.
 1968   *Saturation Evangelism.* Grand Rapids, Mich.: Zondervan.
 1981   *A Theology of Church Growth.* Grand Rapids, Mich.: Zondervan.

Shenk, Wilbert R., ed.
 1973   *The Challenge of Church Growth: A Symposium.* Elkhart, Ind.: In-
     stitute of Mennonite Studies.

Van Engen, Charles.
 1981   *The Growth of the True Church.* Amsterdam: Editions Rodopi.

Wagner, C. Peter.
 1971   *Frontiers in Missionary Strategy.* Chicago: Moody Press.
 1976   *Your Church Can Grow: Seven Vital Signs of a Healthy Church.*
     Glendale, Calif.: Regal Books.
 1979   *Our Kind of People: The Ethical Dimension of Church Growth in
     America.* Atlanta, Ga.: John Knox Press.
 1981   *Church Growth and the Whole Gospel.* New York: Harper & Row.

———, and Dayton, Edward R., eds.
 1979   *Unreached Peoples '79.* Elgin, Ill.: David C. Cook Publishing Co.
 1980   *Unreached Peoples '80.* Elgin, Ill.: David C. Cook Publishing Co.

Watson, David.
 1976   *I Believe in Evangelism.* Grand Rapids, Mich.: Wm. B. Eerdmans.

Waymire, Bob, and Wagner, C. Peter.
 1980   *The Church Growth Survey Handbook.* 2nd ed. Santa Clara, Calif.:
     The Church Growth Bulletin.

IX. Mission and Culture

Bühlmann, Walbert.
 1979   *The Missions on Trial.* Maryknoll, N.Y.: Orbis Books.

Costas, Orlando E.; Jacobs, Donald B.; et al.
 1978   "Conversion and Culture," *Gospel in Context* 1, no. 3, pp. 4–40.

Idowu, E. Bolaji.
 1965   *Towards an Indigenous Church.* London: Oxford University Press.

Jank, Margaret.
 1977   *Culture Shock.* Chicago: Moody Press.

Kraft, Charles H.
 1980   *Christianity in Culture: A Study in Dynamic Biblical Theologizing in
     Cross-Cultural Perspective.* Maryknoll, N.Y.: Orbis Books.

Loewen, Jacob.
 1975   *Culture and Human Values.* Pasadena, Calif.: William Carey Li-
     brary.

Luzbetak, Louis J.
 1975   *The Church and Cultures.* Pasadena, Calif.: William Carey Library.

McGavran, Donald A.
 1974   *The Clash between Christianity and Cultures.* Washington, D.C.:
     Canon Press.

Mayers, Marvin K.
 1974   *Christianity Confronts Culture.* Grand Rapids, Mich.: Zondervan.

Nida, Eugene A.
1954   *Customs and Cultures.* New York: Harper & Row (reprinted 1975 by William Carey Library, Pasadena, Calif.).
1960   *Message and Mission.* New York: Harper & Row (reprinted 1972 by William Carey Library, Pasadena, Calif.).
1968   *Religion across Cultures: A Study in the Communication of Christian Faith.* New York: Harper & Row.
———, and Reyburn, William.
1981   *Meaning Across Cultures.* Maryknoll, N.Y.: Orbis Books.
Niebuhr, H. Richard.
1951   *Christ and Culture.* New York: Harper & Row.
Noble, Lowell L.
1975   *Naked and Not Ashamed.* Jackson, Mich.: By the author.
Richardson, Don.
1974   *Peace Child.* Glendale, Calif.: Regal Books.
Smalley, William A., ed.
1967   *Readings in Missionary Anthropology.* Reprinted 1974 by William Carey Library, Pasadena, Calif.
Stendahl, Krister.
1976   *Paul among Jews and Gentiles and Other Essays.* Philadelphia: Fortress Press.
Stott, John, and Coote, Robert, eds.
1979   *Gospel and Culture.* Pasadena, Calif.: William Carey Library.
Von Allmen, Daniel.
1975   "The Birth of Theology," *International Review of Mission* 44, no. 253 (January): 37–55.
Wallace, Anthony F. C.
1966   *Religion: An Anthropological View.* New York: Random House.
Weekes, Richard V.
1964   *Pakistan, Birth and Growth of a Muslim Nation.* Princeton, N.J.: Van Nostrand.
———, ed.
1978   *Muslim Peoples: A World Ethnographic Survey.* Westport, Conn.: Greenwood Press.
Yamamori, Tetsunao, and Taber, Charles R., eds.
1975   *Christopaganism or Indigenous Christianity?* Pasadena, Calif.: William Carey Library.

X. Mission and Ecumenicity

Abbott, Walter M., S.J., ed.
1966   *The Documents of Vatican II.* New York: Guild Press.
All Africa Conference of Churches.
1972   "Kinshasa Declaration," *International Review of Mission* 61, no. 242 (April): 115–16.
Anderson, Gerald H., ed.
1982   *Witnessing to the Kingdom: Melbourne and Beyond.* Maryknoll, N.Y.: Orbis Books.

Arias, Mortimer.
1975 ". . . That the World May Believe . . ." *International Review of Mission* 64, no. 255 (July): 237-42.
Arlt, Augusto E. Fernández.
1962 "The Significance of the Chilean Pentecostals' Admission to the World Council of Churches," *International Review of Mission* 51: no. 204 (October): 480-82.
Beattie, John.
1952 "Willingen 1952," *International Review of Mission* 41, no. 63 (October): 433-43.
Beyerhaus, Peter.
1972 *Shaken Foundations: Theological Foundations for Mission.* Grand Rapids, Mich.: Zondervan.
1974 *Bangkok 1973: The Beginning or End of World Mission?* Grand Rapids, Mich.: Zondervan.
Bria, Jon.
1980 *Martyria/Mission: The Witness of the Orthodox Churches Today.* Geneva: World Council of Churches.
Castro, Emilio.
1973 "Bangkok, The New Opportunity," *International Review of Mission* 62, no. 246 (April): 136-43.
Cavert, Samuel McCrea.
1970 *Church Cooperation and Unity in America 1900-1970.* New York: Association Press.
Commission on World Mission and Evangelism.
1980 *Your Kingdom Come: Report on the World Conference on Mission and Evangelism* (Melbourne, Australia, May, 12-25 1980). Geneva: World Council of Churches.
DeSilva, F. S.
1957 "The Significance of Prapat," *International Review of Mission* 46, no. 82 (July): 306-9.
Douglass, G. D., ed.
1975 *Let the Whole World Hear His Voice.* Minneapolis, Minn.: Worldwide Publications.
Fenton, Horace L.
1966 "Debits and Credits—The Wheaton Congress," *International Review of Mission* 55, no. 220 (October): 472-79.
Fey, Harold E., ed.
1970 *The Ecumenical Advance: A History of the Ecumenical Movement.* Vol. 2: *1948-1968.* Philadelphia: Westminster Press.
Gaines, David P.
1966 *The World Council of Churches: A Study of Its Background and History.* Peterborough, N.H.: Noone House.
Glasser, Arthur.
1969 "What Has Been the Evangelical Stance, New Delhi to Uppsala," *Evangelical Missions Quarterly* 5, no. 3, pp. 129-50.
Goodall, Norman.
1952 "Towards Willingen," *International Review of Mission* 41, no. 161 (April): 129-38.

1955   "Evanston and the World Mission of the Church," *International Review of Mission* 44, no. 172 (January): 85–92.
1958   "Evangelicals and WCC–IMC," *International Review of Mission* 47, no. 185 (April): 210–15.
1968   *The Uppsala Report 1968.* Geneva: World Council of Churches.

Greaves, L. B.
1958   "The All Africa Church Conference: Ibadan, Nigeria: 10th to 20th January, 1958," *International Review of Mission* 47, no. 186 (July): 257–64.

Hayward, Victor.
1971   "A Survey of National Christian Councils," *International Review of Mission* 60, no. 240 (October): 512–21.

Henry, Carl F.H., and Mooneyham, W. Stanley, eds.
1967   *One Race, One Gospel, One Task.* Minneapolis, Minn.: Worldwide Publications.

Hubble, Gwenyth.
1958   "The Ghana Assembly: A Report on Group Discussion," *International Review of Mission* 47, no. 185 (April): 143–49.

International Review of Missiom (IRM).
1957   "The Prapat Statement: March 1957," *IRM* 46, no. 182 (July): 309–13.
1966   "Wheaton Declaration: The Congress on the Church's Worldwide Mission," *IRM* 55, no. 220 (October): 458–76.
1969   "Renewal in Mission." The Report as Adopted by the Uppsala Assembly. Part 1: "A Mandate for Mission," *IRM* 58, nos. 230–31 (April and July), 145–47; Part 2: "Opportunities for Mission," pp. 354–57; Part 3: "Freedom for Mission," pp. 357–60.
1974   "Meeting in Bangkok," *IRM* 62, no. 246 (April): 135–230.
1976   "The Nairobi Assembly: Implications for Mission," *IRM* 65, no. 257 (January): 1–134.
1978   "Edinburgh to Melbourne," *IRM* 67, no. 267 (July): 249–370.
1980   "Melbourne Reports and Reflections," *IRM* 69, no. 275 (July): 467–574.

Jackson, G. C.
1964   "Report from Bangkok," *International Review of Mission* 53, no. 211 (April): 307–17.

Jacobson, Nolan Pliny, and Winn, William E.
1962   "The Live Centre in Asia," *International Review of Mission* 51, no. 204 (October): 421–23.

Lefever, H. C.
1960   "The Preparation of Missionaries 1910 and 1960," *International Review of Mission* 49, no. 193 (April): 281–90.

Lindsell, Harold, ed.
1966   *The Church's Worldwide Mission.* Waco, Texas: Word Books.

Loffler, Paul.
1977   "The Confessing Community: Evangelism in Ecumenical Perspective," *International Review of Mission* 66, no. 264 (October): 339–48.

Nagpur, John.
1962   "New Delhi, 1961: The Third Assembly of the World Council of Churches," *International Review of Mission* 51, no. 202 (April): 137–52.
Newbigin, Lesslie.
1958   *One Body, One Gospel, One World: The Christian Mission Today.* London: International Missionary Council.
Nissen, Karsten.
1974   "Mission and Unity: A Look at the Integration of the IMC and WCC," *International Review of Mission* 63, no. 252 (October): 539–50.
Orchard, R. K.
1957   "I.M.C.-W.C.C. Relations: A Personal View," *International Review of Mission* 46, no. 182 (July): 299–305.
1957   "The I.M.C. Assembly in Ghana," *International Review of Mission* 46, no. 181 (April): 197–200.
1964   *Witness in Six Continents.* New York: Friendship Press.
Paton, David N., ed.
1976   *Breaking Barriers: Nairobi, 1975.* Grand Rapids, Mich.: Wm. B. Eerdmans.
Ranson, Charles W.
1964   "Mexico City, 1963," *International Review of Mission* 53, no. 210 (April): 137–46.
Setiloane, G. M.
1970   "The Missionary and His Task—At Edinburgh and Today," *International Review of Mission* 59, no. 233 (January): 55–66.
Smith, Eugene L.
1966   "Congress on the Church's Worldwide Mission," *International Review of Mission* 55, no. 220 (October): 457.
1966   "The Wheaton Congress in the Eyes of an Ecumenical Observer," *International Review of Mission* 55, no. 220 (October): 480–82.
Stott, John.
1975   "The Significance of Lausanne," *International Review of Mission* 64, no. 255 (July): 288–94.
Visser 't Hooft, W. A., ed.
1961   *The New Delhi Report.* London: SCM Press.
Wieser, Thomas.
1966   *Planning for Mission.* London: Lutterworth Press.
1978   "Giving Account of the Hope: From Bangkok to Nairobi," *International Review of Mission* 67, no. 266 (April): 127–36.
Williams, Theodore, ed.
1979   *World Missions: Building Bridges or Barriers?* Bangalore, India: World Evangelical Fellowship Missions Commission.
Winter, Ralph.
1973   *The Evangelical Response to Bangkok.* Pasadena, Calif.: William Carey Library.
World Council of Churches.
1967   *The Church for Others and the Church for the World.* Geneva: World Council of Churches.

1974   "Evangelism 1974: A Symposium," *International Review of Mission* 63, no. 249 (January): 96–123.

XI. Mission and Spirituality

Bosch, David.
1979   *A Spirituality of the Road*. Scottdale, Pa.: Herald Press.

Fraser, Ian M.
1975   *The Fire Runs*. London: SCM Press.

Gannon, Thomas M., S.J., and Traub, George W., S.J.
1968   *The Desert and the City: An Interpretation of the History of Christian Spirituality*. London: Macmillan.

Hall, Mary.
1980   *The Impossible Dream: The Spirituality of Dom Helder Camara*. Maryknoll, N.Y.: Orbis Books.

Newbigin, Lesslie.
1972   *Journey into Joy*. Grand Rapids, Mich.: Wm. B. Eerdmans.

Raguin, Yves.
1973   *I Am Sending You: Spirituality of the Missioner*. Manila: East Asian Pastoral Institute.

Reilly, Michael Collins, S.J.
1978   *Spirituality for Mission*. Maryknoll, N.Y.: Orbis Books.

Troutman, Charles.
1976   *Everything You Want to Know about the Mission Field, but Are Afraid You Won't Learn until You Get There*. Downers Grove, Ill.: InterVarsity Press.

XII. Mission: Area Studies

Africa and Madagascar

All Africa Conference of Churches (AACC).
1963   *Drumbeats from Kampala: Report of the First Assembly of the All Africa Conference of Churches*. London: Lutterworth Press.

1969   *Engagement: The Second AACC Assembly, "Abidjan 1969."* Nairobi: AACC.

1974   *Evangelization of "Frontier Situations in Africa:" Report of a Consultation Organized by the AACC, 15–19 December 1973, Nairobi, Kenya*. Compiled and ed. George K. Mambo and Manjiru Matenjwa. Nairobi: AACC.

1975   *The Struggle Continues: Official Report of the Third Assembly of the AACC, Lusaka, Zambia, 12–24 May 1974*. Nairobi: AACC.

Andersson, E.
1968   *Churches at the Grass Roots: A Study in Congo-Brazzaville*. London: Lutterworth Press.

Appiah-Kubi, Kofi, and Torres, Sergio, eds.
1979   *African Theology en Route*. Maryknoll, N.Y.: Orbis Books.

Barrett, D. B.
1968   *Schism and Renewal in Africa: An Analysis of Six Thousand Contemporary Religious Movements*. London: Oxford University Press.

Boer, Jan Harm.
1979   *Missionary Messengers of Liberation in a Colonial Context.* Amster-
            dam: Editions Rodopi.
Boesak, Allan Aubrey.
1977   *Farewell to Innocence: A Socio-Ethical Study on Black Theology and
            Black Power.* Maryknoll, N.Y.: Orbis Books.
Bosch, D. J.
1974   *Missiological Developments in South Africa.* Frankfurt: Janus.
Cassidy, Michael.
1974   *Prisoners of Hope.* Lesotho: African Enterprise.
——, ed.
1974   *I Will Heal Their Land.* Lesotho: African Enterprise.
——; Le Fuevre, Charmain; and Blanc, Anne, eds.
1974   *I Will Heal Their Land . . . Papers of the South African Congress on
            Mission and Evangelism,* Durban 1973. Pietermaritzburg: Africa En-
            terprise.
—— and Osei-Mensah, Gottfried.
1978a   *Together in One Place: The Story of PACLA* [Pan African Christian
            Leadership Assembly]. Nairobi, Kenya: Evangel Publishing House.
—— and Osei-Mensah, Gottfried, eds.
1978b   *Facing the New Challenges: The Message of PACLA.* Kisumu,
            Kenya: Evangel Publishing House.
DeGruchy, John W.
1979   *The Church Struggle in South Africa.* Grand Rapids, Mich.: Wm. B.
            Eerdmans.
Dickson, Kwesi A. and Ellingworth, Paul, eds.
1969   *Biblical Revelation and African Beliefs.* Maryknoll, N.Y.: Orbis
            Books.
Hastings, Adrian.
1967   *Church and Mission in Modern Africa.* London: Burns & Oates.
Hayward, Victor E. W.
1963   *African Independent Church Movements.* London: Edinburgh
            House Press.
Henderson, Lawrence.
1979   *Angola: Five Centuries of Conflict.* Ithaca, N.Y.: Cornell University
            Press.
Ilogu, E. C. O.
1974   *Christian Ethics in an African Background: A Study of the Inter-
            action of Christianity and Ibo Culture.* Leiden: E. J. Brill.
Jacobs, Donald; Milimo, John; Kibicho, S. G.; et al.
1972   *A New Look at Christianity in Africa.* Geneva: World Student Chris-
            tian Federation.
McVeigh, Malcolm J.
1974   *God in Africa: Conceptions of God in African Traditional Religion
            and Christianity.* Cape Cod, Mass.: Claude Stark, Inc.
Martin, Marie-Louise.
1975   *Kimbangua: An African Prophet and His Church.* Trans. Basil
            Blackwell. Grand Rapids, Mich.: Wm. B. Eerdmans.
Mbiti, John.
1971   *New Testament Eschatology in an African Background. A Study of*

the Encounter between New Testament Theology and African Traditional Concepts. London: Oxford University Press.

1973   *Love and Marriage in Africa.* London: Longman.

1975   *African Religions and Philosophy.* Garden City, N.Y.: Doubleday Anchor Books.

Mothabi, Moegethi, B. G.

1980   "The Theory and Practice of Black Resistance to Apartheid: A Socio-Ethical Analysis of the Internal Struggle for Political and Social Change in South Africa, 1948–1978." Unpublished Ph.D. dissertation. Boston: Boston University.

Nyamiti, Charles.

1978   *African Tradition and the Christian God.* Kenya: Gaba Publications.

Oosthuizen, G. C.

1968   *Post-Christianity in Africa: A Theological and Anthropological Study.* Grand Rapids, Mich.: Wm. B. Eerdmans.

Pobee, John S.

1979   *Toward an African Theology.* Nashville, Tenn.: Abingdon.

Saeveras, Olav.

1974   *On Church-Mission Relations in Ethiopia: 1944–1969.* Lunde: Lunde Forlag og Bakhandel A/S.

Sales, J. M.

1971   *The Planting of the Church in South Africa.* Grand Rapids, Mich.: Wm. B. Eerdmans.

Shorter, Aylward.

1975   *African Christian Theology: Adaptation or Incarnation?* London: Geoffrey Chapman.

Smith, Edwin W.

1926   *The Christian Message in Africa: A Study Based on the Work of the International Conference at Le Zoute, Belgium, 14–21 September 1926.* London: International Missionary Council.

Sundkler, B. G. M.

1961   *Bantu Prophets in South Africa.* London: Oxford University Press.

1962   *The Christian Ministry in Africa.* London: SCM Press.

Taylor, J. V.

1958   "Processes of Growth in an African Church." *International Missionary Council* Research Pamphlet no. 6. London: SCM Press.

————, ed.   *The Wholeness of Human Life: Papers Presented at the Ibadan Consultation with Special Reference to African Traditional Religion.* Ibadan: Daystar Press.

———— and Lehmann, D. A.

1961   *Christians of the Copperbelt: The Growth of the Church in Northern Rhodesia.* London: SCM Press.

Turner, H. W.

1968   *African Independent Churches.* 2 Vols. New York: Oxford University Press.

Verstraelen, F. J.

1975   *An African Church in Transition: From Missionary Dependence to Mutuality in Mission.* Leiden: Interuniversity Institute for Missiological and Ecumenical Research. Part I: chapters I–IX and Part II: chapters X–XIII.

Asia and the Pacific

Anderson, G. H., ed.
1976a   *Asian Voices in Christian Theology.* Maryknoll, N.Y.: Orbis Books.
1976b   *Studies in Philippine Church History.* Ithaca, N.Y.: Cornell University Press.
Boyd, Robin H. S.
1974   *India and the Latin Captivity of the Church: The Cultural Context of the Gospel.* London and New York: Cambridge University Press.
Bühlmann, Walbert.
1980   *The Search for God: An Encounter with the Peoples and Religions of Asia.* Maryknoll, N.Y.: Orbis Books.
Caldarola, Carlo.
1979   *Christianity: The Japanese Way.* Leiden: E. J. Brill.
Chang Lit-sen.
1970   *Strategy of Missions in the Orient. Christian Impact on the Pagan World.* Nutley, N.J.: Presbyterian and Reformed Publishing Company.
Cho, David J., ed.
1976   *New Forces in Missions: The Official Report of the Asian Missions Association.* Seoul: East-West Center for Missions Research and Development.
Christian Conference of Asia (CCA).
1973a   *Christian Conference of Asia Fifth Assembly: 6–12 June 1973, Singapore.* Bangkok: CCA.
1973b   *Christian Action in the Asian Struggle.* Singapore: CCA.
1976   *Mission in Asia Today. Papers from Hong Kong, 1975.* Singapore: CCA.
Dawe, Donald G.
n.d.   *Paul Interpreted for India.* Patiala, India: Punjabi University.
Devanandan, Paul D.
1962   *Christian Issues in Southern Asia.* New York: Friendship Press.
Drummond, R. H.
1971   *A History of Christianity in Japan.* Grand Rapids, Mich.: Wm. B. Eerdmans.
East Asia Christian Conference.
1950   *The Christian Prospect in Eastern Asia: Papers and Minutes of the East Asia Christian Conference, Bangkok, December 3–11, 1949.* New York: Friendship Press.
1953   *Christ—The Hope of Asia: Papers and Minutes of the Ecumenical Study Conference for East Asia, Lucknow, India, December 27–30, 1953.* Madras, India: Christian Literature Society.
1957   *The Common Evangelistic Task of the Churches in East Asia: Papers and minutes of the E.A.C.C. Prapat, Indonesia 17–26 March 1957.* Prapat: East Asia Christian Conference.
Elwood, Douglas J.
1980   *Asian Christian Theology: Emerging Themes.* Philadelphia: Westminster Press.

———, ed.
1976   *What Asian Christians Are Thinking: A Theological Source Book.*
        Quezon City, Philippines: New Day Publishers.
Fabella, Virginia, ed.
1980   *Asia's Struggle for Full Humanity.* Maryknoll, N.Y.: Orbis Books.
Foreman, Charles.
1982   *The Island Churches of the South Pacific: Emergence in the Twentieth
        Century.* Maryknoll, N.Y.: Orbis Books.
George, M. V.
1971   *My Lord and My God: An Introduction to Christology.* Kerala, India:
        St. Paul's Book Dept.
Germany, Charles H.
1965   *Protestant Theologies in Modern Japan: A History of Dominant The-
        ological Currents from 1920-1960.* Tokyo: IISR Press.
Hammer, Raymond.
1962   *Japan's Religious Ferment: Christian Presence amid Faiths Old and
        New.* New York: Oxford University Press.
Hayward, V. E. W., ed.
1966   *The Church as Christian Community: Three Studies of North Indian
        Churches.* London: Lutterworth Press.
Hunt, Everett Nichols, Jr.
1980   *Protestant Pioneers in Korea.* Maryknoll, N.Y.: Orbis Books.
International Missionary Council.
1961   *Beyond the Reef: Records of the Conference of Churches and Mis-
        sions in the Pacific Malua Theological College, Western Samoa, 22
        April-4 May, 1961.* London: International Missionary Council.
Katoppo, Marianne.
1980   *Compassionate and Free: An Asian Woman's Theology.* Maryknoll,
        N.Y.: Orbis Books.
Kitamori, Kazoh.
1965   *Theology of the Pain of God.* Richmond/Atlanta: John Knox Press.
Koyama, Kosuke.
1974   *Pilgrim or Tourist?* Singapore: Christian Conference of Asia.
1977   *No Handle on the Cross.* Maryknoll, N.Y.: Orbis Books.
1978   *Waterbuffalo Theology.* Maryknoll, N.Y.: Orbis Books.
1979   *Three Mile an Hour God: Biblical Reflections.* Maryknoll, N.Y.: Or-
        bis Books.
Kraemer, H.
1958   *From Missionfield to Independent Church.* The Hague: Boekencen-
        trum.
Mooneyham, W. Stanley, ed.
1969   *Christ Seeks Asia: Official Reference Volume Asia-South Pacific
        Congress on Evangelism, Singapore 1968.* Hong Kong: Rock House.
Nelson, Martin L.
1976   *The How and Why of Third World Missions: An Asian Case Study.*
        Pasadena, Calif.: William Carey Library.
Niles, D. Preman, and Thomas, T. K., eds.
1979   *Witnessing to the Kingdom.* Singapore: Christian Conference of
        Asia.

Osthathios, Geevarghese Mar.
1980   *Theology of a Classless Society.* Maryknoll, N.Y.: Orbis Books.
Pacific Council of Churches.
1972   *The Fourth World Meets: The Report of the Pacific Conference of Churches Assembly, Davui Levu, Fiji, 1–4 May 1971.* Suva, Fiji: Pacific Council of Churches.
1976   *Report of the Third Assembly: The Pacific Council of Churches.* Suva, Fiji: Pacific Council of Churches.
n.d.   *Market Basket Media: The Report of the Evaluation Conference on Christian Communication in the Pacific, Suva, Fiji.* Honoria: Provincial Press.
1973   *SPADES: South Pacific Action for Development Strategy. A Report of the Conference on Development in Vila, New Hebrides, in January 1973.* Suva, Fiji: Pacific Council of Churches.
Phillips, James J.
1981   *From the Rising of the Sun: Christians and Society in Contemporary Japan.* Maryknoll, N.Y.: Orbis Books.
Song, Choan-Seng.
1979   *Third-Eye Theology.* Maryknoll, N.Y.: Orbis Books.
1982   *The Compassionate God.* Maryknoll, N.Y.: Orbis Books.
Taylor, Richard W., ed.
1976   *Society and Religion. Essays in Honour of M. M. Thomas.* Madras, India: Christian Literature Society.
Than, U Kyaw.
1973   *Joint Laborers in Hope: A Report of the EACC 1968–1973.* Bangkok: Christian Conference of Asia.
———, ed.
1959   *Witnesses Together: Being the Official Report of the Inaugural Assembly of the EACC, held at Kuala Lumpur, Malaya, May 14–24, 1959.* Rangoon: East Asia Christian Conference.
1960   *A Decisive Hour for the Christian Mission: The EACC 1959 and the John R. Mott Memorial Lectures.* London: SCM Press.
Thomas, M. M.
1965   *Religion, State and Ideologies in East Asia.* (With M. Abel.) Bangkok: Eastern Asia Christian Conference.
1966   *The Christian Response to the Asian Revolution.* London: SCM Press.
1969   *The Acknowledged Christ of the Indian Renaissance.* London: SCM Press.
1970   *Salvation and Humanization.* Madras, India: Christian Literature Society.
1975   *Man and the Universe of Faiths. Inter-religious Dialogue Series.* No. 7. Madras, India: Christian Literature Society.
Tippett, Alan Richard.
1977   *The Deep Sea Canoe: The Story of Third World Missionaries in the South Pacific.* Pasadena, Calif.: William Carey Library.
Van Akkeren, P.
1970   *Sri and Christ: A Study of the Indigenous Church in East Java.* London: Lutterworth Press.

Visser 't Hooft, W. A.
1959   "The Significance of the Asian Churches in the Ecumenical Move-
           ment." *The Ecumenical Review* 11, no. 4 (July): 365–76.
Wong, James; Larsen, Peter; and Pentecost, Edward.
1973   *Missions from the Third World: A World Survey of Non-Western
           Missions in Asia, Africa and Latin America.* Singapore: Church
           Growth Study Center.
Worsley, Peter.
1957   *The Trumpet Shall Sound: A Study of "Cargo" Cults in Melanesia.*
           London: MacGibbon & Kee.

Latin America and the Caribbean

Antoine, Charles.
1973   *Church and Power in Brazil.* Maryknoll, N.Y.: Orbis Books.
Arias, Esther and Mortimer.
1980   *The Cry of My People. Out of Captivity in Latin America.* New York:
           Friendship Press.
Atkins, H. L., Jr.
1971   "The Church in the Spanish and French Caribbean," *International
           Review of Mission* 60, no. 238 (April): 192–95.
Barreiro, Alvaro.
1982   *Basic Ecclesial Communities: The Evangelization of the Poor.* Mary-
           knoll, N.Y.: Orbis Books.
Barrett, Leonard E.
1977   *The Rastafarians: The Dreadlocks of Jamaica.* Kingston, Jamaica:
           Sangster's Book Stores, in association with Heinenmann Educational
           Books.
Bastide, Roger.
1971   *African Civilizations in the New World.* New York: Harper & Row.
Beach, Harlan P.
1916   *Renascent Latin America: An Outline and Interpretation of the Con-
           gress on Christian Work in Latin America, held in Panama, 19–29
           February 1916.* New York: Missionary Education Movement of the
           United States and Canada.
Brown, Robert McAfee.
1978   *Theology in a New Key.* Philadelphia: Westminster Press.
Bruneau, Thomas C.
1974   *The Political Transformation of the Brazilian Catholic Church.* Lon-
           don: Cambridge University Press.
Chaplain, David.
1971   "Caribbean Ecumenism," *International Review of Mission* 60, no.
           238 (April): 186–91.
Coleman, William Jackson.
1958   *Latin American Catholicism: A Self-Evaluation.* Maryknoll, N.Y.:
           Maryknoll Publications.
Conference of Latin American Bishops (CELAM).
1970   *Latin American Episcopal Council, Second General Conference of
           Latin American Bishops, Medellín, 1968: The Church in the Present-*

day Transformation of Latin America in the Light of the Council. 2 vols. Bogotá: CELAM.

Costas, Orlando.
1976   *Theology of the Crossroads in Latin America.* Amsterdam: Editions Rodopi.
De Santa Ana, Julio.
1977   *Good News to the Poor.* Maryknoll, N.Y.: Orbis Books.
———, ed.
1979   *Toward a Church of the Poor.* Maryknoll, N.Y.: Orbis Books.
Dussel, Enrique.
1976   *History and the Theology of Liberation.* Maryknoll, N.Y.: Orbis Books.
1982   *A History of the Church in Latin America: Colonialism and Liberation (1492–1979).* Trans. Alan Neely. Grand Rapids, Mich.: Wm. B. Eerdmans.
Eagleson, John, ed.
1975   *Christians and Socialism. Documentation of the Christians for Socialism Movement in Latin America.* Trans. John Drury. Maryknoll, N.Y.: Orbis Books.
———, and Scharper, Philip, eds.
1979   *Puebla and Beyond.* Maryknoll, N.Y.: Orbis Books.
———, and Torres, Sergio, eds.
1981   *The Challenge of Basic Christian Communities.* Maryknoll, N.Y.: Orbis Books.
Erskine, Noel Leo.
1981   *Decolonizing Theology.* Maryknoll, N.Y.: Orbis Books.
Flanagan, Padraig, ed.
1982   *A New Missionary Era.* Maryknoll, N.Y.: Orbis Books.
Griffin, C. C.
1961   *The Enlightenment and Latin American Independence.* Ithaca, N.Y.: Cornell University Press.
Hamid, Idris, ed.
1977   *Out of the Depths.* Trinidad: St. Andrew's Theological College.
International Review of Mission.
1979   "Mission without Missions." Vol. 68, no. 27 (July).
Kadt, Emanuel D.
1970   *Catholic Radicals in Brazil.* London: Oxford University Press.
Kessler, J. B. A.
1967   *A Study of the Older Protestant Churches and Missions in Peru and Chile.* Goes: Oosterbaan & Le Cointre N.V.
Kirk, Andrew.
1979   *Liberation Theology: An Evangelical View from the Third World.* Atlanta, Ga.: John Knox Press.
1980   *Theology Encounters Revolution.* Downers Grove, Ill.: InterVarsity Press.
Kirkwood, Dean R.
1980   *Renewal amidst Revolution.* Valley Forge, Pa.: Judson Press.
Lalive D'Epinay, C.
1969   *Haven of the Masses: A Study of the Pentecostal Movement in Chile.* London: Lutterworth Press.

Lernoux, Penny.
1980   *Cry of the People.* Garden City, N.Y.: Doubleday.
Levine, David, ed.
1980   *Church and Politics in Latin America.* Beverly Hills: Sage Publications.
McGavran, D. A.
1963   *Church Growth in Mexico.* Grand Rapids, Mich.: Wm. B. Eerdmans.
Materne, Yves.
1980   *The Indian Awakening in Latin America.* New York: Friendship Press.
Míguez Bonino, José.
1974   *Doing Theology in a Revolutionary Situation.* Philadelphia: Fortress Press.
1976   *Christians and Marxists: The Mutual Challenge to Revolution.* Grand Rapids, Mich.: Wm. B. Eerdmans.
1979   *Room to Be People.* Philadelphia: Fortress Press.
Ribeiro, Darcy.
1972   *The Americas and Civilization.* New York: E. P. Dutton.
Sinclair, John.
1967   *Protestantism in Latin America: A Bibliographical Guide.* Pasadena, Calif.: William Carey Library.
Speer, Robert E.; Inman, Samuel G.; and Sanders, K. Franks, eds.
1925   *Christian Work in South America at Montevideo, Uruguay, April 1925.* 2 vols. New York: Fleming H. Revell.
Vallier, Jean.
1970   *Catholicism, Social Control and Modernization in Latin America.* Englewood Cliffs, N.J.: Prentice-Hall.
Wagner, C. Peter.
1973   *Look Out! The Pentecostals Are Coming.* Carol Stream, Ill.: Creation House.
Willems, Emilio.
1967   *Followers of the New Faith: Social Change and the Rise of Protestantism in Brazil and Chile.* Nashville, Tenn.: Vanderbilt University Press.
World Council of Churches.
1961   *Christians and Rapid Social Change in Latin America: Findings of the First Latin American Consultation on Church and Society. 23–27 July 1961, Huampani, Peru.* Montevideo: Latin American Commission on Church and Society/Geneva: World Council of Churches.

North American Minorities

BLACKS

Boberg, John, S.V.D., ed.
1976   *The Word in the World, Divine Word Missionaries, '76 Black Apostolate.* Techny, Ill.: Society of the Divine Word.
Bruce, Calvin E., and Jones, William R., eds.
1973   *Black Theology II. Essays on the Formation and Outreach of Con-*

temporary Black Theology. Lewisburg, Pa.: Bucknell University Press.

Cleage, Albert B.
1968   *The Black Messiah.* New York: Sheed and Ward.
1972   *Black Christian Nationalism: New Directions for the Black Church.* New York: Wm. Morrow and Co.

Cone, Cecil W.
1975   *The Identity Crisis in Black Theology.* Nashville, Tenn.: African Methodist Episcopal Church.

Cone, James.
1969   *Black Theology and Black Power.* New York: Seabury Press.
1970   *A Black Theology of Liberation.* Philadelphia: J. B. Lippincott.
1972   *The Spirituals and the Blues.* New York: Seabury Press.
1975   *God of the Oppressed.* New York: Seabury Press.
1982   *My Soul Looks Back.* Nashville, Tenn.: Abingdon.

Haley, Alex.
1976   *Roots.* New York: Doubleday.

Jones, Major J.
1971   *Black Awareness: A Theology of Hope.* Nashville, Tenn.: Abingdon.
1974   *Christian Ethics for Black Theology.* Nashville, Tenn.: Abingdon.

Jones, William R.
1973   *Is God a White Racist?: A Preamble to Black Theology.* Garden City, N.Y.: Doubleday Anchor Books.

Lincoln, C. Eric, ed.
1974   *The Black Experience in Religion.* Garden City, N.Y.: Doubleday Anchor Books.

Massey, James Earl.
1981   *Designing the Sermon: Order and Movement in Preaching.* Nashville, Tenn.: Abingdon.

Massie, Priscilla, ed.
1973   *Black Faith and Black Solidarity.* New York: Friendship Press.

Mitchell, Henry.
1970   *Black Preaching.* Philadelphia: J. B. Lippincott.
1975   *Black Beliefs.* New York: Harper & Row.

Nelson, Hart M.; Raytha, Yokley L.; and Nelson, Anne K., eds.
1971   *The Black Church in America.* New York: Basic Books.

Pannel, William.
1968   *My Friend, the Enemy.* Waco, Tex.: Word Books.
1974   "Evangelism and the Struggle for Power," *International Review of Mission* 63 no. 250 (April): 201–10.
1976   "Discipleship from a Black Perspective," *The Future of the Missionary Enterprise,* no. 17: *Mission in America in World Context.* Rome: IDOC.

Perkins, John.
1976a   *Let Justice Roll Down.* Glendale, Calif.: Regal Books.
1976b   *A Quiet Revolution.* Waco, Tex.: Word Books.
1982   *And Justice for All.* Glendale, Calif.: Regal Books.

Roberts, J. Deotis, Sr.
1971   *Liberation and Reconciliation: A Black Theology.* Philadelphia: Westminster Press.
1974   *A Black Political Theology.* Philadelphia: Westminster Press.
————, and Gardiner, James J., eds.
1971   *Quest for a Black Theology.* New York/Philadelphia: Pilgrim Press.
Skinner, Tom.
1970   *How Black Is the Gospel?* Philadelphia: J.B. Lippincott.
Thibodeaux, Sister Mary Roger.
1972   *A Black Nun Looks at Black Power.* New York: Sheed and Ward.
Thomas, Latta R.
1976   *Biblical Faith and the Black American.* Valley Forge, Pa.: Judson Press.
Traynham, Warner R.
1973   *Christian Faith in Black and White. A Primer in Theology from the Black Perspective.* Wakefield, Mass.: Parameter Press.
Washington, Joseph R., Jr.
1970   *Marriage in Black and White.* Boston: Beacon Press.
Wilmore, Gayraud S.
1972   *Black Religion and Black Radicalism.* Garden City, N.Y.: Doubleday Anchor Books.
1974   "The Case for a New Black Church Style," *The Black Experience in Religion,* ed. C. Eric Lincoln. Garden City, N.Y.: Doubleday Anchor Books.
————, and Cone, James, eds.
1979   *Black Theology: a Documentary History, 1966-1979.* Maryknoll, N.Y.: Orbis Books.
Woodson, Carter G.
1972   *The History of the Negro Church.* Washington, D.C.: Associated Publishers.

HISPANICS

Curti, Josafat.
1975   "The Chicano and the Church," *Christian Century* (March 12), pp. 253-57.
Day, Mark.
1971   *Forty Acres: Cesar Chavez and the Farm Workers.* New York: Praeger.
DeLeon, Victor.
1979   *The Silent Pentecostals: A Biographical History of the Pentecostal Movement among the Hispanics in the Twentieth Century.* Taylors, S.C.: Faith Printing Co.; La Puente, Calif.: Latin American Bible College.
Elizondo, Virgilio.
1975   *Christianity and Culture.* Huntington, Ind.: Our Sunday Visitor.
1978   *Mestizaje: The Dialectic of Cultural Birth and the Gospel.* San Antonio, Tex.: MACC.

1980   *La morenita: Evangelizer of the Americas.* San Antonio, Tex.: MACC.

Godsell, Goeffrey.
1980   "Hispanics in the U.S.: 'Ethnic Sleeping Giant' Awakens," a five-part series, *Christian Science Monitor* (April 28, 29, 30, and May 1 and 2).

Gonzalez, Justo and Catherine.
1980   *Liberation Preaching: The Pulpit and the Oppressed.* Nashville, Tenn.: Abingdon.

Haselden, Kyle.
1964   *Death of a Myth: New Locus for Spanish American Faith.* New York: Friendship Press.

Holland, Clifton L.
1975   *The Religious Dimension in Hispanic Los Angeles.* Pasadena, Calif.: William Carey Library.

Matthiessen, Peter.
1970   *Sal Si Puedes: Cesar Chavez and the New American Revolution.* New York: Random House.

Meir, Matt S.
1972   *The Chicanos: A History of Mexican Americans.* New York: Hill & Wang.

Nieves-Flacon, Luis.
1975   "Puerto Rican Migration: An Overview," *Journal of Contemporary Puerto Rican Thought* 2, no. 4, pp. 5–19.

Orozco, E. C.
1981   *Republican Protestantism in Aztlán.* Glendale, Calif.: Petereins Press.

Rendom, Armando.
1971   *Chicano Manifesto.* New York: Collier Books.

Robinson, Cecil.
1963   *With the Ears of Strangers: The Mexican American in American Literature.* Tucson, Ariz.: University of Arizona Press.

Rogg, E.
1974   *The Assimilation of Cuban Exiles.* New York: Aberdeen Press.

Romo, Oscar.
1974   "Ministering with Hispanic Americans," in *Missions in the Mosaic,* ed. M. Wendell Belew. Atlanta, Ga.: Home Mission Board, Southern Baptist Convention.

Seda-Bonilla, Eduardo.
1972   "Ethnic Studies and Cultural Pluralism," *The Rican: Revista de pensamiento contemporáneo puertorriqueño* 1, no. 1.

Servin, Manuel.
1970   *The Mexican Americans: The Awakening Minority.* Beverly Hills, Calif.: Glencoe Press.

Stevens-Arroyo, Antonio M.
1980   *Prophets Denied Honor: An Anthology of the Hispanic Church in the United States.* Maryknoll, N.Y.: Orbis Books.

Thomas, Piri.
1973   *Savior, Savior, Hold My Hand.* Garden City, N.Y.: Doubleday.

Traverzo-Galarsa, David.
1979   "A New Dimension in Religious Education for the Hispanic Evangelical Church in New York City." Unpublished M.A. thesis. New Brunswick, N.J.: New Brunswick Theological Seminary.

NATIVE AMERICANS

Beaver, R. Pierce.
1977   "The Churches and the Indians: Consequence of 350 years of Missions." *American Missions in Bicentennial Perspective,* ed. R. Pierce Beaver, Pasadena, Calif.: William Carey Library.
Berkhofer, Robert, Jr.
1972   *Salvation and the Savage.* New York: Atheneum.
Brown, Dee.
1970   *Bury My Heart at Wounded Knee.* New York: Holt, Rinehart and Winston.
Deloria, Vine, Jr.
1969   *Custer Died for Your Sins: An Indian Manifesto.* New York: Macmillan.
1973   *God Is Red.* New York: Grosset & Dunlap.
1974   *The Indian Affair.* New York: Friendship Press.
Jennings, Francis.
1975   *The Invasion of America: Indians, Colonialism and the Cant of Conquest.* New York: W. W. Norton.
Katz, Jane B.
1977   *I Am the Fire of Time: The Voices of Native American Women.* New York: E. P. Dutton.
Lurie, Nancy Oestreic.
1961   *Mountain Wolfwoman: Sister of Crashing Thunder.* Ann Arbor, Mich.: Ann Arbor Paperbacks.
McNickle, D'Arcy.
1973   *Native American Tribalism: Indian Survivals and Renewals.* New York and London: Oxford University Press, for the Institute of Race Relations.
Reist, Benjamin A.
1975   *Theology in Red, White, and Black.* Philadelphia: Westminster Press.
Starkloff, Carl F.
1974   *The People of the Center: American Indian Religion and Christianity.* New York: Seabury Press.

PACIFIC/ASIAN

Alika, Clifford.
1976   "The Institutionalization of American Racism in Hawaii." Berkeley, Calif.: PACTS [Pacific Asian Center for Theology and Strategy]. Mimeographed.
1977   "Haole: American Racism in Hawaii." Berkeley, Calif.: PACTS. Mimeographed.

Asian Center for Theology and Strategies (ACTS).
1975   "East Asian and Amerasian Theology," Proceedings of the Second
           Conference on East Asian and Amerasian Theology of Liberation.
           Berkeley, Calif.: PACTS. Mimeographed.
Ben-Dasan, Isaiah.
1972   *The Japanese and the Jews.* New York: Weatherill.
Bird, Frederick.
n.d.   "A Study of Chinese Churches in the San Francisco Bay Area."
           Berkeley, Calif.: PACTS. Mimeographed.
Bosworth, Allan F.
1968   *America's Concentration Camps.* New York: Bantam Books.
Chan, Lillian.
n.d.   *Interracial Marriage: Chinese and Whites in the United States.* Berke-
           ley, Calif.: PACTS. Mimeographed.
Chong, Frank A.
1977   ". . . And It Came to Pass . . . That We Too Came . . . to Share the
           Good News." Berkeley, Calif.: PACTS. Mimeographed.
Fujihara, Toge.
n.d.   "Asian Americans and Blacks." Berkeley, Calif.: PACTS. Mimeo-
           graphed.
Kimura, Ben.
1973   "A Historical and Comparative Study of the Christian Mission in
           Japan and among the Japanese Immigrants in the United States."
           Unpublished doctoral dissertation, California Graduate School of
           Theology, Glendale, Calif.
Kitano, Harry H. L.
1969   *Japanese Americans: The Evolution of a Subculture.* Englewood
           Cliffs, N.J.: Prentice-Hall.
Lee, Robert.
1969   *The Schizophrenic Church: Conflict over Community Organizations.*
           Philadelphia: Westminster Press.
1975   "Chinese-Americans in the United States." Berkeley, Calif.: PACTS.
           Mimeographed.
1980   *China Journal: Glimpses of a Nation in Transition.* San Francisco:
           East/West Publishing Co.
1981   *Faith and the Prospect of Economic Collapse.* Atlanta, Ga.: John
           Knox Press.
Morikawa, Jitsuo.
1976   "Pre-Centennial Celebration Address—Japanese Christian Mission
           in North America." Berkeley, Calif.: PACTS. Mimeographed.
Nagano, Paul M.
n.d.   "Ethnic Pluralism and Democracy." Berkeley, Calif.: PACTS.
           Mimeographed.
n.d.   "Biblical and Theological Statement for the Asian American Baptist
           Caucus." Berkeley, Calif.: PACTS. Mimeographed.
n.d.   "The Asian Americans: Guidelines to a New Community." Berkeley,
           Calif.: PACTS. Mimeographed.
1970a   "An Overlay of So Called 'Yellow Theology' Upon Black Theology."
           Berkeley, Calif.: PACTS. Mimeographed.

1970b   "The Japanese-American's Search for Identity, Ethnic Pluralism, and a Christian Basis of Permanent Identity." Doctoral dissertation, Claremont School of Theology, Pomona, Calif.

1974a   "Is Hate Ever Justified?" Berkeley, Calif.: PACTS. Mimeographed.

1974b   "Declaration of Independence." Berkeley, Calif.: PACTS. Mimeographed.

1974c   "Amerasian Experience and Christianity: The Japanese Experience." Berkeley, Calif.: PACTS. Mimeographed.

1976   "Search for Identity." Berkeley, Calif.: PACTS. Mimeographed.

Park, J. Philip.

1976   "Asian Christians and the Bicentennial." Berkeley, Calif.: PACTS.

Program Agency, United Presbyterian Church, USA.

1974   *A Study of Chinese, Filipino, Japanese, and Korean Populations in the U.S. and Projections.* Berkeley, Calif.: PACTS.

Sano, Roy I.

n.d.   *The Theologies of Asian Americans and Pacific Peoples.* Berkeley, Calif.: PACTS (compiler).

1969   "From Bowed Heads to Clenched Fists." Berkeley, Calif.: PACTS. Mimeographed.

1972   "The Giant Leap and the Long March." Berkeley, Calif.: PACTS. Mimeographed.

1973   "Toward a Liberating Ethnicity." Berkeley, Calif.: PACTS. Mimeographed.

1975a   "Ethnic Liberation Theology: Neo-Orthodoxy Reshaped—or Replaced?"*Christianity and Crisis* (November 10, 1975), pp. 258–64.

1975b   "East Asian and Amerasian Liberation." Proceedings of the Second Conference on East Asian and Amerasian Theology, Feb. 3, 1975. Berkeley, Calif.: PACTS.

1975c   "Asian American Experiences on the Mainland." Berkeley, Calif.: PACTS.

1977   "The Emerging Pacific Basin and Its Implications." Berkeley, Calif.: PACTS.

Shinto, William M.

n.d.   "The Role of Religion in Asian American Communities." Berkeley, Calif.: PACTS.

n.d.   "The Ethnic Church on the Edge—The End of the Edge of Life?" Berkeley, Calif.: PACTS.

n.d.   "The Eccentric Ministry: A Style of Life in the Margin." Berkeley, Calif.: PACTS.

n.d.   "Asian Americans and Higher Education in the Public Sector." Berkeley, Calif.: PACTS.

1977   "Colorful Minorities and the White Majority." UMHE [United Ministries in Higher Education] Monograph Series. Berkeley, Calif.: PACTS.

Index of Scriptural References

Old Testament

New Testament

Index of Persons

Ahlstrom, Sydney, 76, 84ns9-10
Alexander VI (Pope), 59
Alves, Rubem, 39n2, 77, 84n19, 98n2, 125, 170, 173n11
Anderson, Gerald H., 121, 132n8, 161n37, 196, 197, 200, 209, 216
Arbenz, Jacobo, 106
Arias, Esther and Mortimer, 114n1, 219

Barth, Karl, 12, 20n12, 198
Berkhof, H., 17-20n4, 87n5, 99n5
Boff, Leonardo, 12, 13, 20n4
Bonilla, Eduardo Seda, 73, 83n6, 84n7, 173n3
Bosch, David, 147, 160n25, 198
Braaten, Carl, 40n10, 80, 85ns29,32-34, 198
Bühlmann, Walbert, 83, 85n36, 203, 216

Carey, William, 61, 62, 68
Carter, Jimmy (President), 95
Casas, Bartolomé de las, 68, 123
Castro, Emilio, 148, 150, 151
Cole, Allan, 3, 20n14, 148
Cone, James, 79, 84n25, 222

Dayton, Edward, 160n16, 165, 166, 173n6, 206
Dulles, Allen, 106
Dulles, John Foster, 106
Dunn, James, 19n4
Durninger, Abraham, 61
Dussel, Enrique, 133n15, 165, 173n5, 220

Falwell, Jerry, 179
Ford, Leighton, 150
Fraser, David, 165, 166, 173n6, 206
Frigoli, Bruno, 150

Galvez, Miguer, 50, 56n15
Gilbert, Humphrey, 60
Glasser, Arthur, 148, 153, 160n32, 206
González, Justo, 59, 69n1, 199; and Catherine, 123, 133n10
Gorostiaga, Xabier, 64, 66, 70ns15,20, 115n4
Gutiérrez, Gustavo, 119, 129, 132n4, 133n13, 134ns19,22,24

Haig, Alexander (General), 179
Henry, Carl F. H., xviiin5, 40-42n10, 159n7
Hoover, Willis, 48
Howard, David, 151

Izon, Stan, 151

Jenson, Robert, 76, 84ns13-15
John XXIII (Pope), 124

Kasemann, Ernst, 155, 161n38
Kessler, J.B.A., 48, 55n10, 220
Kirk, Andrew, 129, 131, 134ns20,22,25
Kitamori, Kazoh, 10, 20n7, 217
Krass, Alfred, 71, 83n2, 186n2, 206

Lalive D'Epinay, Christian, 50, 56n16, 220
Lernoux, Penny, 106, 107, 115ns5,7,9, 221
Livingstone, David, 64
Lores, Ruben, 80, 85n30
Lovelace, Richard, F., 179, 187n17

Marshall, George C. (General), 178, 179
Marty, Martin, 79, 85ns27-28
Marx, Karl, 132
McGavran, Donald A., 54-55ns2,8
Metz, Johann Baptist, 163, 173n2
Michelson, Wesley, 68, 76, 82, 84ns11,24, 85n35
Míguez-Bonino, José, 47, 55n9, 183, 187n20, 221
Moltmann, Jurgen, 11, 20ns9-11, 98n4, 183, 187ns19,21
Montesino, Luis Antonio de, 68
Morikawa, Jitsuo, 167, 168, 173n8, 207
Muñoz, Humberto, 49, 55n11, 56n24
Murray, John, 39n5

Nichols, Bruce, 148, 153, 155, 160n31, 161n39

Padilla, René, 20n15, 49, 54-55n2, 56n14, 168, 173, 207
Panikkar, Raymond, 44, 55n3, 202
Pannenburg, Wolfhart, 19n4, 20n6
Pinochet, Augusto (General), 50

Index of Subjects

Africa: at Bangkok, 135; bibliography on, 213-15; Christ today in, 13; and David Livingstone, 64; as part of Third World, 118-19; theology in, 117, 132n9; and US Christians, 113

Alienaton: *see* Sin

American Dream, 177-78

American Society: and civil religion, 76-77; economic-technological reality of, 77-78; emerging religious frontier of, 75-76; and ethnic minorities, 72-75; institutional church and theology of, 78-79; as a mission field, 71-72; in the 1980s, 175-81; and the Third World, 71-72, 81-83

Americas, the: and Anglo-Saxon messianism, 107-08; characteristics of, 86-88; kingdom priorities in, 94-98; and the mission of God, 88-91

Antichrist: as oppressive powers, 15, 20n15

Asia and the Pacific: bibliography on, 216-19, 225-27; as part of Third World, 118; religious milieu of, 75, 119-121; theologies of, 132n9

Asians: in the U.S., 73, 181

Associated Press (AP), 107

Bandung Conference of Non-Aligned Nations (1955), 118

Bangkok (Eighth World Missionary Conference, 1972/73), 65, 135-36

Baptists: and American Christendom, 190; and William Carey, 61-62; Particular and General, 69n7

"Barmen Declaration," 51

Bible: and contextualization, 5; and the hermeneutics of Melbourne and Pattaya, 154-57; and liberation theology, 130-31; place in theology of, 21, 33

Billy Graham Evangelistic Association, 136

Blacks: bibliography on, 221-25; and Christ in South Africa, 13; as part of the other American church, 185; as part of the Third World, 119; in the United States, 73, 113, 184

Captivity: in American church and theology, 78-79; of American society, 177-81; as consequence of sin, 22-26; of Israel, 191-92, 193; of Latin America, 34-35; and liberation in the American minority church 184-86; in liberation theology, 126; of the modern missionary movement, 58-70; need to be freed from, for mission, 193-94

Caribbean: bibliography on, 219-22; and Latin America, 86-87; Puerto Rico as part of, xv, xviiin5

Central Intelligence Agency (CIA), 88, 106

Chalcedonian Confession, 17-20n4

Chile: Protestantism in, 48-52

Christ, Jesus: as critical principle of missiological contextualization, 15-16; as the crucified Son, 7; death, resurrection, and lordship of, 7-12; as the God-human, 8-12, 17-20n4; and ideologies, 121-23; as the Incarnate Word, 5; as incarnated in the poor, powerless, and oppressed, 13-15; and Israel, 89; and the kingdom of God, 91-94; as Man, 6; at Melbourne and Pattaya, 138-45, 147, 153-54, 159n5; and the mission of God, 88-91; and outsiders, 188-94; and the principalities and powers, 170-71; and the proclamation of the gospel in the 1980s, 181-85; and salvation, 26-33; and the Trinity, 89; verification of historical incarnation of, 16.

Christendom: and Christian civilization, 14; in colonial Latin America, 35-36, 123; and domestication of mission, 68; as historical project, xvii, 180-81, 189-90; illusion of, in contemporary American society, 179-80; missionary challenge of, 192-93, 194; negative impact on the church of, 190; and new strategy in Latin American Catholic Church, 124

Church: and Christendom, 190; as institution, 167-69; and the kingdom of God, 40-42n10, 45; in liberation theology, 126-27, 128, 131; at Melbourne and Pattaya, 140-42, 148n17, 151-53; nature of, 44; as pilgrim community, 44; of the poor, 184-85